DIGITAL PIRATES

DIGITAL PIRATES

Policing Intellectual Property in Brazil

Alexander Sebastian Dent

STANFORD UNIVERSITY PRESS
Stanford, California

STANFORD UNIVERSITY PRESS
Stanford, California

Printed in the United States of America on acid-free, archival-quality paper

Library of Congress Cataloging-in-Publication Data
Names: Dent, Alexander Sebastian, author.
Title: Digital pirates : policing intellectual property in Brazil / Alexander Sebastian Dent.
Description: Stanford : Stanford University Press, 2020. | Includes bibliographical references and index.
Identifiers: LCCN 2019038803 (print) | LCCN 2019038804 (ebook) | ISBN 9781503611443 (cloth) | ISBN 9781503612976 (paperback) | ISBN 9781503612983 (epub)
Subjects: LCSH: Piracy (Copyright)—Brazil—Prevention. | Piracy (Copyright)—Social aspects—Brazil. | Piracy (Copyright)—Economic aspects—Brazil. | Intellectual property infringement—Brazil. | Video recordings—Pirated editions—Brazil. | Sound recordings—Pirated editions—Brazil.
Classification: LCC KHD1614 .D46 2020 (print) | LCC KHD1614 (ebook) | DDC 346.8104/82—dc23
LC record available at https://lccn.loc.gov/2019038803
LC ebook record available at https://lccn.loc.gov/2019038804

Cover design: Four Eyes | John Barnett

Cover image: Graffiti, São Paulo. Photo taken by the author.

Text design: Kevin Barrett Kane

Typeset at Stanford University Press in 10.5/15 Minion Pro

. . . but objects . . . are "promiscuous" and can move freely between cultural/transactional domains without being essentially compromised. This they can do because they have indeed no essences, only an indefinite range of potentials.

ALFRED GELL

"Vogel's Net: Traps as Artworks, and Artworks as Traps" (1996)

With numbers, everything goes.

FRIEDRICH KITTLER

Gramophone, Film, Typewriter (1999)

CONTENTS

ACKNOWLEDGMENTS
PIRATICAL CONFESSIONS

THE AUTHOR OF A BOOK about piracy should probably cop to all the thieving the project required.

In Brazil, I stole untold acts of kindness from my Brazilian family, Nícia and Ivanil Bonatti and their sons Flávio, Thiago, and Daniel. I have similarly pilfered the Schumaker clan, including Roberto, Teca, and Felipe. I took all kinds of interviews and observational data from numerous police officers, NGO workers, informal economy workers and clients, and pirates—who shall remain anonymous.

Colleagues who work on piracy seem to be unusually lax about keeping a watchful eye on their stuff. In Brazil, I helped myself to the untold generosity of Oona Castro, Ronaldo Lemos, Pedro Mizukami, Pablo Ortellado, Rosana Pinheiro Machado, and Jhessica Reia. In the United States, it isn't difficult to quantify how much I took from Michael Carroll, Sean Flynn, Peter Jaszi, Joe Karaganis, and Susan Sell. I'm going to be cagey about the precise dollar value, but suffice it to say that whatever I took cost millions and prevented them from accessing important oxygen and fresh water. Colleagues at the US Trade Representative (USTR) were also remarkably careless about thoughts, words, and deeds—so I took from them, too, though they shall remain nameless. Mea culpa.

I was excessively light-fingered where I teach, at the George Washington (GW) University. In unguarded moments, I filched from Attiya Ahmad, Catherine Allen, Robert Baker, Joshua Bell, Jeff Blomster, Douglas Boyce, Ilana Feldman, Richard Grinker, Hugh Gusterson, Susan Johnston, Joel Kuipers, Steven Lubkeman, Marilyn Merritt, Barbara Miller, Robert Shepherd, Chet Sherwood, and Sarah Wagner. I also used verbal skills to extort grant money from The George Washington University on numerous occasions; the Office of Research and Strategic Initiatives should check its pockets, particularly Yongwu Rong.

At workshops and conferences, I simply lifted the productive questions and comments of Maria José de Abreu, José Carlos Aguiar, Richard Bauman, Dominic Boyer, Don Brenneis, Carlo Caduff, Amy Chazkel, Gabriella Coleman, John Collins, Rosemany Coombe, Vincent Crapanzano, Shannon Dawdy, Chris Dunn, Marshall Eakin, Falina Enriquez, Alex Fattal, Paja Faudree, Aaron Fox, Laurie Frederik, Ilana Gershon, James Green, Shane Greene, Bridget Guarasci, Zeynep Gursel, Ben Harbert, Charles Hirschkind, Jason Jackson, Kajri Jain, Webb Keane, Chris Kelty, Michael Lempert, Lawrence Liang, Joe Masco, Andrew Mathews, Sean Mitchell, Megan Moodie, Rosalind Morris, Mary Murrell, Paul Nadasdy, Constantine Nakassis, David Novak, Ana Maria Ochoa Gautier, Derek Pardue, Marina Peterson, Fernando Rabossi, Danilyn Rutherford, Matt Sakakeeny, Steven Sangren, Roger Sansi-Roca, Dan Sharp, Jesse Shipley, Patricia Spyer, Rebecca Stein, Kedron Thomas, Anna Tsing, Catherine Verdury, Winnie Wong, Sha Xin Wei, and Martin Zillinger.

The work of my past teachers continues to provide productive sources of plunder, in particular Andrew Apter, Philip Bohlman, James Boon, Manuela Carneiro da Cunha, John Comaroff, John Kelly, Elizabeth Povinelli, Michael Silverstein, and Terry Turner.

A cluster of graduate students at GW have been too generous, in particular, Chloe Ahman, Angelique Baehr, Jorge Benavides, Dana Burton, Jessica Chandras, Schweta Krishnan, Sam Pfister, Devin Proctor, Sarah Richardson, Scott Ross, and Kaitlyn Schoenike; Emma Backe and Raquel Machaqueiro contributed invaluable editing. Undergraduates who helped include Lauren Deal, Amanda Kemble, Briel Kobak, and Sarah Otis.

In DC, music friends who were caught unawares by my wiles include Mark Andersen, Amy Farina, Josh Freed, Chris Hamley, Ian MacKaye, and Avi Zevin.

I have pirated these chapters from previously published work. Parts of this book appeared in *American Ethnologist, Anthropological Quarterly, Cultural Anthropology, Current Anthropology,* and in a volume on cellular phones edited by Joshua Bell and Joel Kuipers and published by Routledge. I am required to thank these journals and publisher: thank you for allowing me to steal from works I wrote (but you helped me to circulate).

My editor at Stanford Press, Michelle Lipinski, has been a tireless supporter, rigorous questioner, and keen critic. I am deeply grateful for her engagement, her knowledge of this subject, and her sharp eye for nonsense.

And finally, why steal exclusively in professional circles? A good pirate is coherent if not always concise. I also stole the love and support of my wife, Kye, and our two boys, Neko and Sloan.

I'd say I owe all of you if that were how a pirate thinks. However, I hope I can genuinely say "thank you" without losing all credibility.

DIGITAL PIRATES

INTRODUCTION
THE JOYS AND SORROWS OF DIGITAL TEXTUALITY

> At first glance, mimesis seems to be a stylizing of reality in which the ordinary features of our world are brought into focus by a certain exaggeration, the relationship of the imitation to the object it imitates being something like the relationship of dancing to walking.
>
> Michael Davis, *The Poetry of Philosophy: On Aristotle's Poetics* (1999)

BAZAAR, SHOPPING MALL, AND CARNIVAL: that's how the downtown informal market in Campinas struck me when I first arrived in the late 1990s. In this city of two million about 1.5 hours northwest of São Paulo, what locals called the *camelódromo*—a term that mixes "itinerant seller" *(camelô)* with "stadium" *(dromo)*—appeared to offer *everything* for sale: sneakers, sunglasses, cell phones, speakers, pens, backpacks, batteries, soccer jerseys, car stereos, videogames, CDs, bananas, and DVDs (Braz 2002). I had begun to visit the place regularly in order to figure out the popularity of Brazilian "country music" (which locals called *música sertaneja*) for my first book on rural performance in neoliberal Brazil (Dent 2009). However, the camelódromo quickly became an autonomous preoccupation for me because of the way it confounded my belief that formal and informal economies ought to be separated by clear boundaries. My experiences in Canada, the United States, and the United Kingdom had not prepared me for this—not even my visits to street markets in New York City.

The stalls in this Brazilian marketplace were of cinder block with metal roll-down fronts that locked at night. Each one measured about ten feet by ten feet and had been officially numbered by the mayor's office when it had sought to "clean up" the downtown a few years before. To protect from the rain, fiberglass and aluminum roofs covered rows of connected "boxes" (the word was often spoken in English rather than Portuguese, indexing, I surmised, a linguistic modernity). These stalls stretched through the sidewalks and streets in an ordered but frantic way, surrounding the bus station a bit like a coiled snake (see Holston 2009 on "insurgency"). Music pumped out of speakers or videos played from many of the individual stalls, creating little orbits of light and sound that projected sensory turbulence when they came together (Cardoso 2019). Most purchases could be made by credit card. The police alternated between behaving like clients, carrying out punitive raids, and as we shall see, investigating murders that were the result of the criminalization of the work that went on there.

When I first arrived, I wasn't sure how to read the goods themselves. Indeed, my temporary confusion, once again an artifact of my experiences in Canada, the United States, and the United Kingdom, led to a developing epistemology of consumption; I learned to understand the profusion and provenance of the goods, and navigate within it (see also Coombe 1998, 2009). At the start, before my localized consumer sense got honed, some goods looked, sounded, smelled, and felt like consecrated brands, such as Nike, Dolce & Gabbana, and Drakkar Noir. Others appeared to poach some of the iconography of those popular brands, offering close approximations: a slightly less curvy swoosh, large gold letters that were not D and G, but that still interlocked while facing opposite directions, that smell from nervous high school dances (see Brenneis 1987 for how aesthetics combine sensory registers). The CDs and DVDs that were my initial focus appeared to occupy a range of formalities—with some taking the shape of briskly burned copies labeled with a marker (informal) and others resting in jewel cases with hologrammed manufacturer "seals" (decidedly more formal). Still other products bore no marks at all, while nonetheless emulating the spirit of brands in color, shape, and smell. Electronics bore names that closely resembled mainstream products, such as HiPhone. Fragrances were always factory sealed in plastic.

At moments, these goods looked like cheap things that might stink, fall apart, or fail to play (perhaps all three). But during my next visit to the market I felt sure that what I had characterized as knockoffs were in fact good deals that would perform like their more expensive counterparts. There were still other times when it seemed to me that these products might in fact *be* the real deal after all—having been either smuggled duty-free or produced after hours in precisely the same factory that had made the originals during the day. Friends told me stories about how these products were "even better" than the "originals" (always the term used to describe an object with pristine provenance); in one case a friend crowed that the dragon on his pair of copied jeans—embroidered by a computerized sewing machine that could digitally reproduce the design of one's choice from thousands of options—was larger, and therefore better, than the embroidered dragon on the original pair. Others railed against the injustice of noncamelô high-priced imports. Still others fretted that cheap sunglasses might permanently hurt their eyes (though they perpetually lost sunglasses, justifying spending little) or that the proceeds of their pirated CD purchase "funded organized crime." The stall owners kept track of their inventories with laptops and, by the mid-aughts, sent email or surfed the Internet while customers browsed—sharing an immense wireless network (see Kelty 2008 on "recursive publics"). The products, their interpretations, and their means of circulation refused to sit still.

I had a series of questions about the camelódromo right away. If I tried to buy something (which I eventually did), might I be expected to barter? (I wasn't.) Or perhaps sellers would sense my foreignness and try to rip me off. (They didn't.) Would there be guarantees if something broke? (There were.) Where did all this stuff *come* from? (China by way of Paraguay, for the most part.) And finally, how was all this legal, or if it wasn't legal, why were the police browsing at a DVD stand selling illegal copies of movies twenty-five yards from where I was interviewing a cell phone repair worker, and how were these police getting cash ready to make a purchase? How did they understand their position as purchasers of the likely illegal goods and arbiters of the market's overall legality *at the same time*?

These sorts of questions animate this book, which is about the way consumers and producers of texts such as movies and music experience the intellectual property (IP) system as profoundly broken. It is also about the way that brokenness indexes past communicative strategies, while calling forth new ones. I argue that the brokenness of the global IP system becomes locally generative as actors engage with IP to produce new modes of action. These, in turn, are contested and reworked by a productive tension with "piracy"—with the entire process conceivable as the kind of "dynamic nominalism" espoused by philosopher Ian Hacking (2002). Hacking proposed that subjects are constantly in the process of contesting the categories into which they fit, at the very same moment in which they rework those categories for future use by them and others. My analysis of this dynamic process is based on extensive fieldwork I carried out in Brazil over a period of twenty-two years.

Research on the book began in 1998 with those initial visits to the camelódromo, driven by my interest in the "pirated" music for sale there. However, in developing an approach to what I came to frame, less normatively, as "unauthorized use," I realized not only that piracy and IP were intimately related to one another but also that this relationship made more sense if I framed it within a field of cultural practice I have come to call "digital textuality" (Bourdieu 1993).[1] Indeed, one of the major arguments of this book is that digital textuality helps us understand not only the productive brokenness of the current IP system but also the centrality of that brokenness to contemporary capitalism.

I should be clear that my interlocutors in Brazil and the United States did not speak about something called "digital textuality" per se. They did speak about digital culture, digital communication, digital media, digital language, digital marketing, digital currency, digital surveillance, digital value, and even digital love—and of course, they spoke continuously about IP and piracy. Across these indigenous terms, I define digital textuality as a mode of *inscription* (Bakhtin 1981a, 1986; Geertz 1973a; Helenius 2016; Ingarden 1973; Kittler 1999; Miller 2001; Ricoeur 2004) that reduces response time, transcends space, condenses communicative modalities, and travels everywhere with its users. In somewhat different words, digital textuality travels fast and far while seeking to encompass the interactive ecologies of its users—incorporating all of their senses. Though my claim is that digital textuality provides new scales of dissemination, enjoining massive enforcement efforts in terms of sums of money and numbers of people involved, I also claim that it is deeply continuous with forms of mediation stretching all the way back to the printing press (Johns 2010). On a micrological level, digital textuality can be elucidated by what performance theorists have called "entextualization"—by which they mean that tendency in acts of communication to pull the current moment away from the here and now and make it portable, and available for future interactions (Bauman and Briggs 1990; Brenneis 1987; Dent 2009; Kuipers 1990). You are doing it now, reader, as you evaluate whether or not you think this is a good introduction to a good book; indeed, all communication relies on entextualization. However, inscription dials it up—making the circulated text highly portable by seeking to fix it in a form that can then be reproduced with varying degrees of fidelity; digital textuality's users frequently aspire to a high degree of fidelity, reducing the level of "noise" to make the "signal" more audible (Larkin 2008). Digital textuality so pervasively entextualizes our contemporary communication—our phone calls, texts, WhatsApp communications, emails, music, videos, pictures, and voice memos (at least)—by accruing an increasing amount of our communication in "inscripts," which are written transcripts that we generate as we interact (Shieffelin and Jones 2015). These traces are simultaneously virtual and material, undermining any pat distinction between the two (Kuipers and Bell 2018). Indeed, digital textuality extends to texts we often take to be unproblematically material—such as crops and clothes (Fisher 2014; "How Fashion" 2018). Another important feature of digital textuality is that its users enjoin "automation" (Kockleman 2017), whereby pieces of disembodied yet active language called algorithms carry out various kinds of work a bit the way Melanesian witch doctors acted upon their crops using spells (Malinowski 1935). In so doing, digital textuality stretches entextualization by stripping out context, creating anxieties about how future instances of a given text will circulate—whether those future iterations will align with an "original" (that term, again) speaker's intentions, or whether they will be put to profoundly different uses. In part as a way to manage these kinds of decontextualizing anxieties, digital textuality enjoins propertization and facilitates enforcement by leaving traces in multiple locations (see Boyer 2003) that can then be inspected by consumers whose sensory apparatus has been trained to gather specific qualia (Dent 2016a). Digital textuality must be considered across scales (another parlance would frame this as both global and local); we must not assume that it simply radiates from a top, "down," or from a center to a periphery (Chan 2014).

Digital textuality must be put into historical context, and not only with respect to the long tradition of discussions of mimesis (Davis 1999). During the period of my research, as I will discuss in more detail in a moment, Brazil was succumbing to considerable international pressure to modernize, and a stricter approach to IP was one way to align itself with the "progress" promised on its flag (along with "order"). Furthermore, during the years of my research, developed nations of the North transformed themselves from industrial powers to economies based on knowledge and leveraged finance, media markets internationalized, and development planning focused on the rule of law and legal reform. My point is not that a move to the digital somehow caused all this to happen; rather, I seek to show that digital textuality plays a crucial constitutive role in all of these processes. Moreover, its centrality to these ongoing injunctions of modernity has gone largely unexamined—at least in a cohesive way that integrates its modes of subjectivity with an empirical site of practice (in this case, Brazil).

I will say much more about digital textuality in the coming pages (particularly in chapter 1), but for now, I should outline my methods by saying that I take an anthropological approach that nonetheless aims at broad issues in the social sciences such as the contemporary shape of capitalism (Marx [1867] 1977; Weber [1905] 1958), the relationship between technology and embodiment (Heidegger [1954] 1993), and techniques of governance (Foucault 1991). This means that I call on interviews conducted with, and observations of, pirates, musicians, filmmakers, salespeople, technicians, policymakers, politicians, and consumers in the southern state of São Paulo, Brazil; throughout this ethnographic process I attend carefully to language. The interviews, observations, and sometimes participation (involving, at times, purchases . . . shhh) reinforce one another. This is because the actions and words of my interlocutors sometimes added up but just as often rendered each other more complex by repositioning, or even undermining each other. By this I simply mean, for example, that police would espouse a strongly antipiracy stance in interviews, but I would later see them browsing and making purchases; I also heard rumors about police who had railed against "pirates" later looting confiscated pirated inventories to find Christmas presents for their families.

Though there are many works on IP and piracy available right now (Boateng 2011; Caldwell and Holt 2018; Castells and Cardoso 2013; Eckstein and Schwarz 2014; Guertin 2012; McLeod 2005; Meuller 2019; Patry 2009;

Philip 2014; Ruen 2012; Sinnreich 2013; Strangelove 2005; and Thomas 2016 are just a few), this one defines its terms by drawing on concepts from linguistic anthropology. I will outline an approach to piracy and IP that treats it as a way of managing "intertextual gaps"—spatial and temporal spaces between circulated texts where we can observe varied institutional practices as well as transformations in the text's mode and meaning (see Briggs and Bauman 1992); I will explain more in chapter 1. I also outline a theory of "publics" in which a public is a self-organizing orientation to the way that texts are simultaneously private and public as we read, scrutinize, or listen to them (Kelty 2008; Warner 2002; see also chapter 5). Where other books focus mostly on producers and consumers, this book puts law enforcement and anti-IP activists at the center of the analysis. Indeed, I believe that we cannot understand digital textuality without all of these varied actors in the mix (see Barney, et al. 2016; Martin 2018).

I hope the book is useful not only to anthropologists but also to all those interested in communication, creativity, and mediation. I want my remarks to be read by policymakers and law enforcement as well, and for this reason have toned down some of my anthropologese without dialing back on theoretical rigor. In terms of what might help police and policy makers, my analysis of digital textuality leads me to argue that the extensive policing of copying neither reduces rates of what some call "piracy" nor improves the lot of producers of music, movies, medicines, or what have you by earning them more. Nor does it improve consumers' lives, because it fails to incentivize novel ideas in the arts, sciences, architecture, pharmaceuticals, or anywhere else. Instead, the increasing global enforcement of IP in the last two decades has pushed piracy right to the center of contemporary capitalism, while forcing piracy's users (that is, most of us) to intermittently cower at the fringes of virtual and concrete spaces—from social networks to cities. It has accomplished this through the increased scrutiny of piracy in the form of public relations campaigns—magazine ads, billboards, "educational" programs in schools, and warnings before, after, and sometimes even during video and sound presentations. Enforcement has also made piracy more intimate by fragmenting once large markets for pirated goods and placing them closer to "home," as I will explore in more detail in chapter 2. I want to underscore this point; in the early twenty-first century, piracy is at the core of our quotidian affairs, but we all have a brooding sense that it is shameful and maybe even dangerous. We have to play at piracy, but complex laws and capricious enforcement tell us we shouldn't.

This whiplash between piracy's centrality and its marginality in the domain of text production and reception has politicized circulation in unprecedented ways. Perhaps most importantly, it has made already precarious populations that much more precarious.[2] Another of this book's arguments is that our failure to understand digital textuality increases levels of violence and suffering around the world—most obviously among the poor and dispossessed but also among the shrinking middle class. This escalation of violence is doubly absurd, since this ineffective IP policing costs a lot of public dollars to carry out, though it is often incentivized by the private sector (as we will see in chapter 3). For these reasons, it is my hope that those participating in the current IP-policing regime—as policymakers, lawyers, producers, consumers, marketers, advertisers, or police—should read this book and then work toward a more humane and realistic approach to the making, movement, and meaning of texts.

In order to carry out this rethinking of the relationship between IP and piracy by way of digital textuality, we should begin by understanding that the policing of IP around the world is not the result of people wanting to "be right with the law"; almost categorically, my interlocutors found IP laws arcane and risible—even the police tasked with enforcing them. This was true despite perceived allegiances between IP laws and discourses of modernity and development. But it is also too simplistic to say that IP policing is just wealthy corporations from the United States, Japan, and Europe imposing their wishes on the poor—whether they be located in American inner cities or emerging economies such as Brazil, India, Russia, and China. In fact, something more complex is taking place. What is happening is that local police find enforcement situationally attractive because IP elicits their localized anxieties about digital textuality.

This statement requires explanation. In more detail, then, a doctrine known as IP maximalism (which I define as the belief that IP should be policed at all costs; see Sell 2003, 2010) dovetails with fears that contemporary modes of communication put subjectivity at risk. What I mean by this is that the speed, distance transcendence, and omnipresence of digital textuality make users nervous about who they are and how they can act in and upon the world. Indeed, as we shall see in chapter 3, it even makes users apprehensive about political boundaries—between nation-sates, for example. If we can understand this, we can begin to unpack the claims by critics of IP policing that enforcement is driven by bribery. The enforcers I interacted with were not hypnotized by money or anything else; they were carrying out something they intermittently believed in. I saw plenty of them taking active pleasure in their work. Perceiving IP policing as the result of either rapacious globalization or alienation ignores a more complex reality—that aspects of digital textuality are frightening to many users but, as we shall see in this Brazilian case, in locally specific ways that ethnography is uniquely suited to uncovering (Chan 2014; Sundaram 2010). In other words, the fears surrounding digital textuality act as an incentive to police piracy—aside from anything large corporations or their NGO representatives might foster. For this reason, piracy policing can be very attractive to a broad array of social actors across race, gender, and social classes. I will examine Brazilian fears about textual production and reception that contribute to piracy policing, rendering IP maximalism momentarily efficacious, though also, as will become clear, harmful to what we refer to as creativity, and often, justice for the dispossessed.

All of this means that this book lacks villains or heroes. Until we step around the current framing of IP that allows a war in its support (resembling the war on drugs), we will remain stagnant in polarization.[3] Until we stop talking about IP as though it were either a kind of sacred protection for new ideas (the way the IP maximalists frame it), or a weapon of the rich for keeping "information" from being "free" (the way IP's critics often frame it), we are going to keep missing what's important—that the way digital texts circulate (or fail to) creates worries about hostile and/or uncontrolled circulation that we need to bring into the open (Philip 2014). I want to be clear that I am not letting a frequently rapacious group of IP maximalists off the hook. Black box accounting practices, obfuscatory public relations campaigns, and attempts to privatize policing have characterized much of this costly IP war. However, the task of calling out these dishonesties has been carried out more competently by others (see, for example, the level-headed work of Joe Karaganis 2019). My point in this book is that our current troubles with IP are not just about particular actors and institutions squaring off against one another—although this, of course, plays a role. Rather, users interact with the affordances of digital textuality—characteristics that seem consistent across a very wide array of usages and that feel inalienable—in ways that contribute to our IP woes (Gibson 1986; Keane 2005).

A Sign's Eye View of Mediation

My support for these arguments draws heavily on cultural comparison that, in turn, relies on what linguistic anthropologist Michael Silverstein (2001, 73) has called "a sign's eye view" of social life. In more detail, I mix semiotics with an interest in the material qualities of sign-related behavior (Keane 2013). The culture-language nexus that I advance here is indebted to much of the cognitive and comparative work on language that began in the 1930s, with scholars such as Franz Boas ([1929] 1982), Eduard Sapir (1949), and Benjamin Lee Whorf (1956); it was in the context of this lineage that we began to see detailed elaborations of the way in which language shaped habitual thought and action. Though adumbrations of the "culture" concept are sometimes viewed as dated, I believe culture to be at the heart of what anthropology has to offer to the social sciences and humanities (see, for instance, Sahlins 1993). For me, culture is best thought of as an interpretive lens—a capacity and exhortation through which human beings categorize the sensory information that comes to them. This definition is crucial for this project due to the ways in which digital textuality involves a kind of quarrel over the senses in the context of consumption (Cox, Irving, and Wright 2016). These interpretive practices are carried out in interaction—in dialogues that have been characterized as *performances* by linguist, literary critic, and philosopher Mikhail Bakhtin (see also Austin [1962] 1975; Bakhtin 1981a; Brenneis 1987; Kuipers 1990). My approach to culture relies on the primacy of performances wherein texts are oriented toward evaluating audiences, and these evaluations have consequences for daily life (Dent 2016a).

In getting to and from producers and receivers, texts must pass through channels. Along those lines, one of my frequent targets in this book will be the state of current thinking about "media" and processes of "mediation," not just in anthropology but also in media studies.[4] On one level, conceiving of textuality and circulation by way of the concept of mediation is salutary. Particularly in domains of social science where textual models reign, analysis can too frequently focus on the text before (T1) and the text after (T2), spending little time on what happens in between. This approach appears in those influenced by the work of telecommunications scholars Claude Shannon and Warren Weaver (discussed by Peters 1999), who pitched a model with a sender, a receiver, a message, and a channel. Broadening our discussion to include the variety of factors that come into play as texts move, transforming their meaning, keeps us focused on the ways in which texts are not unitary and fixed, but are, rather, constructed through interaction (see, in particular, Jakobson 1960).

Treatment of mediation, however, is frequently clouded by a sort of "everything's new" theology that we should interrogate. Indeed, as though the explosion of interest in media weren't enough to broadcast arguments for novelty all by itself, we may often find the term "new" appended. This attachment does not, however, have the effect of historicizing mediation by suggesting that there were once "old" media. Rather, the insistence on newness frequently reinforces the staggering freshness of it all (as critiqued by Sterne 2007). My problem with these theologies of newness is twofold. For starters, processes of mediation are very old indeed—at least as old as the printing press, and probably as old as language itself. As historian Jonathan Spence's *The Memory Palace of Mateo Ricci* unfolds, when the Jesuit and linguist traveled to China in the late 1500s, he brought with him what he thought of as the awe-inspiring virtual architecture known as a memory palace (Spence 1985). Perhaps the Chinese lack of enthusiasm for the Jesuit's "new" techniques reinforces that virtual architectures were neither utterly new nor much better than what the Chinese already had.

The second problem with work on mediation is that it tends towards what literary critic and theoretician Raymond Williams has called "technological determinism" (Williams and Williams 2003), by which he means an overemphasis on the "arrival" of new technologies in the transformation of social orders.[5] Such determinism takes the contemporaneous usage of a form of mediation—often the product of decades of trial and error—and imposes it retroactively on the moment at which that mode of mediation was ostensibly invented: the printing press transformed European society; the cell phone has dismantled conversation (Turkle 2011); and so on. This is not only shoddy history, since, as Williams shows in the case of television, it takes years for a medium's users to figure out the kinds of information it can be made to carry and the modes of circulation it calls forth. Such determinism also enacts a myopic materialism that overly empowers the device itself. It does so in a way that Karl Marx's theory of commodity fetishism sought to critique as the very ground of capitalisms (Marx [1867] 1977). Put somewhat differently, fetishizing what are suddenly perceived to be the speed and efficacy of the circulation of "messages," determinists grant altogether too much power to the "medium" (in language made famous by Canadian media theorist Marshall McLuhan). The point is not at all that the mode of mediation has no capacity to shape the interaction; indeed, this will be my topic in chapter 2. Rather, the point is to see how institutions and social practices interact with technology—in a way resembling Lévi-Strauss's bricolage (Lévi-Strauss 1966; see also Winner 1980)—producing novel needs and processes (see also Karaganis 2007).

Another problem with "mediation" is that focusing upon it sometimes compartmentalizes the specific nature of the processes of transformation (translation and transduction, mostly) that are taking place as the text moves from one semiotic mode to another. Invocations of media and mediation reference modes of conveyance that claim to have done away with the immediately preceding era's mode of conveyance. For this reason, when scholars, documentary filmmakers, musicians, or journalists talk about media, they are actually making a highly specific argument that their use of the term obviates. I will explore this obviation more in chapters 4 and 5, but in the meantime, what I mean by this is that the tablet computer critiques the laptop, which flouted the encumbrances of the desktop, which laughed at the shortcomings of the card-reading mainframe, and so on, backwards. Similarly, the cellular phone critiques the landline, which flouted the encumbrances of the telegram, which laughed at the shortcomings of the handwritten letter. You get the point, which is that the study of mediation needs to look backwards *while* it looks to the future. "And," to quote novelist Kurt Vonnegut ([1969] 2010), "so it goes."

Contemporary Capitalism

I have chosen the term "contemporary capitalism" to describe the moment in which we find ourselves because it seems like the simplest and the most honest. In previous scholarship I focused on neoliberalism—before a flapping of scolds erupted around uses of the term in anthropology (see, for instance, Ganti 2014). Such scolding sometimes results in a preference for "late capitalism." The terminological discussion about whether the capitalism we currently find ourselves writing not just *about* but *in* has ended up being predatory, digital, casino, financial, surveillance, millennial, late, early, or right on time would do best to focus on the central question: What distinguishes current capitalist practice from past forms? If we tune in to this, we can discern some important characteristics. In the 1980s and early 1990s, business owners and many policymakers sought to "free" markets that had once been controlled by bureaucrats, so the story went. This involved replacing government monitoring with corporate self-monitoring, removing regulations, and dismantling institutional oversight. Inspired by thinkers such as Milton Friedman and Friedrick von Hayek, an important pillar of this social and economic reform was the propagation of an ethos of "competition" across a wide variety of social domains (Harvey 2007). This, in turn, required expanding the notion that actors called "individuals" "rationally" chose to maximize their "resources" in a world of scarcity—a world not unlike that of Adam after having eaten from the Tree of Knowledge—except with tall buildings (Sahlins 1996; Smith [1776] 1976).

These "rational choice" theories were compellingly imposed upon domains not previously conceived of as "competitive" by economists, politicians, journalists, policymakers, entrepreneurs, and even consumers.[6] Some of the results of these changes include a dramatic rise of "informal" (or alternative) economies (Centeno and Portes 2006; Fernández-Kelly and Shefner 2002; Leyshon, Lee, and Williams 2003; Lobato and Thomas 2015; Palmade and Anayiotos 2005; Portes and Haller 2005; Soto 1989), an unequal distribution of income as well as space (Caldeira 2001, 2013), and an uneven "development" by trickle down (Cardoso 1989; Saad-Filho 2010; Knight 2011; Schuster 2012; Turner 1996). The combination of these activities has received critiques not unlike those carried out by Max Weber in *The Protestant Ethic and the Spirit of Capitalism* ([1905] 1958)—many of them within anthropology (Gershon 2017; Povinelli 2011; Stewart 1996; Weston 2008), though many outside of it as well (see, most prominently, Berlant 2011; Picketty 2014).

Current practitioners of the policies put forth by neoliberal economists such as Friedman and Hayek—including an array of NGOs propounding entrepreneurial "participation" and "training" for "human capital"—have turned to newer tasks. It is here that IP maximalists and pirates reside. Our current form of capitalism relies on a cluster of interrelated practices—among them, consumption (O'Dougherty 2002), leveraging of risk (Zaloom 2004), and associated dependency with respect to emerging markets (Cardoso 1989, 2001). Across these processes and locations, competition (and its companion, efficiency) remains a core value, and the extension of competition to a broader and broader array of practices serves to further naturalize property. Under these circumstances, the idea of piracy—analogically partaking of what it means to steal a material object on the open seas (Lessig 2004)—gets applied to a whole variety of domains, from the offhand exclamations of fashion mavens and football players to the jottings of software engineers. This rapid expansion of the notion of property to all aspects of social life works hand in hand with the increasing importance of highly individualized consumption to identity formation. Critiques of identity politics have already begun to dismantle the economistic roots of such forms of thinking about the relationship between structure and agency (Turner 2018; Turner 1993), but it bears reinforcing that who we are is frequently determined—for purposes of a joined finance and democracy—by what we buy or vote for. The confluence of finance and democratic politics does not go unnoticed by contemporary market researchers, with accurate prediction as the value orientation of mathematicians and computer scientists alike (Zuboff 2019).

Another important detail is that contemporary capitalists seek to apply "branding" to almost everything (Agha 2015; Nakassis 2013). The notion of the brand finds itself not only useful to manufacturers of clothing, but across scales, to high school students starting a lawn-care business, for example (see Gershon 2011). The idea of branding permeates thinking about self and society—often by providing a way to mediate between the two. An associated practice, consumption, then, rests on a widespread belief in the "magical," even redemptive, qualities of "legitimate" circulatory processes that attend to copyright, trademark, brand, and patent.[7] I call this *filtering* for the provenance of commodities using a carefully attuned sensory apparatus abetted by "circulatory legitimacy" and explore this in chapter 1 (see also Dent 2013).

Finally, contemporary capitalism is defined by an amplification of risk (Zaloom 2004). Within this ambit, an important aspect of the calculation of risk has gone undocumented—namely, the way in which the opportunities for circulation offered by the digital also enjoin dangers to the integrity of the self (Golub 2004). We are prone to hear the risks associated with contemporary capitalism in financial or even political ways, but we should understand the deep interpersonal risks that emerge communicatively—in the production and circulation of texts. It is no coincidence that "paying it forward," "going viral," and "blowing up" are ways of describing communicative vectors in an age of fears about terrorism and boundary-busting infections such as Zika, swine flu, or Ebola. Digital textuality offers payoffs and risks that must simultaneously be sought out and carefully managed—its "propagational vectors" closely monitored (Goodman 2010, xix).

Why Brazil?

Brazil is an important place to study these issues not merely because it is one of a handful of "emerging" economies whose centrality to the United States, Europe, and Japan is poorly understood. I have written elsewhere about Brazil's trumpeting of its propensity to mix traditions (local and other), thereby upending customary expectations in music, food, religion, and even science (see also Collins 2004; Dent 2016b; Mitchell 2013; Moehn 2012; Pardue 2004; Sansi-Roca 2007). Brazil dramatically enlivens the sorts of social tensions and reading practices that characterize the dialogue between piracy and property; this stretches back into Brazil's colonial entanglements with Portugal (Collins 2015). However, the appropriateness of analyzing digital textuality in Brazil extends into the present, with recent events channeling anxieties about the digital circulation of texts, their authorship, origins, and ends. In the early years of the twenty-first century, Brazil has undergone staggering changes while maintaining surprising (and often depressing) continuities (Caldeira 2013; Holston 2009, 2013). Under the leadership of its most popular democratically elected president ever, Lula (Luiz Inácio Lula da Silva of the Workers' Party and president from 2003 to 2011), the nation rapidly expanded consumer credit, manufacturing, and consumption; Lula joked that it took a socialist to bring capitalism to Brazil, a Brazilian friend repeatedly told me. Social class, often discussed in popular contexts in Brazil by way of the consumption of specific commodities (most often cars, refrigerators, and washing machines) began to shift. Many people bought these consumer items because they now had the money to do so and because the prices had dropped. In large part by way of an unevenly policed border with Paraguay, DVD players, computers, and for almost all Brazilians, cellular (increasingly "smart") phones became common household items (we will see precisely how in chapter 4). Big banks issued credit cards in large numbers (Lavinas 2017). In what some analysts read as a ratification of such changes, the nation won the right to host both the 2014 World Cup and the 2016 Summer Olympic Games—a confluence unknown in the history of international sport.

Protests that took place in the winter of 2013 (June–August) highlighted tremendous problems that remained despite the economic transitions (Dent and Pinheiro Machado 2013). Chief among the problems were the income disparities that Brazilians and foreigners alike love to cite as typical of this South American nation; tremendous divides between rich and poor, measured in terms of raw incomes and ratified by the intricacies of Brazil's legal codes, continued unabated. The explosive growth of consumer debt meant many citizens began to declare bankruptcy. Increased levels of car ownership made getting around cities intolerable; policies in which cars had to be kept off the road on certain days led some well-to-do families to buy a second car for the off days, making the traffic problem worse while aggravating class divides and climate change. Perhaps most importantly, the Lula government was rocked by a series of corruption scandals—the worst of which implicated top levels of the administration in a vote-buying scheme of immense proportions (referred to, in the press, as the Big Monthly Payment scandal, or *mensalão*). This ruckus was particularly disheartening for the left, which had hoped that a Workers' Party government might finally attain something called transparency; instead, shameful accountabilities were facilitated by digital traces left in a variety of formats—from emails and text messages to surreptitious voice recordings.

Economic qua political scandals continued after Lula's departure in 2011. Powerful conservative politicians banded together to oust Lula's successor, Dilma Rousseff, on charges that she had manipulated financial information about the Brazilian economy in order to get elected. The architects of what many referred to as this "coup" then fell to corruption investigations of their own, leaving a power vacuum and a broad distrust not only of politicians but of the very possibility of democratic politics in Brazil (Ansell 2018). A far-right candidate named Jair Bolsonaro slouched into Brasília (the federal capital), echoing the jump to the right that seemed to be taking place around the world—most prominently in Austria, the Philippines, Turkey, and the United States. Lula was convicted of accepting bribes in 2017, while many of his right-wing competitors' more serious deeds went unexamined.

The back-and-forth of these victories, losses, and scandals is well documented in Brazilian and foreign news media, often tinged with a North American and European perspective that ignores corruption in Washington, DC, Paris, or London. Frequently, such accounts underscore Northern predispositions about the hopelessness of achieving modernity in Brazil (Goldstein and Drybread 2018). What is important about these affairs for the purposes of understanding digital textuality is the way the anxieties they have channeled were mediated. For example, for the court cases, evidence was gathered from cellular phones, which provided a way to make and circulate recordings of malfeasance while simultaneously providing concrete evidence (extractable by way of digital forensics) for texted and nontexted interactions—the aforementioned inscripts. Digital textuality showed itself to have the potential to bring about accountability, chaos, and large audiences, all very quickly. In the case of Bolsonaro's election, it was greatly assisted by the use of a cell phone application known as WhatsApp, which allowed his team to target specific users, putting out what most scholars and journalists argue was false information about opponents and policies and heaping scorn on women, the poor, and minorities (Pinheiro Machado and Freixo 2019).[8] Anthropologist Leitícia Cesarino (2019) termed Bolsonaro's use of WhatsApp "digital populism" and accounted for his popularity by way of his capacity to create a political ecosystem that was separate from the mainstream media. Bolsonaro's success in doing so depended on his capacity to circulate radically decontextualized messages by "pushing" them to users who believed them to be backed by compelling evidence.

The evidentiary status of digital textuality also played out in spectacular irony through the case of politician, radio host, and economist Eduardo Cunha. Cunha (who bragged about presiding over the adoption of cellular phone technology in Rio de Janeiro in the early aughts as a politician and promoter, and whose tremendous cellular phone bills achieved notoriety in political circles) was dramatically brought down by an old cellular phone of his that was found in his home during a police search. The phone, it turned out, contained records of conversations detailing the use of public institutions for private gains, putting Cunha at the center of what eventually became known as the "Car Wash" scandal that implicated numerous bankers, politicians, and administrators at all levels of local and national government, as well as national and international corporate collaborators.

One need not look far to find further evidence of the tight relationship between redemption and perdition with respect to digital textuality in Brazil during the period that this book analyzes. The aforementioned 2013 protests—by those fed up with expensive World Cup preparations as basic infrastructure was being neglected—began by advocating for a reduction in public transportation fares. For some Brazilians, the notion that soccer might get criticized in any way was deplorable, and mainstream media coverage of the protests in Brazil and abroad suggested that this sacrilege (even if it was directed at the construction of stadiums rather than the sport itself) went hand in hand with "looting" and "rioting." A digital mode of media countercritique took shape in response to these indictments. A group called Media Ninja—a collective of cellular phone users that organized itself through Google documents—targeted mainstream media portrayals of protesters. Piecing together as many as twenty cellular phone videos provided by participants and bystanders, Media Ninja proved that two Molotov cocktail throwers, whom the police used as justification for beatings and arrests, had actually been planted in the crowd by the police. Media Ninja's guerilla theater clearly evidenced a crowd-based, highly digital form of accountability, developed along distinctly Brazilian lines, celebrating durable discourses of creativity and a glorious tendency to flout the "rules"—be they rules of decorum, media production, or individual authorship (Collins 2015). But perhaps more significantly, what Media Ninja's interventions suggested was that much public activity was being recorded somehow, somewhere, using digital means, and in ways that could be broadly disseminated (Otis 2015). All one had to do was piece things together and then use the result to speak truth to power.[9]

Digital textuality, however, was not always celebrated in a Brazilian context. During the period this book examines, criminal gangs came to prominence, intent on carrying out selected state functions (running prisons) while controlling portions of the economy deemed illegal (such as drugs and prostitution). One prominent case is instructive. In the state of São Paulo, a group of prison inmates named the First Capital Command (PCC) formed in the early 1990s around the intent to avenge a police massacre of inmates at the horrendous Carandiru prison in 1992 (Biondi 2016; Willis 2015). In the early aughts, the organization grew tremendously in size and scope, coordinating the sale of drugs inside and outside the prison as well as reprisals against police, judges, and other public officials for enforcement activities carried out against gang members. Brazil's news media seemed to enjoy dwelling on how some of the organizing for these activities was done by gang members, in prison, using smuggled cellular phones (see chapter 5).

Public anxieties about a perceived deterioration in public safety led to an outpouring of public culture about gangs—most prominently the two Brazilian-made *Elite Squad* blockbusters. In these films, and in responses to them, Brazil seemed to be asking itself about the differences between licit and illicit politics, policing, and policy. But more significantly for our purposes, the boundary-transcendence normally touted as a liberating aspect of the cellular phone (in which workers can work "from anywhere") became a curse, allowing gang members to coordinate assassinations from prison and thus transcend the prison's walls. In the opening scene of the second *Elite Squad* movie (*Elite Squad: The Enemy Within,* the 2010 sequel to the tremendously popular 2007 film), gang members use cell phones to organize a war against one another, taking over their prison and then requiring that a sociologist be flown in to negotiate between the factions. The action takes place in real time, over the phone—encapsulating the tensions between digital textuality as a brake on wrongdoing and an incentive for criminality. I will explore the way Brazilian digital publics are elucidated by an understanding of piracy and IP in chapters 4 and 5.

Across these moments, Brazil was the focus of international policy discussions centered around IP. During the period in which my research was carried out, an important treaty penned by the World Trade Organization (WTO) called TRIPS (trade-related aspects of intellectual property rights) sought to globalize the definition and policing of IP—and it was instituted in Brazil with some "success," where success was defined as calming foreign investors that their IP would be protected should they sink money, time, and technology into the nation (Kunisawa 2015).[10] However, from a corporate standpoint, all was still not well in Brazil. TRIPS itself included important "flexibilities" for developing countries, intended in large part to allow them to produce crucial medicines that would support the handling of, for instance, HIV. Other flexibilities were intended to allow emerging economies to make cheaper use of unaffordable technologies deemed crucial to development (Biehl 2006; Petryna, Lakoff, and Kleinman 2006). Many countries failed to make use of these flexibilities due to "TRIPS-plus" pressures applied by developed countries—chief among them, the Special 301 process whereby the United States publicly shamed targeted governments for violations of US IP as a prelude to imposing economically damaging sanctions. Ironically, the USTR's policies involved plagiarizing briefs submitted by large corporations and their representatives (Dent 2013).

In any case, Brazil, often on the Special 301 Watch List, was one of the countries that was able to make use of TRIPS flexibilities by taking advantage of compulsory licensing to manufacture medicines needed to combat HIV (Schwartz 2014). Their success became an international story that embarrassed the US pharmaceutical industry. In part due to this success and in part due to a perception among developed nations that emerging economies such as Brazil's were flouting IP in a whole variety of ways, developed countries—led by the trade associations of big pharma, entertainment, and software—poured their energy into TRIPS-plus treaties. As I began to devote my attention to digital media "piracy" full time, in 2008, a large international trade treaty called the Anti-Counterfeiting Trade Agreement (ACTA) looked as though it might be ratified by a number of countries with large budgets and diverse trading partners (mostly countries dubbed "First World" by Brazilians). This secretively negotiated treaty, which had only begun to appear in the media due to leaks, attempted to establish pancultural and panhistorical definitions for piracy and counterfeiting—exactly the sort of the thing the IP maximalists wanted (Dent 2010).

One of the treaty's intentions was to stop the sorts of processes that were allowing pirated goods to move across borders, processes such as smuggling, bribery, and theft but also illicit importation. If the definition of illegality was universal, and not locally negotiated, then surely policing would be easier. I should trace out this logic just a touch further. Policing would be easier because there would be no localized differences of opinion over what constituted illegality. Law enforcement would not have to discuss niceties because definitions would be clear. This new ease of policing would, in turn, mean that producers and consumers of pirated goods would not bother trying to distribute their wares. Put more abstractly, proponents of contemporary capitalism were seeking coherence by controlling the surfeits of digital textuality.

Due to inadequate support, ACTA was not ratified, but as I was writing this book another international treaty, the Trans Pacific Partnership (TPP), made the rounds with what many of its critics and proponents believed were even harsher penalties for pirates. Withdrawal of US support sank the treaty in 2017. But whatever happens to particular agreements, the fact remains that this book emerges from a desire to grapple with internationalizing, panhistorical, and pancultural approaches to piracy and counterfeiting. Of course, there have been globalized wars fought against pirates before, as we will come to see (Dawdy 2011). And yet, if we compare the scale and coordination of contemporary policing efforts for, say, printing or cassettes to that which currently exists, contemporary efforts appear unprecedented; more people are involved in more highly coordinated operations, with more effort to bring varied governments into the mix. And those who claim that the war on piracy is over are being premature. It is true that, when I poll students in my classes (or look at international numbers), the piracy of physical CDs and DVDs appears to be down from where it was between 1998 and 2008. Many are streaming their music, legally, for example. However, the anxieties over the licit nature of digital texts continues in other forms that I will explore in this book's closing chapters.

The Gringo Effect: Piracy's Intimacies

In discussing the camelódromo, above, I spoke about the way in which it took some time for me to become accustomed to the provenance of goods and services offered there. It also took me some time to figure out how Brazilian policing worked. Throughout the research for this project, I was identified as a North American anthropologist by my interlocutors, and by myself. When my interlocutors would figure out within a few minutes that my accent was not Brazilian, they usually guessed I was European. When participants discovered that I was "American," they were often surprised at my fluency, as they tend to expect Americans to be heavily accented, and also at my interest in Brazil. I often shared the information about what I was up to long before they made this discovery.

When I was writing about Brazilian country music for my last book, I found that what anthropologist Michael Herzfeld calls "cultural intimacy" was germane to many of my interactions (Herzfeld 1996; see also Matory 2004). With this concept, Herzfeld indexes material that is taken to be highly localized and, simultaneously, embarrassing; since he works in Greece, his examples were sheep stealing, plate breaking, and table dancing—behaviors that are sometimes taken to be eminently Greek, but that Greeks revile in conversations with foreigners (and even among themselves). Material that is culturally intimate is usually complicated by the fact that there is a grain of truth to it. In the case of my earlier research, for example, I would find that interlocutors would rant about the absurdities of *música sertaneja*, but after I had gotten to know them better, they would admit their affection for it or I would find records of the genre in their CD collections (or on phone playlists).

Intimacy is something that most anthropologists will encounter in doing long-term, immersive research, and the present study was no exception. I found that being a tall, white gringo—the term is less disparaging in Brazil than it is in Mexico, though it still largely indexes someone from North America (even those born in Canada, as in my case) or Europe—meant that aspects of my conversations were amplified. By this I simply mean that my interlocutors railed slightly more forcefully against the absurdities of the pricing of "legitimate" goods, or were prone to fits of anger about how "all Brazilians are pirates." As we will come to see in the coming chapters, particularly chapter 2, my interlocutors were particularly critical of Brazil's propensity to forget its own history. This troubled them in the context of digital textuality's radical decontextualizing—where texts circulate "promiscuously" without much regard for the device on which they are played and without necessarily paying attention to the intentions of an originator (Sterne 2006). One long-time friend felt that the digital age had necessitated an NGO that would go door to door simply informing Brazilians of their history. He never ended up creating that NGO. Furthermore, in terms of Brazil's desire to orient itself to international developmentalism in the context of TRIPS and the US Special 301 process, my North American identity led directors of antipiracy NGOs to assume I was on "their side." When they discovered that my perspectives on piracy undermined the very notion of "sides," they sometimes became angry, and in one case, refused further contact after a very productive three-year conversation. In the context of my "gringoness," then, the localized effects of digital textuality created particular challenges and opportunities. Throughout the text, I have attempted to highlight these moments so that I might more fully account for the cross-cultural dialogue my research involved. In this way, I have tried to keep the gringo effect out of a confessional mode, and in a culturally analytical one.

How I Came to Write This Book

I have already described how I came to hang out at the camelódromo, seeking to understand the number of people who were actually listening to Brazilian country music. In these early days of CD piracy (1998, to be precise), the stall owners didn't mind my nosing around and asking questions. Their attitudes changed, quite quickly, however, in the space of about a year. During that year, I noticed an increase in the number of antipiracy posters, billboards, and television ads. What looked to be a paradox was forming. Just at the moment when Billboard and other music aggregators were ignoring the sales of pirated music in their popularity ratings, a group of internationally funded NGOs was promulgating fears of piracy and actively gathering "data" on the ways in which sales of pirated goods were hurting licit trades. This was all taking place coincident with the institution of TRIPS, negotiations over ACTA, the increasing use of Brazil's permeable border with Paraguay as a way to bring low-cost Chinese imports into the country (chapter 3), and the selling off of the nationalized phone company in preparation for Brazil's cellular phone boom (chapter 4). In this way, the unfolding of the chapters in this book maps onto a narrative ark beginning back in the late 1990s, and stretching into the present.

To provide a sequential map of the book: Chapter 1 further explores what I mean by digital textuality by elaborating on the notion of intertextual gaps. I accomplish this by analyzing the way positions shift on piracy and IP between the informal market in Campinas and a particular NGO's attempt to restore the "magic" of consumption through what I call *circulatory legitimacy.* It is here that I will begin to further question simple divides between the digital-virtual and the real, since circulatory legitimacy requires sensory training (so that consumption may be "correctly" embodied). Chapter 2 explores the materiality of the digital through analysis of the policing of informal markets. Here, I will examine the ways in which police training regimes map onto local ideologies of "dirty" and "promiscuous" to indict digital textuality's incitements to forget—deemed particularly problematic in Brazil (see Gell 1996). Chapter 3 scrutinizes the border with Paraguay and the way in which its permeability both facilitates digital products entering Brazil cheaply *and* represents the spatial and temporal slipperiness of that most digital of spaces: the Internet. Chapter 4 seeks to understand the role of cellularity in digital textuality, unpacking the ways in which cellularity's modes of public address bring about anxieties with respect to lurking as well as fantasies of hypermobility. Chapter 5 continues to consider cellularity, but here I address

Brazilian anxieties about cellular phone "cloning" and how those map onto concerns about the (in)efficacy of the state. The book's conclusion considers Brazil's approach to digital textuality in a broader frame, asking what it means when "the Indians won't jump."

1 "MAGICAL" CONSUMPTION AND THE VIOLENCE OF INFORMALITY

BULL RIDER DANIEL[1] had heard only a few songs by country music duo César Menotti & Fabiano when he decided to buy a "pirated" copy of their first album at a bus station kiosk in the interior town of São José do Rio Preto in 2004. It was a kiosk much like those at the camelódromo in Campinas, though considerably smaller, and Daniel paid just two reais (about one US dollar, at the time).[2] His reason for consuming piracy was simple. He wasn't sure he would like the entire album, and the "official" price was high. A few songs were good, sure—he'd heard them on the radio. But he had bought plenty of records based on hearing one good song on the radio and had ended up angry that he'd wasted his money when the rest of the songs turned out to be bad.

When he put César Menotti & Fabiano into his truck stereo and listened to them during his long trips to buy livestock or to coach young bull riders, he ended up loving every track. Confirming his own impressions of just how authentic the duo was, song after song from the album went on to become a hit on the radio. The duo's insistence on using traditional country instruments in live shows drove home Daniel's liking for the group and its CD.

When Daniel decided to give the disk to a friend as a present, instead of repeating his pirated purchase, he spent twenty reais on an official copy bought at the licit shopping mall. He wanted to give something "of good quality," and giving an illegal copy as a present was, he reported, inappropriate. When I pushed him on what might be inappropriate about it, he explained that the unlabeled pirated CD, with its copied cover, would look "disposable" to the gift receiver; she would be able to see and feel the difference between the two—even if, given the reliability of digital reproduction, she would not be able to actually hear that difference.

Most consumers in Brazil and elsewhere navigate their lives such that piracy is inevitable in some places, but unacceptable in others. Daniel's first purchase suggested that it was alright to pirate for himself when he wasn't sure of the overall quality of the product. He described a natural distrust of most commodities in this day and age, musical or otherwise, which so often claimed to be more than they turned out to be. When Daniel did know that the prospective purchase lived up to the licit sale price, and when he wanted the object to be a gift for someone else, however, the CD's provenance suddenly mattered. Rewarding whichever seller had produced the CD in the most efficient way (i.e. most inexpensively) no longer applied, which meant that he no longer found piracy acceptable.

This incident, and many others throughout my fieldwork in Brazil, made me realize how participant roles in consumer economies shift—sometimes accepting piracy, and at other times rejecting it. This multiplicity seemed to be the case for everyone I talked to in the context of a national economy where informal markets offer goods of varying type and origin, whereas formalized shopping malls strive for goods with clear provenance. My interlocutors frequently referred to piracy as simultaneously central to national character and at the same time embarrassing. The fact that I was a gringo, albeit with fluent Portuguese, sometimes augmented this back-and-forth. Once they got to know me well, even those who primarily occupied either a pro- or an antipiracy position stepped out of character to offer the opposite argument once in a while. For example, one worker at an antipiracy nongovernmental organization (NGO) lauded pirates as Brazilian geniuses in their capacity to provide large numbers of units cheaply and quickly. On the other side of the coin, purveyors of copied CDs would sometimes fret to me over the impurity of their "Third World" occupation—flowing from the fact that the majority of the population could not afford the "real thing." Whatever the case, within the context of contemporary capitalism at the end of the twentieth century and into the twenty-first, piracy seemed both problematic and inevitable, both central to Brazilian capitalism and proof that Brazil resided at capitalism's periphery. Consumers were caught in a web of competing moral, legal, and economic claims.

As a way to understand this experience of feeling caught, this chapter analyzes the space between Daniel's two texts: the two CDs he purchased—one pirated and the other legitimate. "Intertextuality" provides a way of analyzing the multiple locations of digital textuality. Digital textuality relies on subject positions (consumers) learning to evaluate texts of various sorts for their "circulatory legitimacy"—a measure of a text's proximity to, or distance from, a "rights holder." Allow me to explain these terms in detail.

Intertextuality: Policing Only Certain "Gaps"

Much of the contemporary discussion of the relationship between piracy and intellectual property is freighted by normative assumptions—where piracy leads to either damnation or redemption. But it is more accurate to understand piracy as an interruption in a set of expectations for how a text will and should circulate. Beginning with a broad definition of what constitutes a text (a spell or a bell, a car or a star), the example of a popular song (a hypothetical one that might play on the radio or the Internet with some regularity) illustrates the nature of that interruption. As I trace this example, please notice that anxieties about copying emerge in several intertextual gaps. Significantly, only certain gaps become contentious in the context of discussions of piracy. I will elaborate more on this in a moment.

A contemporary pop song most often begins its existence as an idea that a songwriter assembles. We'll call this T1. This earliest version of the song, which may take the form of the union of notes on a piece of paper with short recordings, eventually coalesces into a full-fledged draft, T2. This version may get worked out in practices with a series of other musicians, creating T3. Eventually, after some live performance of the song, it may get recorded in a studio, creating T4. T4 will eventually be sent for "mastering," a process that prepares the song for play in a diversity of spaces (cars, cellular phone speakers, and movie theaters, perhaps) by maximizing its volume and making the balance of its various layers more precise. T5 will then be placed on streaming services such as Spotify or iTunes, where it can be purchased by users, or it may be "pressed" to CD or vinyl that may then, in turn, be purchased. In all of these cases, to get to T5, the user, or listener, pays for her version of the text. Sometimes this purchase involves a physical object (in the form of a CD or vinyl LP). Sometimes it is simply a version of a file on a device such as a smartphone or laptop.

So far, so good. One value of such an approach to tracking the development of a song is that we can analyze what takes place between versions of the text, as it moves from place to place. This process-oriented approach seeks to keep power relations in view, as well as forms of social identification and institutional affiliations (Briggs and Bauman 1992). To demonstrate, what happens between T1 and T2 is that the songwriter fleshes out the initially fragmented idea, turning it into a relatively coherent idea, and in so doing, claiming a particular orientation as the originator of that text. Between T2 and T3, others get involved—a band, for instance, or perhaps producers; there may well be more recordings taking place in this intertextual gap, and aspects of the authorship of the song may or may not be parsed out. It is at this point that the pop star for whom the song was written may get involved. Between T3 and the next version of the song, a recording studio enters, with an engineer (in charge of the recording equipment) and a producer (charged with aesthetic choices, such as instrumentation and playing styles). Between T4 and T5, a mastering engineer enters the picture, with a whole new set of equipment. Customarily, the mastering engineer does not receive any rights to the song, but is paid for her labor. And at T5, a record company distributes the text through varied means—CDs, radio, television, vinyl, and the major music streaming services.

This is a radical simplification of the contemporary production of a "hit" (see Seabrook 2016 for more details). There may well be more, or fewer, versions of a song text as it progresses from a notion to a fully realized song. Also, in a traditional popular music model, a record company may get involved before T5 by paying for earlier stages—hiring songwriters to fashion songs, paying for studio time, hiring musicians to help mold an idea, and so forth. We can also notice that at the earliest phases of this process, copyright protections certainly apply; should one of the band members attempt to steal the primary songwriter's idea, a lawsuit might well occur in which that primary songwriter's handwritten notes or early recordings might be used as evidence. As anthropologist and legal scholar Rosemary Coombe has argued, "no system of authentication is ever free from alterity and difference" (1998, 198). Unauthorized use is certainly possible at all phases of this production. For the purposes of understanding the relationship between piracy and IP, however, the attention of policymakers and enforcement is focused almost entirely on what happens between T4 and T5. It is in this intertextual gap that IP maximalist expectations for reproduction get undermined. Previous steps become exponentially less important. Record companies, and sometimes artists as well, want any and all possible forms of T5 to be fully paid for, with that money going back to the record company to distribute as it wishes (and where some percentage returns to the artists). In this sense, IP involves the circulator of the song taking concrete steps to ensure that that right price is paid and that that money goes where they want it to go. This stage of purchase is where piracy interrupts that set of expectations. The pirate seeks not to pay the recording company, either making the text available for free or charging a reduced price.

What an intertextual understanding of piracy reveals is that IP and piracy are opposed strategies for managing a particular gap between one version of a text and another—as well as the incumbent finances and morals associated with that gap. A focus on IP by and large elides other gaps where unauthorized use might occur. In more detail, IP and its policing concern the preservation of a relation with rights holders, while piracy seeks to violate that relation. Notice the institutional and circulatory specificity of the situation. It is worth spelling this out, since there are other paradigms in which acquiring a song for free might not be called piracy—situations in which, say, the recorded text might be distributed for free as promotional material to get people to buy tickets for future live performances. Along these lines, Brazilian media scholars Ronaldo Lemos and Oona Castro (2008) document the way *technobrega* (which roughly translates as technotacky) CDs are given away in Northern Brazil as enticements to buy tickets for an evening party where the artist will then play. Notice, then, that the focus by IP maximalists on the gap between T4 and T5 shows that contemporary anxieties about piracy revolve around a particular aspect of digital textuality—the way in which large numbers of high-fidelity reproductions can me made quickly. In other words, digital textuality, in increasing the speed with which a text might circulate and extending the distance it might travel, creates anxieties for rights holders (in the case of our example, record companies) who work hard to promulgate the notion of "circulatory legitimacy" as a way to protect this gap. Getting this gap right, from the perspective of IP maximalists, requires a sensory recalibration in which consumers must be taught to sense circulatory legitimacy. Furthermore, the failure of Brazilians with respect to this now essential apparatus becomes shame inducing and a way to attempt to align the nation more closely with policy interventions such as TRIPS.

Digital Textuality

All of this begs an important question. Possibilities for piracy certainly existed between T4 and T5 in an age of analogue cassettes (Manuel 1993). Indeed, large numbers of pirated cassettes still circulated in the early years of my study, before CDs had entirely replaced them (circa 1998). We could go even further back, in that media piracy existed in the age of the printing press (Darnton 2003; Johns 2010).[3] So what explains the heightened anxieties about piracy in an age of digital textuality, along with the increased scale of policing? One quick answer, returning to cassettes, is that the speed and fidelity of digital reproduction are quite different from the analogue forms that preceded them. Cassettes took considerably longer to reproduce, and the resultant sound was diminished when compared with the originals. You knew you were listening to a copy, once upon a time creating a pirate aesthetic (as in Larkin 2008).[4] However, despite the fact that speed and fidelity are indeed important aspects of digital textuality, we must go deeper than this, and consider not only the devices upon which digital textuality depends but also the broader social practices that are involved in its practice (see Williams and Williams 2003).

As I am about to show, digital textuality applies broadly, working its way into how we conceive of communicative processes writ large—working its way even into our understanding of face-to-face conversations. In this sense, digital textuality operates like an episteme (Foucault 1971), an ethos (Weber 1958), and an aesthetic (at least in the sense of the term adumbrated by Adorno 1989). On the simplest level, by this I mean that "digital textuality" refers to more than just films and music. In the introduction, anxieties surrounding the illicit reproduction of sunglasses, jeans, perfumes, and running shoes appeared in the same group as those surrounding films and music; we are about to hear more of this. Another way of framing this encompassment is that digital modes of circulation saturate contemporary consumption in all its forms (Barney, et al. 2016).

Along these lines, the simplest way to conceive of the digital is as a kind of "on" or "off" switch—a zero or a one. Indeed, these zeros and ones make up the binary code involved in the storage and reconstitution of most contemporary information (Lessig 1999). Binaries operate in other domains as well—phonology, for example, where a given phoneme can be either nasalized or unnasalized, voiced or unvoiced; or even the pre-Columbian system of string notation used by the Inka (Urton 2003). Digital textuality, however, applies binary decomposition to an extremely wide array of textual genres and object types, imbricating itself in such a broad range of social life as to appear simultaneously banal and ingenious (Coleman 2010). Despite the fact that consumers of digital texts—even texts that are only designed, manufactured, priced, shipped, and sold by digital means such as food and clothing—do not come into direct contact with binary code, the experience of digital textuality relies upon the knowledge that contemporary texts are decomposed into much smaller units (numbers) and then recomposed for the purposes of manufacture and consumption. This making small and then large is most easily captured by way of the metaphor of the "sample," which refers to a process whereby tiny pieces of information are grabbed from a larger "signal," stored, and then reconstituted—sometimes as an ultraclose approximation of the original and other times in a rather different configuration (Katz 2004). For example, 44,100 kHz expresses the fact that 44,100 samples per second are being drawn from a given signal: the "sound quality" of a CD is expressed using such a number, and since this is a relatively large number of samples, CDs are deemed to be a "high-fidelity" medium (McCartney 2016; Schafer 1993). This underlying knowledge unites a very wide variety of text types that might be less easily ascertainable as "digital," such as agriculture (Aoki 2008), fashion (Thomas 2016), house keys (Greenfield 2017), and currencies (Maurer, Rea, and Nelms 2013), but that are, nonetheless transformed by digital textuality. All of this reinforces myriad claims from journalists, scholars, and artists of various types that we are living in an age of "remix" culture. The way in which knowledge can be compressed and moved briskly facilitates a "cut and paste" approach to the construction of future texts (in his book *Remix* [2009], Lessig also calls this "read/write" culture, which he opposes to "read-only" culture).

None of this, however, is sufficient for explaining the distinctiveness of digital textuality, in part because these kinds of arguments are frequently technologically deterministic (explaining social change by recourse to technology; once again, recall Williams and Williams 2003). We must go, yet, deeper. Another of digital textuality's primary properties revolves around its "promiscuity." In his analysis of the MP3 as a file format that seeks to compact texts in ways that a hypothetical listener's ears will not notice, Jonathan Sterne notes that the makers of this file format wanted it to be usable on as large an array of devices as possible (Larkin 2014; Sterne 2006; Thomas 1991).[5] The designers of the MP3—this digital tool for compressing musical texts so they could travel faster and further and be amassed more copiously—sought as many sources of playability as possible. It is this promiscuity of digital textuality (in the sense advanced by Gell in the opening epigraph of this book) that also facilitates its encompassment—the way in which its designers seek to create devices that will shape as much of our communicative activity as possible. We will see this in detail in chapter 4. In his broad analysis of the role of mediation in the context of modernity, Friedrich Kittler indexes this promiscuity with a hint of doom:

> And once optical fiber networks turn formerly distinct data flows into a standardized series of digitized numbers, any medium can be translated into any other. . . . Modulation, transformation, synchronization; delay, storage, transposition; scrambling, scanning, mapping total media link on a digital base will erase the very concept of medium. Instead of wiring people and technologies, absolute knowledge will run as an endless loop. (Kittler 1999, 2)

In his inimitably impressionistic provocativeness—Kittler has perfectly captured an anxiety about digital textuality: that it will erase mediation altogether.

This negative fantasy is overblown. In fact, digital textuality involves something more complex. Its users are simultaneously afraid of the unification of all mediation, at the same time that its compression and reconstitution root their practices in contemporary sensory matrices (Connor 2001). Another way of saying this is that fundamental aspects of digital textuality—compression formats for visual and sound files, for instance—are, as Sterne has also argued, designed with human perceptive faculties in mind (Sterne 2006). The MP3 file format anticipates what the listeners will pay attention to and what they will ignore. The algorithm-dependent format (more on this in a moment) then reduces the complexity of the file according to what will *not* be paid attention to. It is this aspect of compression formats that leads Sterne to argue that it is not a listener that plays an MP3, but the MP3 that plays the listener. In this way, digital textuality is profoundly rooted in the way contemporary listeners choose to apprehend texts, not only in semiotic ways, but in simultaneously material and embodied ones as well (Kuipers and Bell 2018). Digital textuality is, as media theorist Mark Poster has argued with respect to human-machine interfaces, a deeply interactive process, whereby meaning is co-constituted (Poster 2006). And this, too, must be localized. As the work of both Ravi Sundaram (on "pirate modernities" in India; 2010) and Anita Chan (on "networking the nation" in Peru; 2014) reveals, digital textuality is far from pancultural and panhistorical. Digital circulation is a dialogic process, in which globalizing ideologies pull some localized practices to the fore while pushing others into the background (Tsing 2011).

Digital textuality has a number of other entailments that move beyond technological determinism and place it into a historical context. When programmers, movie viewers, phone users, journalists, and many others use the term "digital," they are pointing to a particular field of institutions, actors, objects, and practices (Bourdieu 1993; Dent 2009). This field includes businesses, governmental agencies, NGOs, and CEOs—the most obvious corporate entities, as of this writing, comprising the FAANG companies: Facebook, Apple, Amazon, Netflix, and Google. (In Europe, the term is often GAFA, and excludes Netflix.) The precise companies we include in such a digital power structure will no doubt shift in the coming years, though corporate control of important aspects of digital textuality will likely remain without entirely monopolizing the space—thanks in part to the interplay between IP maximalists and pirates. Many spaces in this field are decidedly material, such as mainframes that must be cooled and powered, high-capacity microprocessors for moving through data briskly, or sizable devices for the storage of code—be they hard drives or even smaller means.

Digital textuality refers to a particular aspect of what we might call the publicness of texts, by which I mean the way a text gathers a kind of community by virtue of addressing interlocutors. As literary theoretician Michael Warner has argued in his work on the centrality of publics to modernity, contemporary texts are simultaneously outward facing—in that large numbers of people may be addressed by them—and deeply private—in terms of the specificity of experience that the text may index (Warner 2002). This is a fancy way of saying that that song playing on the radio can be simultaneously "your song" and "everyone else's song" at precisely the same time. We imagine the circulation of these close-distant texts (Mazzarella 2014) using metaphors from associated circulatory process (as in Kelty 2008; see also Feld 1996 on reverberation). It is no coincidence that, for example, a broadly circulating video clip should be referred to as having "gone viral." With respect to its circulatory vectors, our mainstream media frames disease, success, "memes," and terrorism in nearly identical ways—in terms of their potential to "spread" from person to person, reader to reader, listener to listener, viewer to viewer, as captured by a branch of quasi-evolutionary cultural transference theory qua corporate practice called "memetics" (see Goodman 2010).

But there's more, because, digital textuality multiplies this attribute of the modern publicness of texts through automation. Algorithms beyond our control—beyond even our knowledge because they are kept secret *as* IP—replicate "content" in unexpected ways, scuppering financial markets, bringing unanticipated blog posts to the top of searches, and making countless unexpected copies of private files (Besteman and Gusterson 2019). The automated substrate of much digital textuality means that its products frequently contain embedded subroutines that perform tasks such as gathering information, anticipating preferences, maintaining continuity, and calculating probable actions. Digital textuality makes use of anticipatory equations, predicting listening and viewing habits in order to compress large pieces of information—as in the aforementioned MP3s. In more concrete terms, roboprocesses suggest what books you should buy next, trace your voting behavior, or anticipate your parking habits (see, for example, Kockleman 2017; Striphas 2015).

These combined attributes mean that digital texts risk a more complete stripping from their contextual surroundings than previous text types—a concept critical theorist Walter Benjamin attempted to capture by way of "aura" in an age before digital reproduction (Benjamin 1968a). This removal of something from its originary context of circulation produces considerable anxiety for users of digital textuality (recall—pretty much all of us these days; see Delueze and Guattari 2004 for a suggestive framing of "anxiety"). Digital textuality—and the political, economic, and social tasks carried out through and by means of the digital—frequently strips a great deal of the originary circulation away. To use literary philosopher Roman Ingarden's phrase, digital textuality ramps up the "incompleteness" of a text—and assures that the concretization of an "original" can be profoundly malleable (Ingarden 1973). Digital textuality often assures that the text you lay down is potentially recruitable to a whole series of projects—some of them welcomed by you as that text's creator, others distinctly unwelcome. For example, that video of you singing goes viral and can make you a star (hello Justin Bieber) or it can render you a global laughing stock (I'll leave the innocent unnamed, though prominent examples are not difficult to find; once again, see the critique of Feld 1996). In this context, the form in which texts may circulate and the platforms through which they may circulate become mutually dependent. It therefore makes perfect sense both that subjects seek to circulate texts as widely possible and that they should feel nervous about where those texts might end up and what work they might do when they arrive.

With digital textuality, the stripping away of context together with the scale of circulation means that those in a given public become knowable by way of adulation or malevolence. Intertextual gaps under digital textuality contain worshippers and murderers. Digital publics are experienced by myriad participants as being replete with potential fans and lurkers—in sum, those who would seek to remediate the text again (and again) in a way that could either elevate us or do us permanent harm. Indeed, the contemporary use of the term "stalker" shows how fans and lurkers often bleed into one another, underscoring the way worship mixes with threat in a mode that often gets colloquially described as creepy by users of social media. This mixture profoundly shapes digital publics in particular. In this sense, philosopher Bernard Stiegler's understanding of the digital as a pharmakon applies—as something that is "both a poison and remedy, a benefit and a problem, a promise of emancipation as well as a form of subjection" (quoted in Barney, et al. 2016, and prefigured in an epigraph). In part because of the portability of the devices we use to circulate our thoughts and statements (frequently, these days, cellular phones), digital textuality also involves the recruitment of an increasingly large portion of what might once have been thought of as private to openly public spaces and purposes. This leads to the mutual dependence of celebrations of convenience and plangent premonitions of doom (such as Zuboff 2019).

Circulatory Legitimacy

Armed with this understanding of digital textuality and the role that intertextual gaps play in processes of circulation, we can return to one of the central projects of IP maximalism—training consumers to filter the qualia of commodities (their phenomenally materialized attributes) for circulatory legitimacy (on qualia, see Harkness 2015). One of the challenges for IP maximalism is that it is often not immediately apparent to consumers precisely how adherence to circulatory legitimacy improves their act of consumption. This is especially true with music, film, videogames, and software. Pirated music and movies can almost always be experienced precisely like their authorized counterparts. Around the world, the camcorder pirated film is becoming increasingly uncommon, and "bootleg" recordings of live music are vanishingly rare, too. Instead, most media piracy involves copies of digital files with pristine video and audio (see chapter 2). How, then, do IP maximalists attempt to turn circulatory legitimacy into a consumer-oriented ethos under such circumstances, particularly when consumers may buy identical quality for less money? When consumers look to price as a way to distinguish between two products that are, in important ways, similar (if not identical), how can potential sellers impress upon their customers the importance of the rights holder? And more broadly, what can we learn about subject formation under contemporary capitalism by the competing legal, economic, and political contexts of digital textuality?

In order to answer these questions, I focus on two sites where the dialogically related subject positions that digital textuality gives rise to begin to emerge clearly: IP maximalist versus pirate. The first site reveals an argument for the sanctity of legitimately circulated products within the context of individuated consumption. Here, piracy constantly threatens what I call "circulatory legitimacy" and, consequently, identity formation itself. This site embodies an ad campaign against the purchase of what are called "pirated products," a deliberately diverse group of goods intended to blur distinctions between the copyrights, brands, patents, and trademarks meant to "protect" them. The campaign thus may be seen as part of a kind of semantic warfare that seeks to apply the term "pirated" to as broad a range of goods and services as possible, even to those goods and services that might, in the past, have been labeled "generic" (such as medicines) or simply "aftermarket" (in the case of auto parts). We should notice two things about this concatenation—first, that it blurs types of IP usually conceived of as distinct (trademarks and copyrights, for example). Second, the union of these various kinds of texts under a banner of "circulatory legitimacy" indexes the way digital textuality unites a broad array of textual forms and incumbent modes of production: food, fashion, and phones all become understandable as digital. In supplementary interviews with lawyers, economists, public relations consultants, retired police officers, advertising executives, and lobbyists, piracy's minions are portrayed as exploiting brand loyalty, which in turn is thought to muddy the capacity of a commodity to make its purchaser feel whole (magically). Piracy is said to put the individual consumer and, more generally, society at risk by supporting, say, drug and gun smugglers, pimps, and racketeers.

In this chapter's second site, piracy is understood as a way to be economically "competitive." Workers in this ethnographic example—a street market—include: those who have recently lost manufacturing jobs in the formal business sector; small business owners who have grown weary of restrictive state regulations governing licit businesses; church and community organizers supplementing their salaries; and those who might view themselves as students headed toward more formal careers in education, law, or even medicine, but who have so far been unable to enter university—mostly due to cost. Sellers and buyers at this second site celebrate their "informal" occupations as antidotes to Brazilian underemployment and corporate price gouging. Circulatory illegitimacy nonetheless hovers, since disagreements over how to formalize the market can lead to violence, and sometimes murder.

Despite the fact that these two sites would seem to be philosophical and practical opposites with regards to piracy, we will observe the ways that social actors go back and forth between various subject positions. Each site has absorbed the critique of the other, responding to contradictory injunctions to buy cheaply while preserving the exclusivity of IP.

Losing (and Regaining) Magic

Brazil, the land of mixture qua hypersexuality (Edmonds 2010; Goldstein 1999; Kulick 1998; Matory 2004; Parker 2009), is a veritable minefield of unclear categories, IP maximalists informed me repeatedly. The redemptive "magic" of legitimately circulated goods in the country is continually beset by thieves, with ostensibly disastrous consequences for the Brazilian consumer and hence, the story goes, for society writ large. We clearly see this sort of argument on the set of an ad campaign sponsored by Brazil's media meganetwork *O Globo,* and an NGO that I will call the National Antipiracy and Illegality Forum (NAIF).[6]

NAIF is one of several antipiracy NGOs currently operating in Brazil, but it became most visible in antipiracy classroom pedagogy and government lobbying in the early twenty-first century. When I first began to study the organization it was headed by Roberto, a lawyer, economist, and business school professor. Roberto's law practice, he proudly informed me, frequently brought him to New York City, oddly presented by him as a mecca for respect of the branded and copyrighted. The absurdity of this contention underscores Roberto's embarrassment at Brazil's particular penchant for piracy (i.e., piracy's cultural intimacy—the way it is perceived to be both embarrassing and important for national self-identification). Or perhaps, on his trips to New York, he managed to avoid New York's omnipresent street markets and the mixed-tape practice that surrounds its hip-hop scene. His discourse certainly made me reflect on his perception of my own subject position as a North American champion of IP—a perception I regularly problematized. At NAIF, Roberto is logistically supported by a small team of public relations experts and advertising consultants, as well as financially supported by organizations from Europe, Japan, and the United States, including the International Chamber of Commerce.[7]

For the ads I analyze here, Roberto's team assembled representatives from seven Brazilian industries that consider themselves vulnerable to piracy. These include music and movies, sunglasses, sneakers, printer cartridges, dishwashing detergent, and auto parts, among others. Notice, once again, the uniting of text types typical of digital textuality. In a cavernous studio in the city of São Paulo, a group of actors, producers, makeup artists, and customer relations representatives gathered on three nights in October of 2008 to assemble seven thirty-second videos condemning "piracy" that began airing on national television in January 2009.

Since NAIF believes that piracy is both a constant threat and a sore temptation in a world of digital textuality, the organization seeks to teach consumers to buy products through legitimate processes. Goods thus purchased are the only ones that can be "magical," meaning that they perform as their advertising promises they will, and that their circulatory legitimacy is intact. To return to our example of the hypothetical song, above, "magical" consumption minimizes the gap between T4 and T5, while maintaining institutional ties with rights holders in that process of minimization.

Each of the seven ads follows a similar structure: a magician in a tuxedo attended by a woman in a red dress proposes to use "pirated products" for various purposes. His voicing lays out the dialogic nature of the subject positions we are analyzing, because his discourse cuts two ways. In introducing each ad, the magician plants the seeds of his own failure, but he does so *excitedly.*

For example, at the opening of the auto parts ad in the series, he proclaims: "And now, an old *trick* of vehicular maintenance—using parts of *doubtful origin* in this particular vehicle" (my emphasis underscores the pejorative terms being pronounced with a joy that will soon dissipate). Meanwhile, the female assistant lasciviously removes a tire from a tiny car piloted by a grinning simpleton whose acceptance of a piracy-based repair appears carnally motivated. This is a stereotypical Brazilian seduction. Here, the need for piracy manifests itself not only in the old-fashioned search for a deal but also in the celebration of Brazilian mixture; the counterfeit auto parts are not only cheaper but "just as good," locally made, and sexy to boot. True to form, the magician's tone continues to belie his content, splitting him, for the moment, in two. He is stating with excitement that he is using "tricks" and parts of "doubtful origin." In this way, the short's producers argue that the consumption of pirated products divides the consuming Brazilian into one who *wants* to believe in the less costly product and one who *suspects* that it is about to malfunction.

At the beginning of each piratical modality represented in the series of ads (auto repair, pressing "print" on your computer, or playing a DVD, for example), the assistant looks on with anticipation. The magician's promise pleases her. Yet, after the puff of smoke meant to produce the desired effect, something untoward occurs: the car's engine bursts into flames, or after pressing "play" on the DVD player, the TV intones that this illegal copy will directly fund "organized crime." The magician's expression then becomes one of embarrassment and disgust. He has failed to perform for his assistant. He then reverses his previously excited stance, and his delivery now aligns with the negative vocabulary he used before. To finish the ad, he wags his finger, scolding: "With pirated products, there's no magic." The real magic is in the fully consummated act that comes from buying a licit good—an act that piracy's temptations have foreclosed.

The message here is that consumers must be on guard against a constant threat, not only of the informal economy with all its copying and theft but also of their own impulse that they are getting a locally made and even sexy "deal," allied with the common tendency in Brazil to ignore boundaries—in this case, the boundaries that define legitimate consumption. Here, as a buyer, the mixing so often touted as a Brazilian virtue in discussions of music, food, and religion brings nothing but trouble.

Another dimension of NAIF's ad campaign forefronts this trouble with boundaries. In one commercial, the magician proposes to transform his "lovely assistant" into an even prettier "doll" by placing her in a black box with a pair of "pirated" sneakers, some sunglasses "made with contaminated raw materials," and a few pirated soccer jerseys. Once again, the appeal is sexual. The magician winks at the camera to signal his anticipation of his already lovely assistant's soon-to-be enhanced attractiveness. She understands what's in play, leering at the camera. The box turns, and we hear "abracadabra." The assistant then emerges covered with cuts and bruises, wearing a torn dress, a pair of glasses containing eyeballs hanging from springs, and a shredded tennis shoe. She limps and wobbles, far too disoriented for intimacy, and requiring assistance from the now repulsed magician. This act of mixture has produced a jumbled monster as from the pages of Brazilian social science classic *Rebellion in the Backlands*, in which nineteenth-century essayist Euclides da Cunha describes a miscegenated and stunted backwoods people who fall under the sway of an absurd but dangerous apocalyptic preacher railing against the state (Cunha [1902] 1944). By being let down by piracy, we come to know what good and just consumption ought to feel like. The claim being made in this commercial is that piracy has real physical risks, especially for women. The beauty product–induced deformity that the magician's assistant sustains receives added impetus in the context of a nation where plastic surgery is relatively common (Edmonds 2010). Buying the real thing becomes knowable through the disappointment that lurks in taking the fake, as the act of piracy becomes sexualized according to gender stereotypes.

The ending that caps off all the shorts further underscores piracy's threat to Brazil writ large. The magician, now dressed as a civilian, sits on a sofa in a living room with his spouse (the assistant—this time dressed modestly in jeans and a sweater). Their daughter sits between them. The room is orderly, and the mood is now chaste. The absence of piracy has transformed the scene from sexualized chicanery to domestic calm. When the contraband DVD finally refuses to play, the husband qua magician, who succumbed to the temptation to consume piracy, looks embarrassed, while his wife looks angry. There has been an infidelity by way of consumption. NAIF's logo and hotline for reporting piracy flash on the screen as a narrator entreats:

"Don't make your life into a *show* for piracy." In this retreat to the domestic, piracy has mixed Brazilian anthropologist Roberto DaMatta's "street" with the "house," bringing disorderly and dangerous pirated goods into the living room (DaMatta 1997). For DaMatta, the street was the domain of the general populace and of disorder, whereas the house was the domain of the family and of order. The goods have violated the house's emphasis on monogamy and have thus denied the possibility of a consummated act of consumption with its redemptive magic. In the context of DaMatta's arguments, wherein the house becomes the synecdoche for the body politic, the disagreement we have just witnessed is much more than just marital strife. We should have seen the danger in accepting the illusions of this two-bit magician and his sexy sidekick. But we didn't.

If we consider what is taking place at the margins of the filming of these ads, however, this advertising campaign is far from coherent. It contains contradictory offstage celebrations of the illicit use, sale, and copying of products. One experienced TV producer who helped organize the filming praises an employee he once worked with on a different advertising campaign, an employee who "copied" objects needed for filming ads: enormous brand-name pens (Bic) that write, oversized women's shoes (Nike), and tiny cars (Ford). Cinematic requirements often call for these violations of scale, he explains. The "artist of the copy" who performs these violations is surely a pirate, too, the producer excitedly announces to his appreciative audience of customer service representatives, who giggle at the meticulousness involved in reproducing a brand-name car down to its tiny hubcaps.

Later, in even stronger support of the piratical, the makeup artist working on the ads wonders to me what on earth the multinationals *thought* would happen when they went to Asia to cut costs, taking jobs out of Brazil while continuing to charge outrageous prices? For starters, she continues, they fired thousands of Brazilian workers, making them poor and angry. But they also engaged the Asians' sense of profit. *Of course* those overseas factories that normally make licit goods also make goods for informal markets after hours. Those multinationals *deserve* to be pirated for being so cheap, she finishes, quietly. Luckily for her employer that evening, her opinions are not captured while the camera is rolling.

By way of these on-the-set remarks, this NAIF ad campaign briefly doubles back on itself to actually promote the pirated, evidencing the simultaneity of seemingly opposed subject positions that digital textuality allows us to see. In this zone of apparently unitary opposition to piracy, it becomes clear that positions are subject to competing claims: the knowledge that piracy produces impotency, female deformity, inefficacy, and personal qua national ruin attempts to distance itself from—but cannot obliterate the desire for—piracy, coupled with the sexiness of boundary violation, the urge to get something for less, and economistically defined notions of efficiency. In this context, circulatory legitimacy allies itself with sexual continence.

The contestation involved in this back-and-forth emerges as well in the camelódromo of Campinas, where piracy is by and large a social good (a way for the unemployed to be "productive," for example), though it sometimes harmonizes with the ideologies we have just explored (a potentially dangerous embarrassment).

"Working in Peace": Circulatory Legitimacy from the Other Side

In our second site—the same place where this book began—the sense of circulatory legitimacy that the previous site's ads sought to inculcate does its work in a different way. The Popular Shopping Center (camelódromo) of Campinas presents an ideal location for exploring Brazil's propiratical discourses.[8] This is because its business owners, workers, shoppers, and suppliers espouse "entrepreneurship," pride in "hard work,"[9] *brasilidade* (Brazilianness), and good economic sense (see also Lindtner 2014; Lippman 2014; Simone 2006). This aligns with what Sasha Newell (2012) has described in Côte d'Ivoire as a kind of "modernity bluff," where the latest brands foster a sense of economic and social participation.

The sense that buyers and sellers at the camelódromo are not attending to circulatory legitimacy as they should manifests itself in fierce disagreements over how the market should formalize itself. In addition, throughout the market, digital textuality is in evidence not only in how the shop owners control their inventories and transactions but also through the hierarchical system that organizes the market. Devices that circulate digital texts—such as smartphones, videogame consoles, DVD and CD players (yes, *still* in 2020), speakers, and computers—have the largest profit margins. This means that "box" owners who sell these digital devices have more influence in group decision-making and more financial influence with local government and law enforcement. Furthermore, sellers communicate that the capacity to copy all manner of goods quickly (from shirts to videogames) comes from computers. Finally, as we will see in more detail in the next chapter, illegal copies of DVDs, videogames, software, and CDs are almost categorically the excuse offered by law enforcement for entering the market space and beginning punitive raids. These raids often begin with these obviously digital texts but soon spread to other less obviously digital ones, such as clothing.

The camelôs and their clients describe the Popular Shopping Center as being "disorderly," but they would qualify this by claiming that Brazilians are comfortable with disorder; let the riotousness of Brazilian nature take its course. Thus, camelôs and their clients merge their activities with Brazilian creativity and inattention to boundaries. This useful failure to attend to regulations has allowed Brazilian consumers to discover rule-breaking solutions to the problem of how to get name-brand and popular items cheaply. "Do you think for a minute I'm going to pay those ridiculous prices across town?" one university student asked me rhetorically, referring to the high-end shopping mall in Campinas. By asserting that things can be done more cheaply, the camelô indicts the high cost of goods and services in Brazil (particularly cell phones—see chapter 4). Nor is the high cost of consumer goods in Brazil the only ill tackled here. Customers and sellers continually restate the way in which this informal economy solves high unemployment. We would all be "on the streets" if we were not here "being good businessmen," I heard repeatedly. For these sellers, being good at business means running an organized stand with a strong guarantee and good-quality products. It does not require carrying branded goods, though some do.

Buyers and sellers meet the notion that the licit shopping mall across town offers conveniences and protections unavailable at the camelódromo with scorn. The means of payment at the camelódromo is frequently digital. If you don't have the cash, just pay by credit card, since many of the kiosks have the same credit card machines found at the mall. But there is also a personal touch. Contrary to NAIF's ugliness-inducing explosions, if something bought at the Campinas camelódromo breaks, it can often be returned for an instant exchange—a process I witnessed time and again. As Marcos of box 384 tells me, as he stamps my DVD purchases (don't tell anyone) with the name and number of his stall, shop owners take pride in their "guarantees." If something doesn't work, he'll burn me a new copy on the spot. His stamping suggests to me that he wants me to know where to find him if something goes wrong, plus he also wants my return business. Similarly, the owner of a nearby electronics kiosk informs me that now he can even take things back all the way to the original stores where he bought them in Paraguay—the location where most of the illicit goods come from (see chapter 3). These guarantees are often confirmed by those who purchase goods. Shoppers inform me that if, for example, they had to deal with Sony's customer service representatives when their digital camera broke, they'd be waiting for weeks. And they would be disappointed at the end of the process. Here, however, they simply return to the booth where they bought the offending product and exchange it for a new one. The flexibility of the system ends up serving Brazilian consumers more effectively than in an official context. This is a significant critique of customary arguments to support IP, which state that IP protection maintains the "goodwill" of consumers (Bannon 1990; as argued, for example, by Schechter 1927). Here, it is piracy that maintains goodwill.

Store owners will go far to obtain "customer satisfaction." Antônio, a retired university administrator, described dropping the digital camera he had recently bought at the camelódromo. Naturally, it stopped working. Feeling somewhat guilty, he nonetheless returned to the kiosk where he had bought it, feigning ignorance of what might have caused the problem. The owner asked no questions and put in a new memory card for free, saying, "I think this will work, but if it doesn't, bring it back next week." Antônio has not returned, since the camera is working fine. The consequences of such return and repair policies go beyond mere efficiency in service. Numerous shoppers questioned in visits to the camelódromo between 2000 and 2015 claimed that they "establish a relationship" with "their" shopkeeper that is much closer than any they could establish at the impersonal mall across town. The warm embrace of the camelô thus dovetails with discourses of "cordiality" as fundamental to Brazilian social relations, an idea advanced by

Brazilian sociologist Sérgio Buarque de Holanda in 1936 and widely discussed to this day as the foundation of *brasilidade* (Holanda 1995). Buyers and sellers explained to me that the camelódromo system in Brazil resembles the formal economy in developed countries, where big companies such as Sony actually pay attention to individual customers. "Sony doesn't care about us here, so we improvise."

Another feature touted by stall owners is that their economy, in its digitization, is fast and responsive. "We can follow trends more quickly than the regular stores," one owner informed me. Purveyors of music and movies have computers in the back where they can burn whatever a customer wants. "If there's no copy already out on display, *ask*," I was told repeatedly. "I can make it for you."[10] Even for the clothing, sneakers, and sunglasses, sellers reference their digital technology in more than inventory control and credit card purchases. Their sense of being able to quickly respond to style changes comes from their awareness that computers facilitate design and manufacture. As one seller phrased it, "when that new soccer jersey comes out, someone snaps a digital picture, and the machines make it."

As in the case of the antipiracy ads, the dialogic tension in the camelódromo between circulatory legitimacy and piracy requires constant vigilance—though in this location it is vigilance of a slightly different sort. Over each entrance, in addition to the suggestion that you smile because "you are being filmed" (yet another index of digital oversight, since the system backs up to hard drives), another sign states, "we are Brazilians. . . . We will never give up" (see figure 1.1). Another sign states, "We want to work *in peace*" (my emphasis). This second sign appears courtesy of "the workers of the informal economy of Campinas," known as STEIC.[11]

"Peace" is not being used metaphorically. The presence of violence in the camelódromo requires that shopkeepers, suppliers, and even consumers remain watchful, since the state (in the form of the civil and sometimes military police), other shopkeepers, or increasingly, criminal gangs might do something rash at any time. The violence perpetrated by the state in the marketplace against buyers is directly blamed on NGOs such as NAIF, which push local police to make raids, punishing violators of IP, while encouraging competing stalls to "inform" on one another through antipiracy hotlines

FIGURE 1.1 Campinas *camelódromo*, October 2011. Photo by the author. The sign over the entrance (obscured by a white Volkswagen bus) reads, "We are Brazilians. We are *camelôs*. We will never give up!"

(like NAIF's). During the raids, people may get hurt or, more seriously, have to spend time in notoriously dangerous prisons. Products get confiscated, too, which is expensive for the stall owners. The justification for such raids continues to be "piracy," but once again, we should notice that it is piracy of the most explicitly digital texts (DVDs, CDs, software, and computer games) that largely provides the initial justification for raids that ultimately confiscate a broad range of goods. Local papers reinforce raids by lauding the destruction of large numbers of pirated goods found within the marketplace. Here, therefore, the conflict for sellers especially lies in believing that what they are doing makes good economic sense, while knowing that a system that ostensibly supports such good sense does not support them.

The violence between shopkeepers within the camelódromo is more personal in cause and more fatal in effect than punitive police raids. Intrashopkeeper violence is the result of a struggle over whether, and how much, to formalize wages, working conditions, and health benefits, as well as what shape that formalization should take. For instance, many camelódromo shopkeepers agree that they want to pay taxes and have wanted to do so for some time. This would increase their "legitimacy" in the eyes of government and tourists. They also believe that paying taxes would result in an improved infrastructure, such as more convenient bathrooms, and allow them access to better health plans. But the precise nature of the formalization process is contested, with two factions vying for control. On one side, a community organizer named Carol heads a "society" of workers, and her dominion stretches back into the late 1980s. She collects weekly "dues" from each stall but is unable (or unwilling) to tell anyone precisely where these dues go. The few willing to discuss the matter speculate that such fees are most likely given to local politicians and police, since stall owners who oppose Carol are often raided by police the day after an argument. On the other side of an increasingly entrenched battle, a workers "union" (described to me as "new" in 2008, officially recognized by the state and supported by one of Brazil's two largest labor unions) struggles for transparency. Its members complain that fear of Carol, who has been hegemonic in the market for so long, keeps membership numbers in the union low. In fact, leaders on both sides were fatally shot due to their involvement in the unionization battle between 2006 and 2010.

Unfortunately, internal violence within the camelódromo reinforces the perception of piracy as dangerous, completing a vicious circle. State planners informed me, off the record, that they were unable to formalize the camelódromo more fully because of the presence of "pirated products" there, as though these pirated products were an unfortunate annoyance rather than the substance of the camelódromo business model. They noted that the presence of such products causes police raids. These raids, in turn, create fear and a greater desire for acceptance, which more formality might bring. Yet the desire for formality itself causes violence, since owners and workers disagree about what form it might take.

Finally, with the increasing dangers associated with circulating illegally copied products (music, films, software, and computer games in particular—though increasingly clothing, shoes, and sunglasses), criminal gangs have become more directly involved in the informal markets as providers of protection against other members of the informal economy and against police. One organizer named Maria, associated with the newer and more aspirationally transparent labor union, told me the story of two young men being sent by a prominent gang to kill her. The prospective killers decided not to carry out their charge because, when they showed up, one of them realized he had grown up with one of Maria's best friends—who talked him out of carrying out the assassination on the spot. She continued to fear for her life, however—since she was at the center of an effort to turn the informal economy into a union, officially empowered by local and state governments. A series of meetings I attended with her suggested that her prounion collaborators are engaged in a delicate balancing act between layers of political processes (mayoral, state, and national) such that elected officials are constantly being convicted on corruption charges, and who are, then, suddenly out of the picture. As I worked with her over time, she gradually came to control my note taking and picture taking in the market—and on the last visit to the camelódromo I was allowed only to talk to owners and sellers (no notes or pictures). I happily complied, fearing for her safety should I slip.

The stakes of this dialogue between piracy and IP are high. Though it is not their explicit aim, NAIF's ad campaigns make life more precarious at the market *through* circulatory legitimacy. Though the workers and customers of the camelódromo may be proud of aspects of their piracy, treating it as a kind of social banditry that counteracts the price gouging of international corporations (Hobsbawm 2000; Schneider and Schneider 2008; Wilson 2003), they strive for formalization. Their differing perspectives also reveal themselves in other moments. Despite their pleasure at receiving cheaper goods and often better service, customers are beginning to have reservations about buying from the camelódromo. Lest NAIF's ads appear solely as corporate ideology, more buyers at the camelódromo over the last decade have described a "sad" feeling about their pirated purchases, fearing that they are stealing from their favorite rock band or robbing a "legitimate" manufacturer.

Circulatory legitimacy at this ethnographic site also appears in the ways that buyers and sellers describe what they are doing at the camelódromo. The commodities consumed there constantly beg the truth of people's claims about the commodities' provenance. We will see this in more detail in the

FIGURE 1.2 Campinas *camelódromo*, October 2011. Photo by the author. Let the chaos of Brazilian mixture reign!

next chapter. Here, among the camelôs, the pirated good is often described as "just as good as" the legitimately circulated one. Some go further, claiming their goods are "even better than the originals." But such arguments always position themselves in opposition to claims to the contrary. The buyers and sellers of "pirated products" continually strive for "good quality." At the same time, they know that the actors and institutions affiliated with NAIF—and the state apparatuses that both support NAIF and take bribes from the camelôs—believe the production and consumption of pirated goods is not only cheap but potentially dangerous. The position taken by a camelô is therefore inherently defensive and divided. In this way, just as those producing NAIF's advertising campaign momentarily support piracy, the camelôs increasingly pine for commodities whose magic derives from attentiveness to IP. This leads to their imitation of aspects of branded behavior, such as warranty and customer satisfaction, while attempting to improve upon it by making it more affordable. And arguments for the magic of "original" products are not hard to find. Looking up from the central intersection of Campinas's camelódromo, passersby can see a large advertising surface on a nearby building, which, since I began research in Campinas in 1998, has presented glossy ads for foreign cars (Hondas, Fiats, and Fords), high-end shampoos (Vidal Sassoon), and digital cameras (by Sony).

For English Eyes, Divided

We have heard accusations on all sides. For the NGOs, except in revealing lapses, the villains are those who facilitate "piracy": buyers, sellers, suppliers, thieves, smugglers, and clandestine manufacturers. The mindset of the NGOs is often reflected in the Brazilian state apparatuses and the media, which attack piracy. For the camelô—except, once again, for telling slips in which pure products are exactly what their advertisers claim them to be (cheap, or frequently, as we shall see, "Paraguayan")—the villains are instead presented as foreign-funded NGOs that seek to malign their honest work, corporate monopolies insulating themselves from competition, and governmental agents who assist in these processes, frequently lining their own pockets in the bargain. For the camelô, these are pirates of another sort. So, everyone is calling everyone else a pirate, which gives weight to the claim of historian Adrian Johns, who, in a massive analysis of the cyclical nature of the piracy "wars," from "Gutenberg to Gates," asserts that piracy seems to be "the definitive transgression of the information age" (Johns 2010, 5).

My argument is that digital textuality makes current piracy different from previous uses of the concept. In the twenty-first century, digital textuality has led to an expansion of IP monitoring and policing, making piracy the indexical ground on which contemporary consumption rests. Piracy is not some sideshow. It *is* the show. IP's proponents—property lawyers, pharmaceutical companies, music and film companies, and so forth—seek to apply IP to as broad a range of communicative practices as they can, claiming that such an extensive definition and application of IP is a transcultural right (Boateng 2011). We see here, however, that circulatory legitimacy can be used to fashion an ethics of accumulation—a moral scheme for deciding who gets to maximize economic potential (in the form of wages for workers and savings for consumers) and who does not. These days, IP proscriptively distinguishes the formal (legitimate) from the informal (pirated) by means of both discursive and logistical supports. These distinctions have substantive outcomes for safety, given that people are being attacked or killed in the informal sector typically affiliated with piracy.

The subjectivities on display here reveal a central paradox of contemporary capitalism. Consumers, producers, and suppliers oriented toward consumer goods are constantly required to do two things at the same time: to use their trained senses to filter commodities, and then buy only those that have genuflected to circulatory legitimacy; and, precisely because trickle-down economics hasn't worked, to buy as cheaply as possible. As an added insult, this quandary often gets spoken about by IP maximalists as a "choice." While it is tempting to view these opposed positions as the reflex of global forces, a notion seemingly abetted by the knowledge that NAIF's funding comes almost entirely from abroad (see chapter 2), the evidence here returns us to the local roots of digital textuality. Both intimate (it's a Brazilian embarrassment) and critical (it's Brazil's finger in the eye of multinationals), stances on piracy approach the practice as a decidedly local failure or success, grounded in durable discourses of mixture, sexuality, and purity. In the case of the NGOs, the argument is that people in other countries actually value IP; people don't steal from one another. North Americans, for instance, leave intact the appropriate boundaries between forms of production and circulation, and thus they provide incentives for invention and creativity (recall Roberto's idealization of, of all places, New York City). This is part of the reason given by Brazilian business owners and investment bankers for why Brazil ought to demonstrate its adherence to TRIPS. Among the camelôs, the average Brazilian's propensity to enact a creative solution to high prices and poor access by violating boundaries provides the necessary response to international monopolies, their local collaborators, and global trade treaties that seek uniformity. The camelô asserts that this is how Brazilians avoid paying the ridiculous prices that citizens of First World countries can actually afford.

A Brazilian expression meaning that something is done to the letter of the law, *só para inglês ver* (only for the English to see), illustrates these localized tensions over boundedness, as well as the ways in which piracy brings these tensions to the fore in current capitalist times. Folk etymologies of this expression differ (Fry 1982). Some say it first occurred in the 1800s during the British blockade off the Brazilian coast of slave ships that had been disguised as regular trading vessels. Others say the idiom was born in the Brazilian interior when British rail companies watched over their laborers. Current invocations channel the tacit assumption that things will get jumbled in Brazil, and the fact that corners will be cut and mingling will take place is simultaneously embarrassing (since it indexes an inability to do things "properly") and locally appropriate. Brazil's need for piracy is something that foreigners (like you, gringo) just won't understand. Thus, foreigners are shown something that seems to fit their rules instead.

The simultaneously "culturally intimate" and "critical" poetics of recognition in the expression "only for the English to see," emplotted within late colonial practice but invoked today to describe phenomena such as the NAIF ads and the formalizations of the camelódromo, underscore piracy's current significance. Digital textuality reinforces a tension between purity and its violation. Piracy thus helps us trace the local limits of practice on which contemporary digital textuality grounds itself. Piracy creates the possibility of both impotent and consummated exchange. The policing and materiality that help to fashion the anxious space between the two will be our next topic.

2 THE MATERIALITIES OF DIGITAL TEXTS

THE SCRUTINY OF PIRACY that antipiracy NGOs and their governmental collaborators have undertaken in the late twentieth and early twenty-first centuries has altered piracy's flows while increasing its reach. In Brazil, by fragmenting piracy and pushing it into smaller locations on less-trafficked street corners—outside apartment buildings and inside residential areas—IP policing has also increased piracy's intimacy: its integration with daily life close to home. In light of this combined dispersion and intimacy, what makes policing of informal economies possible in local terms? When the prices of legitimate, "original" goods are so high, what justification might the government and police have for enforcement of IP? The question becomes even more protracted since Brazilian consumers already complain about what they characterize as the absurd prices of most imported goods.

The answer to why Brazilians might want to police piracy is not exclusively about the imposition of "foreign" IP maximalism onto "local" contexts ill-suited to it, though this does play a role (Boateng 2011; Brown 2003; Coombe 1998, 2009). And as the last chapter showed, the policing of IP is also not simply a question of big business versus the consumer. A more complete answer to why piracy gets policed begins with digital textuality. Such an answer shows how Brazilian approaches to garbage *(lixo)* and processes of cleaning *(limpeza)*—not just of the streets but also social cleaning—are elicited by IP maximalism. Furthermore, proponents of circulatory legitimacy scrutinize object provenance in ways that resemble the worship of relics, with quite particular outcomes in Latin America (Gillingham 2010). Recall the "magic" of consumption from the last chapter. Finally, piracy brings forth anxieties about memory in a nation many Brazilians, in rueful moments, describe as a place of repetitive forgetting with violent consequences.

(Il)legitimacies

In early December of 2012, Edilson—a consumer from Campinas whom I've been interviewing about his purchases of pirated goods since 1999—told me he wanted to expand my horizons, by which he meant my knowledge of informal economies. Over the years, Edilson presented himself as a connoisseur of the camelô. He had, for example, spent many hours at the camelódromo. He understood that I was a gringo who not only did not disparage Brazil for its pirated goods but was in fact fascinated by them.

Edilson could afford branded goods, but he chose instead to get "the best deal," and he always knew where that deal could be found, even in the context of the already cheap informal economy. On this particular research trip in 2012, I spent considerable time with him processing my findings at large, centrally located informal markets in the cities of São Paulo and Campinas—previously, some of his favorite shopping spots. But they no longer were. This was in part because police had forced the removal of CDs and DVDs, as well as brand-name clothing, from the camelódromos; instead, these centralized locations had largely become places to buy a pirated cellular phone or have one repaired, a subject I turn to in chapters 4 and 5. This apparent removal of one policed object in favor of another that was not being policed (the cell phone), however, did not mean that what Edilson conceived of as piracy's equitable pricing scheme was dead with respect to music and movies. Far from it. To illustrate, he invited me to get into his car and head to some of the working-class peripheries of Campinas.

Less than ten minutes from his home, we arrived at a busy intersection where about twenty sellers of pirated CDs and DVDs, as well as knockoff clothing, shoes, sunglasses, and watches, had set up tables on the dirt by the side of the road. Shoppers bustled past, stopping to browse and buy precisely the materials that had all but disappeared from the more centralized markets such as the one in Campinas described in the last chapter—markets with a higher degree of formalization with respect to infrastructure and selling practices. "You see?" he asked excitedly. "No police here." Over the next few hours, he took me to three similar locations around the periphery of Campinas as a way of illustrating his point, and he later directed me to similar spots in the city of São Paulo. In response to policing, the pirated economy had by no means disappeared. It had shifted venues and split up into smaller units, essentially transforming scale and spatial distribution tactics.

Over the last decade (2008–2018), the informal street markets of São Paulo (both city and state) have transformed. During these years of intensifying social and economic reform—many of them led by a left-leaning Workers' Party government and characterized by the contraction of government services together with a widespread promulgation of "entrepreneurialism" by policymakers, NGOs, and lenders—several of the most visible markets that were once home to an immense trade in pirated goods have been almost entirely stripped of their unauthorized copies. This has, in part, been the result of Brazil's observance of TRIPS and its incumbent modernities. Yet the trade in illicit goods continues unabated in other locations because, these days, individual DVD stands now dot residential streets and line prominent intersections in what Brazilians call the "periphery"—by which they mean the largely working-class suburbs (Pardue 2004). How can we understand this capricious policing of only the most visible street markets while residential neighborhoods and peripheries are left alone? And what does this shift in the distribution of pirated media to smaller-scale, less centralized sites mean for police, pro-IP activists, and informal economy workers and consumers in Southern Brazil?

My answers to these questions draw on fieldwork among the buyers, sellers, and suppliers of several large informal street markets in the city of São Paulo—specifically, the Feira da Madrugada (Dawn Fair) and on the avenue named Rua 25 de março (25th of March Street). As one of the largest sites for media production and consumption in Latin America, as well as the region containing most Brazilian antipiracy NGO headquarters, the area including and surrounding São Paulo and Campinas is an optimal location for these inquiries. Another site of particular importance is the Brazilian Film and Music Antipiracy Association (FMAA), a secretive NGO that was funded largely by the Recording Industry Association of America and the Motion Picture Association of America and was operational between 2005 and 2015.[1] Interviews and observations at this NGO provided local framings, in addition to observations of how FMAA interfaced with Brazilian law enforcement. These studies supplement my work with NAIF, analyzed in the last chapter, which promulgated the "magic" of legitimate consumption. Workers in these NGOs viewed their efforts as complementary.

Material Purities

Beginning in earnest in 2005, as international businesses became frustrated with what they considered to be ineffective antipiracy measures, these multinational corporations supported the formation of NGOs to aggressively recruit public law enforcement. In so doing, they sought to protect what they portrayed as their rights. With the support of lobbying groups such as the International Chamber of Commerce, the International Federation for the Phonographic Industry, and the Business Software Alliance, companies such as Nike, Time-Warner, Universal, Microsoft, and Apple provided NGOs in target economies with both money and the doctrine of IP maximalism. Nationally embedded NGOs imbued with this doctrine hired former law enforcement personnel and embarked upon the activities that are the subject of this chapter: training police to recognize and confiscate unauthorized goods; incentivizing enforcement agencies and governmental institutions to apply the strict IP rules already on paper; and publicly destroying contraband goods. This set of procedures seems to be going on all over the world, and in this sense, these practices appear to be uniform—from Boston to Beijing, Buenos Aires to Bali.

As uniform as these practices appear to be around the world, however, the ability to recruit enforcers is not uniform. Rather, enforcement relies upon local approaches to circulatory legitimacy; that is, localized beliefs about the ways in which putative "origins" are (or are not) indexed in the movement of an object or an idea into the material realm—its concretization. Religious relics provide an informative example, in that their spiritual power is derived from an object's ties to its saint of origin (Turner and Turner 2011). In the context of IP maximalism, circulatory legitimacy suggests that objects should reflect aspects of their circumstances of production as they move and change hands. As we shall see, Brazilian approaches to circulatory legitimacy are shaped by IP maximalist arguments that some things are legitimately circulated, while others are decidedly not. This dialogue takes place in pro-IP NGO training sessions, as well as in press releases that get picked up by frequently uncritical reporters at major news media outlets in Brazil. Versions of this dialogue then find expression in the way law enforcement officers discuss all this on the street, with each other, and with the buyers and sellers they encounter.

In this chapter, I focus in particular on the material aspects of digital textuality. In this ambit, IP maximalism argues that, without careful policing, digital textuality produces illicit markets that, in Brazil, are described by law enforcement and the news media as *sujo* (dirty) and *perigoso* (dangerous). A consumer who fails to attend to circulatory legitimacy enacts a kind of forgetting—a failure that we shall see takes a particular form in Brazil. What frightens IP maximalists is how promiscuous listening and viewing (without regard for the origins of the text) reinforce dirty and dangerous modes of materialization; it might not matter to some users how a song file becomes hearable—whether by way of a CD, a portable USB drive, an MP3 player, a cellular phone ringtone, a movie soundtrack, a Web log, an Internet radio station, a handheld videogame, and on and on. This fear of "promiscuity" in consumption (Gell 1996; Larkin 2014; Sterne 2006; Thomas 1991) is exacerbated by the high quality of reproductions available today. Once upon a time, copied films looked grainy or were even framed by the movie theaters in which they had been filmed (sometimes with camcorders, by hand); the grainy quality became part of the "infrastructure" of illicit media noted in the work of Brian Larkin (2008) in the context of the Nigerian film market.

This is no longer the case in most parts of the world where digital piracy is practiced. These pirated hearings and/or viewings are increasingly not experienced as having been degraded in the act of reproduction. Digital reproduction's instability with respect to the mutability and mobility of its textual form, then, coupled with its reproductive fidelity, makes many participants in consumer economies twitchy. In this context, corporations, governments, and often the news media work hard to communicate the notion that some forms of digital textuality are degraded due to their flouting of circulatory legitimacy, while other forms seamlessly integrate with brand, copyright, trademark, and patent, thus guaranteeing "magical" consuming experiences. In this ambit, IP maximalism calls on subjects to distinguish legitimately materialized texts from illegitimately materialized ones. By understanding how certain forms of digital textuality might come to be classified as aberrant—particularly the unauthorized use of movies and music—we can understand how digital texts of all kinds require significant vigilance to remain both viable and valuable. This vigilance, in turn, requires scrutiny—and it is this requirement that helps to explain why members of law enforcement participate in punitive raids and harassment.

IP protection does not seem to be carried out because its helpers just want to be "right with the law" while dutifully aspiring to a "culture of respect," as is frequently argued in policy documents—often supported by research in economics and political science (Bica-Huiu, et al. 2007; Danino 2006; Kleinfeld 2006). Nor is it the case that law enforcement officers are moved by hyperbolic claims such as the statement that piracy in Brazil is now "more lucrative" than the market in illegal drugs and results in the "loss" of two million formal jobs, as well as R$30 billion in taxes (about US$15 billion at that time; FMAA 2008)—the sort of statement that is promulgated by antipiracy NGOs.[2] In the course of my research, not one police officer or antipiracy worker brought up such justifications, and such claims were rejected when I raised them myself. And accounting for the severity and uniformity of antipiracy policing in terms of bribery doesn't explain much, either. While NGOs representing the interests of the big consumer-goods companies have, indeed, multiplied around the globe in the last decade, and bribery—used extensively during the 1990s by the film and music industries to secure confiscations—most likely continues, the informal economies in which the naughty goods circulate also pay a great deal to be left alone (much of it coded as "bribery," but bearing the same characteristics as the payments given by IP maximalists to local police).[3] Furthermore, IP policing increasingly requires coordination between politicians, law enforcement, urban planners, and lawyers—a coordination that is frequently carried out with brutality and relish.[4]

So, to return to this chapter's original question, what can explain this expansion of policing in visible zones, together with a seemingly paradoxical relaxation in residential neighborhoods and peripheries in Brazil? The whole process certainly begins with international pressure exerted through NGOs. The precise way international pressure manifests itself in concrete action remains to be enumerated; this is where digital textuality comes in. In what follows, I will analyze how piracy policing unfolds by attending to Brazilian approaches to "dirt" (DaMatta 1979; Douglas 2003), together with attached notions of "cleaning"—conceived of as the kind of social cleansing that goes along with either rendering invisible or killing socially undesirable types such as drug dealers, the homeless, addicts, prostitutes, and, sometimes, leftists (Green 2015; Taussig 2005; Thomas 2015; Willis 2015). I will further root these approaches to cleanliness in the Brazilian dictatorship's acts of censorship between 1964 and 1985 (Allison 2000; Carneiro 2002; Kushnir 2004; Reimão 2008; Sheriff 2000; Smith 1997). Finally, I will elaborate on the relevance of "promiscuity" (Bandyopadhyay and Nascimento 2010; Caulfield 1993; Gell 1996; Kulick 1998; Larkin 2014; Nazzari 1996; Parker 2009; Rebhun 1999; Thomas 1991) under the banner of embarrassingly repetitive forgetfulness (Collins 2004; Dent 2009; Herzfeld 1996; Matory 2004). Throughout, I will track attempts to establish salubrious and polluted modes of digital textuality.

Dirt, Garbage, and "The Street"

In an interview with Officer Machado on the 25th of March Street (Rua 25 de Março, one of the largest street markets in Latin America) he reported, "It took *us* [the Military Police] to clean this place up." We were standing in the middle of the busy market on December 8, 2012. Just three years earlier, this spot had been the site of one of Latin America's largest informal trades in all manner of illegal products, from DVDs to batteries and backpacks. Nowadays, in place of wandering sellers, orderly kiosks sold only braided jewelry, generic clothing, and seasonal trinkets—ladder-climbing Santas today, pumpkin-headed costumes the last time I had been there, and Easter bunnies on a previous visit. Though trade in the street was a fraction of what it

FIGURE 2.1 Rua 25 de Março, December 2012. Photo by the author. In a nation without chimneys, Santa must use a ladder.

had been only two years ago, the local news media nonetheless reported that business in its storefronts, selling less controversial wholesale fabric, tools, building materials, and clothing, continued to boom (Genestreti 2012).

Machado paused toward the end of our conversation—which had proceeded much like others I had had with police officers at the 25th of March Street market—and looked down, seemingly wondering how best to sum things up. "Do you know what piracy is?" he finally asked. I nodded to say that I did, but please go on anyway. "It's against the law. It's illegal. So all those guys that used to sell that sort of garbage? We cleaned all that up. It's just so much safer now." An identical question-and-answer format about piracy-as-dirt, coupled with safety, was repeated to me hours later by different officers blocks away.

FIGURE 2.2 Rua 25 de Março, December 2012. Photo by the author. Inoffensive braided jewelry. No piracy here!

We should notice in Machado's statements, reinforced by his law enforcement colleagues in supporting interviews, that dirt and its associate, garbage, referred not at all to the American television shows and ultrapopular Brazilian country music that once circulated so copiously here in unauthorized forms. Quite to the contrary, he watches the former, and listens to the latter. While some Brazilian TV or music critics might refer to much of the public culture that once circulated here as "trash"—the term *lixo* was frequently applied to the country music that had been the subject of my first book—this was not Machado's sense of the term.

In his celebration of shutting down the dirt of the 25th of March Street market, Officer Machado was espousing the censorship of form rather than content. Specifically, what triggered the censorship were certain signals that indicated a text's failure to originate with an authorized producer—a quite particular problem viewable by way of intertextual gaps. Pirated texts were therefore dirty, as were the people who sold them. The sense of "dirt" that Machado and his fellow officers were employing brings together three important senses of the term. First, recall Brazilian anthropologist Roberto DaMatta's opposition between an orderly and clean "house" and a chaotic and dirty "street" from the last chapter (DaMatta 1982). Mary Douglas's somewhat different sense of dirt as "matter out of place" is also useful (Douglas 2003). Though she does not explicitly flag the temporality of dirt in her analysis, Douglas alerts us to the way a seemingly spatial difference derives, at least in part, from a temporal one. Dirt, in place, isn't dirty—or at the very least it is not disruptive when it is properly placed. This can be explained by reflecting on another classic social theorist—Pierre Bourdieu, whose analysis of gifts suggest that they mean different things as they move (Bourdieu 1977). Bourdieu used Lévi-Strauss's engagement with the notion of a gift to argue against what he perceived to be structuralism's blindness to time.

Returning to the Brazilian consumer economy, certain kinds of objects (of the house) masquerade as orderly while actually representing disorder (the street). And it is their seemingly clean, digital presentation—their capacity to play without errors—that facilitates this chicanery. When these objects—pirated objects, to be clear—insinuate themselves into the house, they create tensions and anxieties of the sort that we saw in the last chapter at the end of NAIF's television spots. In the ad attempting to raise consumer consciousness about the evils of pirated CDs and DVDs, a family sits down to watch a pirated CD—but what comes out of the television is, "If you want to watch something of terrible quality, while supporting organized crime, press 'play.'" IP maximalism here attempts to reinscribe claims about "terrible quality" that all Brazilian consumers understand to be patently false. Furthermore, the husband's desire to get a movie cheaply has put the family at risk by bringing matter out of place into the home.

A fourth sense of "dirt" in Brazil plays an important role in understanding digital textuality. There is a long tradition among police forces and mainstream politicians in Brazil—and in Latin America more broadly—of framing "cleaning" as the removal of unwanted social types such as the homeless, drug dealers, addicts, leftists, the dark complected, and the poor. The idea behind these modes of social cleanliness is that these types of people should be taken out of prominent social spaces—either by killing them or by forcing them into less visible zones. Here, discourses of security and cleanliness dovetail with governance in Latin America and specifically in Brazil—such that killing may be done in public ways that display the proximity of the killed to the forms of dirt and garbage their crimes are meant to have indexed. What this means is that the dead bodies of murdered people, framed as dirty, are ceremoniously disposed of in locations strewn with garbage, a confluence that is lost on neither the detectives charged with solving the cases nor the killers themselves, nor even those meant to witness the act of cleaning—as can be seen in anthropologist Graham Willis's analysis of policing and organized crime in contemporary Brazil (Willis 2015).

In Brazil, the notion that digital textuality tempts users into acts of unauthorized use, in turn classifiable as dirt or garbage, is not hard to find. Take the rhetoric of antipiracy NGOs, police officers, policymakers, and other antipiracy workers so frequently reproduced in conversations and at the level of enforcement. In his presentations to governmental policymakers, the president of NAIF referred to pirated and counterfeit materials as "monstrous" forms of "poison," concluding "piracy turns the decades-old evolution of the fight for the sacred rights of the [Brazilian] consumer into garbage" (personal correspondence). Such evidence appears in quotidian policing practices, too. For example, back at the 25th of March Street market, three years before the interviews with Machado and other officers with which I opened this chapter, on July 15, 2009, the market was typically packed with buyers and sellers in the early afternoon. Illegal products still abounded then, though on this occasion, as a kind of prelude to the salubriousness of 2012, all illicit commerce was constantly being policed by the Metropolitan Guards (the municipal police) without ever being fully halted. A white van with two officers walking in front and two behind traveled slowly from one end of the street to the other. The sleeves of the officers were rolled up to reveal muscled arms, though it was difficult to know if the officers carrying out this job had been carefully selected for the rigor of their workouts. Whatever the case, the officers at the back of the van grabbed ambulant sellers who failed to get out of the way quickly enough, bundled their presumably illicit wares into white plastic garbage bags, and tossed those garbage bags into the back of the truck with a flick that resembled the technique of trash collectors. Once, an officer punched a seller a few times for reasons that were not clear to me. When I asked about the hitting later that day, these officers told me that certain sellers had initially refused to hand over their goods (hence, the punching) and that all confiscated materials would be destroyed—a process I will come to in a moment.

This treatment of pirated digital media as trash jibes with observations and interviews at the FMAA, located off highbrow Avenida Paulista in São Paulo. Mauro, a retired police officer now working as "Head of Operations" at FMAA, informed me that part of the "help" his organization offers to law enforcement involves teaching officers how to package and transport the offending pirated goods once they have been confiscated. This help extends to providing the actual packaging itself. When the police lack containers to haul away the product (an inevitability, he knowingly reports with a wink I do not return), the FMAA provides white plastic garbage bags. After the raid, the FMAA catalogues and then publicly destroys the materials.

This destruction extends the notion that illicit digital textuality is dirt. One of the chief ways the FMAA communicates the success of its antipiracy operations is through photographs of these acts of destruction. Between 2008 and 2012 (the height of the FMAA's operations), such pictures were emailed to a list of subscribers (including me) as well as posted on the organization's website, together with press releases. These pictures were also forwarded to news agencies in the form of press releases, and many publications simply reprinted them (without citation, mind you). The images of wrecked DVDs most frequently contained a construction vehicle such as a bulldozer or roller compactor crushing a mass of disks on a street. From time to time, the FMAA also used images of disks being held to a tablesaw blade in motion.

Such images of the aftermath of piracy raids have become de rigueur in contexts of enforcement all over the world, but recall that in Brazil the destruction of these disks in the street ends up keeping them where they belong—outside the home. The destruction carries out an act of *limpeza*. But it is in the semiotics of this destruction that we can uncover an important aspect of the struggle over digital textuality that piracy lays bare. The FMAA's strategy in these acts of destruction and accompanying press releases reduces all of these ostensibly singular titles (all the individual CDs and DVDs) to a sameness that is not handled by the precise, laser-dependent devices normally employed in interacting with such texts inside the safety of the living room. Instead, these NGOs employ the sort of machinery used to move earth or cut wood. These images of the bulldozer tell us that the true nature of these illegitimate texts that might appear legitimate is revealed through contact with construction equipment. The tablesaw renders the materials uniform by treating handfuls of disks like wood. The calculatedly brutish display, together with the (albeit limited) public nature of the acts of destruction themselves, are meant to "raise consciousness" about the harm that piracy causes—to borrow language that appears throughout the FMAA's emailed weekly updates (language that was reiterated in interviews). These acts of destruction can be compared to the book burnings that, though rare, took place during the authoritarian regime of Getúlio Vargas (1930–1945; Carneiro 2002; Silva 2001), demonstrating an ostentatiously destructive form of censorship. Here, though, the FMAA and sympathetic IP maximalists render piracy as improperly materialized digital texts—texts that pose as individuated copies of films and CDs but are actually (the story goes) an unclean mass. Put these things into a landfill, not into your DVD and CD players.

The mirror image of the FMAA's disk-destroying has been misleadingly presented in Brazil's most-read weekly newsmagazine—not quite in the form of a cup of sewage being poured into a CD player, though close. In August of 1999, a text box with no listed author appeared on the penultimate page of the magazine *Veja* (which translates as "See!"), just as the antipiracy NGOs this book analyzes were being formed. The article rather precisely mirrored a billboard I had seen weeks before in Campinas, one that had been paid for by the FMAA. In the aforementioned text box, the magazine argued that pirated CDs and DVDs would hurt your CD player, much like putting a gritty LP record on your record player once upon a time would have hurt its needle. If you use these unclean media, your CD player will break and require expensive repairs, the apocryphal report alleged ("CD pirata" 1999). (The president of NAIF made a similar claim to me in an interview.) Here, we can see clearly how the promotional efforts of IP maximalists converge with Brazilian notions of dirt to facilitate enforcement. Anyone familiar with how a CD player worked could easily have refuted the claim. CDs do not work the same way records do because a laser, not a needle, reads the disk. Nothing is coming into direct contact with the CD, meaning that pirated CDs can in no way damage the player. There is a chance the disk might skip, nothing more. But let us take *Veja*'s claim seriously, for a moment—a claim repeated by both NGOs and the police officers they had trained. Even if it wasn't the CD or DVD player, perhaps something was being broken in the process of consuming pirated material. But what?

Promiscuity and Forgetting

As noted, boosters of digital textuality often point to the fact that "files" can materialize in a variety of forms and locations. But according to IP maximalists, in the digital age, some of these texts are authorized by the large corporations taking responsibility for them, while others are decidedly not authorized. And too often, the maximalist story continues, Brazilian consumers don't seem to care much about the form their movies and music come in—where, recall, form is conceived of in circulatory terms, such that the text must index its authorized distributors. For this reason, Brazilian IP maximalists feel that they must instruct police on ways to distinguish between good and bad material instantiations of the digital text—a particularly difficult task when the experience of that text does not suffer from the same evidence of copying (hissing noise or graininess) as it did in the days of analogue piracy. In analyzing this pedagogical enterprise, we begin to see how these acts of policing are shaped by Brazilian approaches to promiscuity, here applied to the illicit materialization of digital texts and linked by a lack of regard for the past.

In late January of 2011, Marcelo, director of the FMAA, proudly announced in one of São Paulo's most-read newspapers that punitive raids on pirated digital media kiosks in Brazil were up 110 percent from the previous year. The future looked bright: "If we can clean up the filth of illegal content, it's just logical that the [film and movie] industry will have more space to sell its products." In an interview I had conducted the year before with him, he had echoed this sentiment, informing me that his suitability to lead the NGO lay in his having had a previous career in law enforcement that was "completely clean—impeccable." His invocations of both dirt and cleanliness—represented by correctly materialized digital goods together with reliable policing—underscore the importance of *limpeza*. In the case of "clean" goods and services, users can be confident that the origins of the object or practice in a designer, brand, or author, are reinforced in the physical form that the object takes. These are the sorts of things we can bring into our homes with confidence. Similarly, clean policing is policing that avoids bribery by organized criminals and that, in this way, provides stable claims about its aims and efficacy.

This polarizing discourse that opposes filth to cleanliness emerges with particular clarity in the classrooms where the FMAA teaches police officers the difference between pirated and legitimate texts. Adriana, the FMAA's Head of Public Affairs (and a communications major in college), who spends most of her workday leading its police officer trainings, has considerable practice narrating her company's "training" PowerPoint. Sitting at her desk by the NGO's front door, and giving me a private run-through, her delivery is polished. She has presented this countless times in her classes in all the policing districts of the city of São Paulo. Working at desks nearby, the three support staff members who assist her with the trainings nod approvingly as she explains, offering contextualizing remarks. In subsequent interviews, they, too, refer back to these slides.

The slides in question—taken from the FMAA's manual, "A Step-by-Step Guide to Identifying CDs and DVDs"—are divided in half; the left side is light gray and accompanied by a thumbs-up icon (meaning *tudo bem*, or "everything's cool," in Brazil), while the right side is red and stamped by a skull and crossbones (the universal symbol of piracy). This dialogic, facilitated by iconic reference to the maritime piracy of yore, pervades the presentation and takes us deeper into the logic of IP maximalism. The first slide contains pictures of both an "original" and a "pirated" disk of the same movie, and seeks to establish the visual and tactile differences between the two. The original has "its own case, the name of the manufacturer, the identity of the recording company or studio, the federal tax number, etc." The pirated copy, by contrast, has "primitive packaging, in plastic, and a printed insert of bad quality."

Subsequent slides underscore the contrast by reference to origins, distinguishing clean and modern "manufacturing facilities" from messy DVD "burning" stations in dark apartments. The "original" has a screen-printed picture on one side, and its other side is "almost always silver (or gold, in a few cases)." By contrast, the side of a pirated disk where the information is stored is "colored (like a blank CD or DVD)," hinting at a racial typology by way of precious metals and underscoring the way in which consumers of piracy are more often poor and people of color. The pirated, or "burned," disk "lacks the artist or film's name, or has the name written by hand . . . [and] rarely uses graphics [pictures from the film]." Two slides are devoted entirely to close-ups of the numbers printed beside the stacking rings of original CDs and DVDs—which, I am instructed, are master codes, injection codes, catalogue and fabrication numbers, and barcodes. The purpose of these numbers is explained by neither Adriana and her support staff, nor the slide. Apparently, numbers merely provide authorization, as has been argued by Ian Hacking ([1975] 2006); they do not require it.

The pedagogy that Adriana and her coworkers articulate is at pains to establish the individuality of legitimate goods as opposed to the homogeneity of pirated ones. This helps us to further understand the above "reading" that the bulldozers provided to illicit DVDs and CDs. In the case of the FMAAs pedagogy, the uniformity of pirated disks is accomplished through a contrastive description of the process through which they are produced. The "legitimate" CD is made by being "stamped" specifically for the purposes of that particular sequence of songs or film, whereas the illegal CD or DVD is "burned" onto a blank medium that could have been used for any record or movie. The term "virgin," as a descriptor of the pirated CD, is sometimes employed ironically, indexing the medium's promiscuity (Gell 1996). Furthermore, the paper used for the illegitimate disk's shoddy label could have been used for any movie or music.

This focus on the physical properties of originals and copies underscores an earlier point about the increasingly seamless nature of pirated consumption—the fact that contemporary pirated movies and music look and sound no different from authorized copies when watched on the home television set or computer. The FMAA believes that the organization must, therefore, distinguish good materialization from bad. Precisely because the media involved in the production of pirated public culture were once "virginal" but are now "burned," they then become promiscuous—an index of willingness to receive any text that happens to be thrust upon them. The legitimate CD was made specifically for that particular movie: stamped and bonded through all eternity. The pirated DVD makes itself available to all comers—indeed, with the right equipment you might be able to burn additional information onto that pirated movie you bought, I am told as a way of reinforcing the impermanence of things pirated.

In the Brazilian context, notions of promiscuity are rooted in a common fear of oblivion. The sexually promiscuous female is sometimes referred to as a *piranha* (piranha fish) who consumes men by way of her unruly appetites—a usage documented in the work of numerous ethnographers of Brazil and a few historians (Bandyopadhyay and Nascimento 2010; Caulfield 1993; Gell 1996; Kulick 1998; Larkin 2014; Nazzari 1996; Needell 1987; Parker 2009; Rebhun 1999; Thomas 1991). This sexist caricature creates the figure of women who have refused monogamy, taking multiple partners—though the truth of the matter often is that multiple partners have forced themselves upon her. In any case, this multiplicity of partnerships is often portrayed as a problem of memory, as we shall come to understand—an incapacity (or refusal) to recall the primacy of a previous union. It is little wonder, then, that the anxieties associated with digital textuality find themselves translated into these idioms—using both garbage and promiscuity to naturalize enforcement, as we will now see in further detail.[5]

DisAppearances

São Paulo's Dawn Fair (Feira da Madrugada), occupies approximately ten square blocks in the city's working-class Brás neighborhood. Once upon a time, one seller informs me, shoppers, largely economic refugees from the Northeast of Brazil, used to travel to the market on tour buses very early in the morning before work: hence the invocation of dawn. Various sellers and clients tell me that over the years, however, the market has become

FIGURE 2.3 Feira da Madrugada, December 2012. Photo by the author. One of the main entrances to the fair.

equally active at all times of the day, and nowadays shoppers are as likely to cart off enormous shopping bags with all manner of commodities at 4 p.m. as at 4 a.m. Increasingly, between 2005 and 2015, the market simply became a low-cost shopping mall for working-class residents of the city of São Paulo and its environs, regardless of their origins. Many buyers live in the surrounding neighborhood and appreciate the low prices.

Three rounds of interviews and visits to the Dawn Fair over a five-year period revealed that, by December of 2012, a number of things had changed. As at the 25th of March Street shopping area discussed above, illicit digital media were absent by 2012. This absence had a specific history, which emerged more clearly in the case of the Dawn Fair than that of the 25th of March Street. In early October of 2011, the police in São Paulo cracked down on both markets. The mayor mobilized military police with the stated aim of ridding the markets of ambulant sellers—workers without a fixed physical presence in the form of a rented metal kiosk, complete with a number on the front and an operating license inside. These ambulant sellers and their goods were figured as *sujeira* (dirt) because of their ostensible clogging of traffic inside the market and on surrounding streets.

The cleaning away (once again, *limpeza*) of these "ambulants" then became the pretext for suppressing media piracy's "filth" writ large. Once the police had rounded up the ambulant sellers, they moved quickly to root out all violations of IP in the fixed kiosks as well. Sellers attempted to fight back. At The Dawn Fair, local workers took to the streets with signs that read "HELP! Ambulant sellers are not thieves! Enough of this repression!" and "Ambulant workers want to unionize! We generate jobs and have the support of society." Their language sought to counter their portrayal as filth, arguing instead that they were legitimate participants in an economy—"we are potential union members!" The situation remained explosive for two

FIGURE 2.4 Feira da Madrugada, December 2012. Photo by the author. The banner reads, "The Dawn Fair will never end."

weeks, with as many as eight mounted police officers at the ready near the entrance to the Dawn Fair and continual patrols of the space within and in surrounding blocks. Eventually, the ambulant sellers simply left the area, moving to the decentralized locations Edilson revealed to me in the introduction of this chapter.

Yet, the results of this policing continued to be manifest in December of 2012, beginning with the market's central square. Strikingly, instead of the usual pirated goods, this zone now contained a cluster of museum-ready objects able to tout the veracity of their own claims about their origins. For the month of December 2012, Hudson, of the Luiz Gonzaga museum (normally located in the airport of the Northeastern Brazilian city of Recife—Gonzaga's home when he was alive), had been invited by the Fair's management to present his exhibition. Luiz Gonzaga (1912–1989) was a famous accordion-playing songwriter and performer who recorded numerous albums and broke rural Northeastern music into mainstream circles throughout Brazil. At the market during the heavy shopping of the Christmas season, Hudson had been able to put just a tiny fraction of his relics on show. Here, he has just twenty-five square meters, whereas in Recife he has about three hundred, he tells me. He has nonetheless hung up reproductions of most of Gonzaga's record album covers. He takes me on a brief tour of "ExpoZaga's most important features"—the objects, in four glass cases, that Gonzaga actually owned and used. Among these are a radio, dinner plates, and musical instruments.

Hudson emphasizes two cases in particular. "You see those sunglasses?" he says, pointing to a pair in a case together with some shoes, a watch, a chamber pot, and a lantern. "Those are the glasses he wore for that record cover's picture, over there"—he points to the wall. And sure enough, the resemblance looks tight. Hudson enacts similar proof of his objects' veracity by pointing out a green-and-yellow leather hat that also appears on a record cover. "These were his personal effects," he concluded proudly.

I would like to be clear that I do not at all intend this description of Hudson's objects as mocking, but take his claims quite seriously. The qualities objects and practices are able to bring with them in processes of circulation have been endlessly debated in Brazil by literary theorists and sociologists (Ortiz 1999), often within the context of anxieties about cultural imperialism.[6]

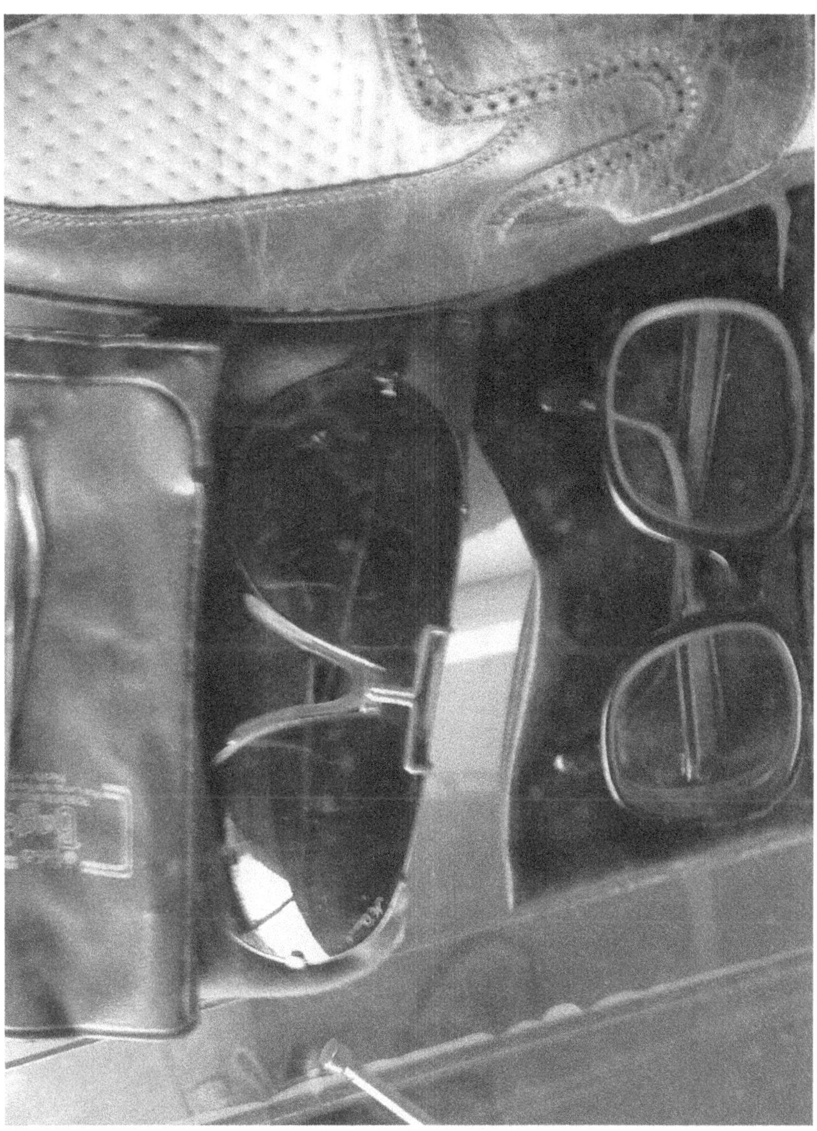

FIGURE 2.5 Feira da Madrugada, December 2012. Photo by the author. Luiz Gonzaga's very own sunglasses.

FIGURE 2.6 Feira da Madrugada, December 2012. Photo by the author. Luiz Gonzaga's very own sunglasses on Luiz Gonzaga's face, pictured on Luiz Gonzaga's record cover—reproduced and framed for ExpoZaga's São Paulo stint.

It has frequently been the case, for instance, that Brazilian elites have sought to reinforce local hierarchies by prominently consuming items from Europe and the United States. One historical example comes from belle époque Rio de Janeiro, where elites insisted on going about town in heavy British woolens that they purchased in transplanted European stores, as revealed by historian Jeffrey Needell (1987). In this context, French sociologist and anthropologist Pierre Bourdieu's conception of "distinction" helps us see how piracy might be threatening in particular ways in Brazil (Bourdieu 1984).

Bourdieu argues that social class is not only maintained through the material means of production but also by way of the symbolics of social capital. In other words, social class is maintained through taste. It is clearly the case that European and American practices and objects must be interpreted in a local context, and not merely dismissed as "foreign." Nonetheless, belle époque Carioca (Rio-based) elites believed that their European goods and practices held local value in shoring up their position in part *because* they came from Europe. Their alterity was the point. In this way, local ideologies about objects and practices clearly standing for the conditions of their production played a crucial role in maintaining local power structures and social capital. So, to return to the beliefs about pirated digital media espoused by the FMAA in the training sessions discussed above, digital textuality is threatening because the multiplicity of its physical forms reveals an ease of reproducibility and—from the perspective of "form"—an unclear connection to a point of origin. Digital textuality's combined promiscuity and inconstancy make it impossible to pin down, and therefore, to trace. In the ambit of piracy, we might begin to lose track of where things "really" come from.

Texts with such problematic gaps (lacking the capacity to clearly demonstrate their ties to IP) have been prominently suppressed in other parts of the 2012 Dawn Fair, too. Departing from the central square, with its temporary museum, I find numerous sealed kiosks. Interviewed officers are proud of the "cleaning" evidenced by these sealings. Walking through the aisles, with their present absences in the form of "boxes" (recall the use of the English word) that have been taped shut and labeled "sealed," is somewhat like looking at a reproduction of a two-dimensional topography from Brazilian history. During Brazil's military dictatorship (1964–1985, but particularly 1967–1975), a practice known as "prior" censorship often redacted the pages of prominent newspapers, magazines, and weeklies, leaving black boxes or white space (though sometimes apocryphal gardening tips, poems, or recipes).

The comparison turns out to be more than cursory, underscoring the ways in which distrust of the unstable materialities of digital textuality arises from distrust of unreliable, inconstant forms of mediation more broadly. According to prominent members of the military in charge of the enactment of censorship in the 1960s, the press had to be controlled not because the specific content of particular news might get out, but because of the news media's inherent unreliability. (Recall that, according to interviews of police and antipiracy NGO staff, it's not the American movies that are garbage, but the forms in which they are materialized.) General Meira Mattos explained the military's views of the news media in an interview in 1990. His opinions did not seem to have changed much since his nation's emergence into democracy five years before: "I don't like the press. I don't talk to the press. They're incapable of reproducing what you say. The goal of the press is sensationalism, not truth. Official decrees should be sufficient. Anything that needs to be disseminated should be announced, and that's that" (Smith 1997, 60). Chief of the Federal Police during the dictatorship, Moacyr Coelho, stated that an uncensored press, "published everything without proof or source" (Ibid. 173). And finally, channeling urgency in a mode that resembles the panics surrounding digital textuality, Special Advisor Helio Romão, who collaborated with Coelho in reading every newspaper every day, excused censorship by saying the dictatorship "was a period of exception" (Ibid. 172). Taken together, these sorts of Brazilian anxieties are directly engaged by IP maximalism in order to naturalize IP policing. Just as digital texts are potentially untrustworthy, the press cannot be trusted to mediate reliably between a source and its publics. These arguments for censorship once again contrast "clean" mediation (the decree, or the museum-ready object) with dirty mediation (sensationalism, or the pirated good), and argue that the unreliability of the middlemen in this context creates a state of emergency that necessitates repression.

We should underscore what is at stake in these disappearances (of pirated goods) and appearances (of Luiz Gonzaga's personal effects). Objections to illegitimate forms of digital textuality are not about the content. Rather,

FIGURE 2.7 Feira da Madrugada, December 2012. Photo by the author. Lacrado (sealed).

the physical presence of the object in what might have been any number of material forms—none of them authorized by the companies claiming responsibility for the origins of the text—is what is deemed slippery. And this slipperiness of form in turn derives from the text's failure to adequately police its gaps through attention to circulatory legitimacy.

Sexuality, History, and Cleanliness

Well-intentioned critiques of the increasing hegemony of IP maximalism have often focused on the uniformity of policing, arguing that this uniformity is the result of the imposition of North Atlantic ideologies onto a Global South (Ferreira, et al. 2012; Sa 2011).[7] In this context, for example, trade treaties seeking to universalize the linkage of illegality with piracy (the now defunct Anti-Counterfeiting Trade Agreement and the Trans-Pacific Partnership, for example, as well as TRIPS) clearly play an important role—suggesting a conflict between international regimes and smaller-scale, "local" ideologies of circulation. Such understandings appear, for example, in texts seeking to elucidate a Brazilian desire to avoid impersonal rules through personal relationships.

In the context of such arguments, the idea is that Brazilians are pirates at heart because of their propensity to strive for the simple solution involved in a workaround often called the *jeitinho* (DaMatta and Hess 1995; Duarte 2006; Ferreira, et al. 2012; Sa 2011).[8] The *jeitinho* literally means "little way" and emerges in situations in which a subject encounters a law or policy that she would like to avoid. The person subject to the imposition of a fine or penalty might start a conversation with the enforcer, attempting to find common ground (we're from the same town, we like the same music, or, best of all, we know the same people) and then use that common ground as a way to avoid the application of the law or policy. In this piratical context, the invocation of the *jeitinho* might lead Brazilian consumers to ask: "Why pay full prices when we can just sidestep the law?" Journalists and cultural critics often trot out the *jeitinho* as proof of Brazilian creativity in the face of constraint.

Such framings of piracy and counterfeiting are only partial pictures, because the Brazilians I talked to simply do not see themselves categorically as pirates— nor as consumers, nor as producers. If we are going to trace the back-and-forth between the institutions seeking to inculcate IP as the correct way to approach digital textuality and those seeking more "open" models (including, but not limited to, the pirates themselves), we must attend not simply to impositions of beliefs dubbed "foreign" or "Western;" rather, we must scrutinize the ways in which IP maximalism activates intertextual gaps in the locations in which it is instituted as well as associated ideologies of sexuality, subjectivity, and cleanliness. This activation creates a hyperattention to the circulatory aspects of form—framed as indexes of those authorized to circulate the given text (rights holders). Such an approach elucidates the ways in which the contemporary unfolding of IP maximalism—beyond just coercion and bribery—sometimes involves international collaboration. Understanding this, in turn, opens us up to a fuller understanding of the current imbrication of policing and governance with mediation—the way in which IP becomes a powerful tool for managing participation in local and national economies.

Dirt, promiscuity, object biography (relics), and censorship can be linked by a historicity that disregards selected aspects of the conditions of production of the text. This is why we must understand the historicity that circulatory legitimacy calls upon. In this context of localizing material purity, consider, again, the work of Brazilian literary critic and theoretician Roberto Schwarz (1992), who argued that much of Latin America is subject to a crisis of authenticity because, since 1920, the national is arrived at by eliminating all that is perceived to have a foreign influence. Schwarz cleverly calls this phenomena "nationalism by elimination." He goes even further by arguing that this crisis of authenticity derives not only from the process of elimination itself but also from the deeply repetitive nature of that process. We Brazilians do this nationalism by elimination again and again, he argues in his essay. This is paired with the aforementioned destructive force of boundary-breaking collaborations in dance, music, food, and religion. The result is a compounded incapacity to remember where things came from—an endemic inconstancy that becomes all that much more disturbing because it is repeated.

A final incident illustrates this point about the ways circulatory legitimacy—as indexed by sexuality, subjectivity, and cleanliness—may be analyzed under a broader rubric of historicity. Such an analysis, in turn, points us to the temporal aspects of intertextual gaps not just in Brazil, but wherever IP maximalism is enacted. During a 2009 lunch interview with Roberto—the lawyer whose work frequently took him to the United States, who taught economics at a private university in São Paulo, and who was at the time president of the antipiracy lobbying group NAIF—he lowers his voice in the somewhat expensive restaurant he has selected for our meeting. He leans forward so that I alone can hear him and tells me in hushed tones about a shopping mall in São Paulo whose owners were exposed for paying the police not to confiscate the pirated goods that were circulating there—among them, fake handbags and sunglasses as well as illicit CDs and DVDs. A very powerful family owned the shopping mall, he tells me, and that family's trickery was eventually brought to light. Stories were printed about the controversy online and in newspapers, and even made it to TV newscasts. "But the problem," he tells me, leaning back and speaking somewhat more volubly, is that

"Brazilians have no memory. They don't care where an object comes from. And when there's a scandal, that scandal just disappears. The dirt just goes away." Much like the hypothetical improper user of a digital file who fails to attend to the circumstances of that file's production, the facts pertinent to understanding who this family might be simply disappear. The family just goes right on running the mall and making money, and very quickly, "people forget. . . . And that," he tells me with finality, "is why we have to fight piracy."

3 BORDERING, THE INTERNET, AND PARAGUAYAN HORSES

THE DIVERSE FIELD OF CULTURAL PRACTICE known as the Internet lies at the core of digital textuality—as the space in which texts of various sorts are produced, given value, and circulated. It is also a space in which notions of national and Net-related citizenship are established, undermining any pat distinctions between the virtual and the real (Postill 2011; Lindtner 2014). One of the central problems for the governance of the Internet therefore lies in the challenges posed by its location in time and space. Where is the Internet, exactly? Everywhere? Nowhere? And *when* is it, as well? In news media outlets, scholarly journals, coffee shops, and blogs, the Internet is frequently indexed by descriptors derived from water—a networked network with amorphous boundaries that are always moving. Terms such as "flow," "depth," and "stream" get recruited to myriad tasks by devotees and dilettantes alike—with the English-language terms frequently prevailing regardless of local language. It won't sit still. Sometimes the Internet becomes positively gaseous, as the now common term "cloud" suggests. Indexes with too much solidity are often unwelcome, as was the case with US Senator Ted Stevens's now famous "series of tubes" gaffe (Mitchell 2006). The idea behind mocking him was not only that the Internet was not nearly so material but also that it was much more complicated.[1] When the *New York Times* ran a series of articles in September of 2012 on the physical structures that support the cloud, information on the cloud's pollution and power consumption came as a shock to many readers (see comments attached to Glanz 2012). The Internet didn't simply float out there, somewhere?

Frequently, an inability to grasp the Internet's locations make it not only "difficult to police" (Davison 2012), somewhat like the high seas, as has been remarked in other anthropological work (Dawdy 2011; Dent 2012), but also like the informal economies I have analyzed in previous chapters. No one quite knows where the boundaries lie. These anxieties are in some ways not new. Consider the novel and movie *Jaws,* and with it, the terror that a large, but nonetheless quick and unfettered predator was supposed to produce in a liquid medium (Benchley 1974); the shark is right beneath you, and you don't even know it. Or consider Adventure Comics supervillain, Mist, who could change himself into a living gas, making parts of himself suddenly material at will (Bester and Burnley 1941). Both liquid and gaseous anxieties continue to play out in contemporary public culture. In the Disney film *Wreck It Ralph,* the villain, called Turbo (aka King Candy), leaves his own videogame when his popularity wanes, destroying the games he attempts to inhabit together with the one he has left. His passage from one game to another takes place through the wires that connect the gaming consoles to the electrical grid, which together provide him with a kind of fluid network. The film's message is clear. In failing to stay put, Turbo ruins both games.

In the last chapter, I examined how localized approaches to intertextual gaps play an important role in the policing of IP. We also saw how IP maximalism connects production and consumption of piracy with problems of memory that have long been the subject of public discussion in Brazil—more specifically, Brazilian shame over forgetfulness by way of sexuality, culture, and history. I have underscored the ways in which IP maximalism is not merely imposed on Brazil from the outside, but must work through Brazilian approaches to dirt, promiscuity, censorship, and relics.

This chapter continues to specify digital textuality by asking how we can place boundaries around the text when the fixity of the speaker in time and space is called into question. I also wonder what happens when the boundaries around the text are called into question by its mode of circulation, while I inquire into situations in which identification itself revolves around precisely that lack of fixity. In more detail, I argue that if we are going to understand how particular groups of people—in this case, Brazilians—are conceiving of the Internet as a lawless space that seems powerful and efficacious but is often ephemeral and dangerous, we should consider local precedents (see also Postill 2011). In this ambit, then, I consider practices of bordering (Fassin 2011; Galemba 2017)—in particular the border between Brazil and Paraguay as manifest at the triple border between Brazil, Argentina, and Paraguay. This border is further complicated by Paraguay's role in negotiating an even further border with a noncontiguous entity, China, since Paraguay has become one of the most important paths through which Chinese goods enter Brazil—at least in popular parlance.[2] Paraguay is significant in this case because it is the location where the pirated or knockoff computers that Brazilians used to begin accessing the Internet were purchased in the late 1990s. Indeed, without Paraguay's supply of cheap digital technology during this period, Brazil's relationship with the Internet would have developed much more slowly.

In the context of these relations, I also wish to consider a Brazilian critique of rapaciousness enacted mostly by intellectuals, media critics, and left-leaning politicians that portrays corporate actors as being capable of entering and leaving the lives of common citizens without warning. In this rendition of Brazilian society, corporations come and go as they please, toying with powerless consumers, and, crucially for the Brazilian case, collaborating with international actors to benefit wealthy Brazilians while the poor languish. Significant in this respect is the work of Brazilian sociologist Euclides da Cunha, whom I discussed briefly in chapter 1 in the context of anxieties about unhealthy mixtures. However, in this context, we must consider da Cunha's indictment of Brazilian institutions (in his case, government and the army), which are characterized as small-minded, incompetent, and murderous (Cunha [1902] 1944). These negative sensibilities currently extend to Brazilian government and business in ways that will become clear—putting into question the very possibility of bounding texts, speakers, and receivers.

This chapter begins with Brazilian approaches to policing the Internet in relation to IP, as well as with a critique of corporate control of society enacted by pro-Internet activists on the left. More specifically, I analyze permeability, appearances, and subterfuge on the Internet, which Brazilians largely accessed starting in the mid-1990s by way of low-cost products that came from Paraguay. Next, I consider Paraguay more broadly as an imaginary that helps define Brazilian digital textuality, showing how nations and their bordering practices in turn shape mediation. We will also see how Paraguay offers a way of thinking about Brazilian greed and the policing of IP.

The Internet(s)

We can learn about the properties of a Brazilian Internet by looking at a debate over its policing, which was only just resolved in 2016. Back in 1999, a then senator (now a congressman) from the state of Minas Gerais, Eduardo Azeredo, drafted a law that sought to control what he portrayed as the Internet's unruliness. The law went through a series of revisions and was never passed, but was trotted out again in 2009 when virtual attacks on banks and hacked presidential emails made headlines. The dormant "Azeredo Law" was suddenly propelled by the run-of-the-mill urgency typical of Brazilian developmentalist speech genres (namely, that Brazil is "behind" other nations and needs to catch up). This time, current criminality added impetus—a form of criminality, mind you, supported by cellular communication from gang leaders behind prison walls (see chapter 5). The law's passage seemed imminent, as Azeredo was voted chair of the national government's Technology Committee. Taking too long to discuss the niceties of Internet policing would make us "overly late," Azeredo argued in the press (Cardoso 2012). The version of the law current in 2009 sought to impose order by criminalizing forms of behavior perceived to be particular to digital environments, among them, implanting viral code, seeking to make use of personal data for purposes other than those for which it had been entered, and either uploading or downloading copyrighted materials. Even those willing to accept that such behavior predated the digital era (and there weren't many) were nonetheless alarmed by what they saw as its unprecedented scope and scale.

Across approaches to IP, many could agree that the acts addressed in the law were undesirable. But the form of policing proposed in the law immediately led to controversy. According to Azeredo, Internet service providers (ISPs) would have to stockpile information on the activities of their clients for at least three years—in case that information should be needed in prosecuting future cybercrimes. Attached to this stockpiling, Internet providers would be held responsible for how their clients were using the Internet—including the veracity of the data their users gave out and also its legality (in cases of the exchange of "pirated" texts). Azeredo and his supporters felt that the Internet was a zone in which criminality had not yet been defined, and hence, it was a zone of impunity. It was, as we shall see, a kind of Paraguay. Sometimes the English term "Far West" was used to describe both the Internet and the neighbor (Paraguay). Furthermore, by way of these proposals, the framers of the Azeredo Law indicated their sense that the Internet was a place in which taking or assigning responsibility was fraught by difficulties. Texts traveled so far and so fast that origins became punishingly difficult to ascertain. Finally, the law's framers also were convinced that policing the Internet's space (however it was constituted) would best be accomplished through private means and that the ISPs themselves—not some external authority established by the state—ought to be in charge of making sure users were being well behaved. The state would simply make the policies that private companies would carry out. This mode of explication was classic neoliberal cant, in that it assigned private responsibility for public concerns.

Many of these proposals were not distinctive to the Brazilian case and had been either tried or debated in North America and Europe. But what was more unusual was Azeredo's next proposal—that users would have to identify themselves before beginning any operation on the Internet that involved interaction with other users, including sending emails, participating in chat rooms, creating blogs, or downloading data. In other words, users would have to furnish their name, telephone number, and general registry number (their RG—the Brazilian equivalent of a Social Security number in the United States) before doing anything online. The monitoring of this, once again, was to be privatized. ISPs would be responsible for the compilation and maintenance of records on each user, and access would be granted only when identity had been confirmed by the provider. This process would, in turn, necessitate that the provider have copies of the identity documents of actual users on file, or else that each provider subcontract this storage to someone else. The law's authors argued that this was the best way to keep hackers out of the system. Access without identification would be punishable by banning the user from the Internet for two to four years, and possibly prison if an actual crime was committed. This proposed policy tells us that its framers believed that the Internet lacked clear spatial and temporal borders and was a zone in which the subject became overly mobile, ephemeral, and perhaps even unknowable. In other words, according to Azeredo et al., the Internet was characterized by epistemological incertitude with respect to subjectivity. It was an omnipresent and lawless zone in which the boundaries between the self and the other were dangerously unclear. Circulatory legitimacy would be almost impossible to maintain since intertextual gaps could not be policed. Strong laws were needed in order to establish the clarity that is apparently enjoyed in regular, face-to-face, interactions—the standard for evaluating all human interaction (of course; see Lee 1997 for an examination of the power of face-to-face ideologies).

The Azeredo Law received substantial support, and the way in which that support was phrased contributed to a sense of the Internet in Brazil as lawless, poorly demarcated, and ubiquitous. Using dramatic language, one columnist proposed that the Azeredo Law "disciplined" the Internet by imposing "order on the existing laws, in order to avoid that crimes in the virtual world should cancel out its incalculable value" (Medioli 2009). The columnist then continued in starker language, complete with damnation, death, and chaos. Apparently the stakes were high, and the choices, clear:

> The Azeredo Law limits the possibility that the Internet should become debased and a living hell for the well-intentioned. It is oriented by a preventative intuition, much like the construction of a bypass before dozens of people get run over in that spot. We know that there, the number of victims will rise very soon, and that moving quickly will prevent heartache and tears. Obviously, we can't leave the most democratic and economical mode of access to knowledge to the mercy of anarchy—this tool that is used, after all, by those who work, be they large or small, rich or poor. (Ibid.)

And finally, the columnist concludes that the lack of fixity of the Internet that leads to democracy and equality also creates dangers: "Delinquents gravitate to the Internet for its ease of robbing banks, commercial establishments, committing fraud, blackmailing without leaving home, destroying reputations and maintaining anonymity since one can so easily lose oneself in the abyss of the system" (Ibid.). Here, then, was the ultimate fear, and the necessary support for Azeredo's requirement that everyone identify themself—that the Internet had created a kind of fourth dimension through which criminals could enter our lives and then disappear without a trace: a personalized trapdoor into our homes that they could efface upon leaving. In sum, an unregulated Internet—an Internet without the Azeredo Law—allowed the boundaries between real life and this new virtual world to remain unpoliced, and it did so by allowing real life and virtual life to mix not indiscriminately—but in a way that was controlled by the wrong sort of people. By way of this poorly demarcated Far West, criminals could get into your home without having to leave theirs. You'd never even get a good look at them.

The Corporate Ether

Support for the Azeredo Law was far from unanimous. Those opposing it worried about a brutish oligarchic state (represented by Azeredo and his corporate supporters), in some cases, a state that was portrayed as totalitarian. Critics of the law began to refer to it as the Digital AI-5 (Institutional Act number 5), comparing it to the harsh antipress and anti–free speech act passed by the bureaucratic authoritarian government during the darkest years of Brazil's military dictatorship (1968–1978). In this historical comparison, the Internet of today was being compared with the news media of yesterday, and also with the right to free assembly and speech.[3] Others proposed that Azeredo had absolutely no understanding of how the Internet functioned, that his attempts to ascertain the identity of users would only work on the already law-abiding; hackers could easily sidestep information requirements. One series of scolds was not directed at the law at all, but made use of the trope of Brazilian civil society I explored at the end of the last chapter—that Brazilians were themselves to blame for such a draconian policy because they were forgetful and ill-informed. This, in turn, meant that Brazilian laws were made "in deafness."

In another discourse quite typical of Brazilian indictments of governmentality, one group of critics, among them literary theoretician Idelber

Avelar, claimed that Azeredo was guilty of plain old Brazilian-style corruption (Avelar 2006). This claim was abetted by Azeredo's recent implication in a vote-buying scandal in the Senate, from which he was forced to step down, only to be elected later as a Congressman. Avelar's worry about the Azeredo Law was that the companies that would authenticate users were, in part, owned by Azeredo, though mostly by his close friends. The sudden requirement for a massive authentication industry that the law promised thus stood to make Azeredo and his friends extremely rich. The Internet could thus be rendered familiar in quite local terms—by way of censorship under military dictatorship, through the ignorance of *o povo* (the people), and as a means by which local politicians might line their pockets in ways that were deemed common for Brazilian politicians and corporations.

In one particular voicing of this anxiety, a group of young, left-wing advocates for freedom of digital communication at Rio de Janeiro's Freenet Foundation appropriated the figure of the lurking hacker that symbolizes the Azeredo Law, reversing the figure's customary associations in order to criticize the proposed legislation. For these critics, it was greedy corporations lurking in the ether who were the attackers of digital citizens, not hackers. Such critiques of Brazil's vulnerability to external influences had their roots in theories of "associated dependent development" (Cardoso 1989), but received further support from comedy—in the form of political cartoons (as seen, once upon a time, in political cartoon and essay magazine *Bundas*, and more recently in popular sketches by YouTube comedy sensation *Porta dos Fundos*; Romero 2013), which often lampoon corporations taking advantage of Brazilians with the support of politicians.

Just such a comic-critical approach was on display during a conference on IP justice hosted by Rio de Janeiro's Getúlio Vargas Foundation in 2013. At the end of the first day, participants gathered for a gala to celebrate not only the conference's successful kickoff but also the tenth anniversary of the open-licensing platform Creative Commons. The platform had been created by a small group of activists and scholars in the United States as a way to make copyright more transparent, but had received almost instantaneous support from activists and scholars based at the Getúlio Vargas Foundation. A few of the American framers were there to lend their support to the celebrations.

In a warehouse a few miles from the conference, participants listened to speeches about the global reach of Creative Commons and the many ways the platform had addressed the expectations of its framers: allowing producers of "content" to take charge of how their work would circulate, while sidestepping the pointless complexity and obfuscation of the copyright process. After these initial speeches had been completed, Freenet took the stage to inject the event with more explicitly local material. The conference organizers had explained the inclusion of Freenet in the program as an attempt to show that important, globally focused, activism was happening in Brazil, too, not just in the United States. Members of Freenet explained their recent completion of a set of videos designed to "raise consciousness" about a series of threats to global communication (recall that "raising consciousness" was the strategy of NAIF, from chapters 1 and 2; here we see that strategy turned to different ends). Some of these videos, spokesman Marina explained, were aimed at a Brazilian audience. But they all referenced threats that Internet users faced all over the world. The problem, as Marina saw it, was that the Internet, conceived of as a fundamental communicative modality and, hence, as a human right, was being encroached upon by Brazilian corporations in cahoots with international ones—all of them unconcerned about the rights of the average consumer.

In the first film Marina played for the conference audience, a somewhat dark-complected hairdresser at a salon lectures her two lighter-skinned clients, both of whom are oblivious about how absurdly overpriced their Brazilian Internet service is. This price gouging is something that people in the First World would never accept, the hairdresser intones (indicating, I think to myself in a culturally intimate moment, that she has never had a brush with American cable companies). The hairdresser becomes increasingly animated as she rails against the evils of Brazilian corporations jacking up the price, frantically teasing the whiter woman's hair into a tangle that more closely resembles her own by the end of her screed. Her interlocutors, one of them being worked on in the chair, the other waiting for her highlights to come in, exchange a worried look as the hairdresser begins to use complex terms about Internet functionality and pricing. In the end, it does not appear that the hairdresser's clients are impressed, or even care much about what she has been saying, though they do appear to be disgusted by the experience they are having at the salon. The video is clearly meant to index the complacency of the Brazilian middle class, while inverting a customary racial topology in which the white are the knowledgeable. Here, they're dolts.

In another video, a young man gets home from traveling and the first thing he does is pick up the phone to try to get his Internet turned back on. Upon connecting with customer service, he discovers that the company has created a pricing scheme that divides up all the different features that he might want online, with tiered charges. If he wants to download content from other providers, he has to pay more. If he wants email, he pays more. He is incredulous, and repeats, numerous times, that the Internet is "all one thing. You can't carve it up this way." Finally, outraged, he threatens to post the text of this entire conversation on his blog as a way of exposing this Internet nonneutrality, shaming the company. "Oh," the woman interrupts. "*O senhor* [the kind sir] has a blog? Well, if you want to contribute to a blog, you will require our deluxe package, which is R$289 a month." The video ends with the youth's expression of total defeat. We can easily imagine him simply having to pay. Both of these videos enact a critique of Brazilian corporations that shows the powerlessness of the consumer. In the first Freenet video, the hairdresser's clients are nonplussed, and far from persuaded. In the second, the young man seems resigned to forking over the cash.

A third video most clearly argues for ways the despatialized and detemporalized properties of the Internet provide opportunities for corporate bad actors to hide. In this piece, a young man walks around the city being filmed by a hidden camera while a narrator talks about all the information that is being gathered on him. As he walks down the street, stops to buy a newspaper, gets on the metro, and continues walking, he is everywhere and at all times followed by a surreptitious handheld camera. On-screen information flashes about the man's habits and preferences. In this video, then, the villains are corporate raiders trying to get money from consumers by profiling them. At the end of the video, the narrator suggests that this information could easily be used to accuse people of political crimes and even terrorism. But we should notice that in this video, the risky liquidities of the Internet are identical to those that were feared by Azeredo and his supporters. At any moment, a hand could reach up out of the pavement and grab the innocent passerby, defying space, time, and common sense. For the Freenet Foundation, the rhetoric is of "transparency" but nonetheless adds up to an aspiration for fixity very much like that of the Azeredo Law. We need to be able to "see" what these corporate bad actors are doing, because as it stands, we can't. Currently, the Internet provides these corporations with a space in which they can appear and then capriciously disappear—an environment of blind spots and smoke screens. This is amplified by the way that, in Brazil, these corporations collaborate with international bad actors to grow the wealth and power of Brazil's richest while diminishing the capacity of the poor to advocate on their own behalf.

These critiques of the suitability of Brazilian corporate raiding to the amorphousness of the Internet have, in many ways, fueled the recently instituted Civil Code of the Internet, or Marco Civil (signed into law in 2014). Instead of seeking to give structure to the Internet by enumerating the crimes that may be committed within it, privatizing its policing, and forcing its users to make their identities concrete, this document instead operates from a human rights perspective, aiming to protect the free speech and freedom of association rights of users of the Internet.[4] Without being explicit about it, the document assumes that these rights need to be protected from the likes of Azeredo and his big-business collaborators, who are currently able to hide, too easily, within the Internet's diaphanous spatiality and temporality. Under the Azeredo Law, criminality on the Internet was to be determined not by intentions, but by association. The ISPs become guilty of supporting piracy whether they knew about the material their users had been illegally posting or not, and "pirates" could be kids who simply shared a song without thinking about the larger repercussions. Under the Marco Civil, one had to have intended to perform a criminal act in order to be held responsible for it (notice the primacy of an ostensibly autonomous individual's "intentions," as critiqued by Rosaldo 1982). We can therefore notice that this argument for concretizing the individual (by forcing someone to have an identification number) carries with it a particular communicative ideology—wherein some acting subject, identifiably rooted in time and space, establishes intentions that, in turn, permit acts to take place.

The drafting of the Marco Civil availed itself of some of the Internet's redemptive qualities by soliciting public feedback online. Anyone with a computer and an Internet connection could post, and the comments were collated by staff of the Getúlio Vargas Foundation of Rio de Janeiro. At the drafting phase, these comments were uploaded to a common page, and many were then incorporated into the policy document. What is noteworthy here is that, despite the very different political orientations and institutional affiliations of this relatively new Brazilian Internet law, it still relies on fixing an acting individual in space and time, defining behavior as criminal only when it is "intentional." So—once again—the Internet's unruly potentialities are to be circumscribed by firming up a user with rights in a particular time and space—in this case, Brazil.

But what, precisely, might we mean by "Brazil" in the context of digital textuality?

Paraguay(s)

In Brazil, Paraguay isn't just "out west." It appears in speech genres associated with nationhood, sport, and shopping as a way of commenting on the unpredictability of Brazil's western border, the inadequacy of soccer teams that suddenly play terribly after seeming to play well, and the conundrums of consumption. But importantly for our purposes, Paraguay's omnipresence in Brazil has increased tremendously alongside the growth of the use of the Internet—in large part because the technology used to access the Internet was acquired *through* Paraguay in the 1990s and into the early 2000s (Rabossi 2004, 2007, 2012; Pinheiro Machado 2017). Under such circumstances, and because of the almost identical terminology used to describe both the spatiotemporal irregularities of the Internet and those of Paraguay, I will explore, in some detail, the way Paraguay surfaces in Brazil in quotidian discourse, and importantly, the ways this discourse has changed over the period in which "piracy" becomes hyperscrutinized.

First, nationhood—a way of conceiving of Brazil's neighbor that has remained relatively stable over the course of the twentieth century: Paraguay appears in every elementary school textbook as the aggressor in the bloody War of the Triple Alliance (1864–1870), in which it attempted to expand its border by carving a route to the sea through the territories of Brazil, Argentina, and Uruguay. After a few dramatic victories, Paraguay ended up getting trounced. Brazilian historian Boris Fausto—normally a practitioner of value-free prose—tells it this way, emphasizing the long-term repercussions of Paraguay's defeat in dramatic language for a nation (Brazil) that sometimes unironically proclaims "order and progress" on its flag:

> Paraguay was devastated by the conflict, and lost parts of its territory to Brazil and Argentina. It also lost its future. Its process of modernization became a thing of the past, and Paraguay itself became an exporter of products of scant value. The most reliable estimates suggest that half of Paraguay's population died in the struggle. . . . Most of the survivors were old people, women, and children. (Fausto 1999, 126)

In many Brazilian contexts, Paraguay holds the status of the gruesomely beaten, and hence, of the subsequently undeveloped and lawless—a place where laws and procedures simply are not in effect: the sort of place where escaped Nazis could hole up for ages not only because of myriad sympathizers but simply because no one can find them (Manzo 2011). In a sense, popular Brazilian treatments of Paraguay suggest that it still hasn't recovered from the beating it received way back when. The War of the Triple Alliance continues to populate contemporary usage. For instance, though the origins of this particular application of Paraguay are apocryphal, the term *cavalo paraguaio* (Paraguayan horse) is sometimes applied to soccer teams that unexpectedly win at the beginning of a tournament and then self-destruct on the field. One recent ESPN-Brasil sports forum asked a prominent commentator to discuss, with fans, his opinions on the biggest *cavalo paraguaio* soccer team of all time, for instance. A wide variety of teams from particular eras were nominated, on the air and in subsequent comments (ESPN Brasil 2014). Apparently, the notion of a Paraguayan horse, complete with potential nominees, was on the tip of many tongues.

The relationship between Paraguay and disappointment has intensified since the 1990s, populating other ways in which Paraguay circulates in Brazil. This linkage is tied to some important socioeconomic variables. In the late 1950s,

Paraguay declared its eastern portion of the country—with particular emphasis on Ciudad del Este—a duty-free zone, and by the 1980s, Ciudad del Este became one of the largest entrepôts in the world for all manner of goods, from clothing and perfume to CDs and electronics (Rabossi 2004; Pinheiro Machado 2009; Aguiar 2010; Rabossi 2012; Schuster 2012). In times when travel to Europe and North America was too expensive for Brazilians, Ciudad del Este became the low-cost shopping zone of choice, as its suspension of taxes allowed it to offer prices many times lower than the national averages. At its height, tens of thousands of Brazilians visited Ciudad del Este every week, and for a short time, it was reported by *Forbes Magazine* to be the third-largest urban economy in the world (Seri 2012, 81). This growth went along with an expansion of informal street markets selling knockoffs and pirated goods within Brazil—all of them supplied by way of Paraguay, and several of them subsequently referred to as "Paraguayan markets." These are the informal markets I first encountered in Brazil—the ones with which this book opened.

Ciudad del Este's piratical importance to Brazil has shrunk somewhat since the passage of the Mercosul Agreement between Brazil, Argentina, Uruguay, and Paraguay in 1996, in which trade barriers to China were largely regularized across the four Southern Cone nations. This agreement has made direct importation from China just as good an option for supplying local goods as bringing them in through Paraguay. Paraguay's brief expulsion from Mercosul (in 2012) temporarily reinvigorated its thoroughfare economy. Despite the low cost of Chinese imports directly into Brazil, the importance of Paraguay as a site of low-cost importation nonetheless continues, as thousands still shop at its stores and kiosks and bring products into Brazil. Whenever the Brazilian currency weakens, Paraguay's popularity as a shopping site surges (because of the rising cost of imported goods for Brazilians and the rising costs of travel). Furthermore, Ciudad del Este ostensibly remains an important source for the smuggling of drugs, guns, and even human beings into Brazil—or so the myriad news reports on the porosity of the border would suggest. For those traveling by legitimate routes, rather than through the nearly unmapped forests and rivers so plentiful on Brazil's western border, traffic jams on the famed Ponte Internacional da Amizade (Friendship Bridge) are still legendary. The quickest way to get across the bridge is to hitch a ride with one of the many motorcycle taxis that, somewhat like hackers on the Internet, are able to find space between conventional vehicles in ways that make a passenger unaccustomed to such needle threading nauseous. Here, we can see the importance of a porous border that indexes a power differential—in which Paraguay's destroyed status and subsequent lawlessness continue to make it useful as a supplier of Brazil's modern consumptive habits—particularly in electronics. It is important to understand that some of the lower-cost goods that flooded Brazil in the 1990s, and which continue to circulate on a massive scale, were not only smuggled products with unpaid duties. They were also low-cost copies of more expensive items such as the latest cellular phones, TVs, stereos, and MP3 players. Almost without exception, these pirated or knockoff goods were made in China. Sometimes, they were just plain counterfeits (phones with the Motorola name, but without the same quality control or brand support, for example).

It is in this way that, in the late 1990s, Paraguay became one of the most powerful indexes of a localized approach to consumption grounded in circulatory legitimacy. Recall from chapter 1: buyers can choose to get a good deal through a pirated product while avoiding high duties and taxes, or pay much more while enjoying the magic of a diminished intertextual gap. This tension of price, quality, and IP emerges in quotidian conversations in which consumers interact with the objects they have bought—most often when those objects break. Disparaging something that malfunctions or works unpredictably as "Paraguayan" is extremely common.

The reproachful term is also applied to things that might appear to be expensive but are, on closer examination, cheap. One contemporary Brazilian fashion blog, *Glamour Paraguaio*, preserves the English term "glamour" in its title. The blog's author offers the following baptismal moment for its name:

> One day I found a nostalgic keepsake from my childhood, a 24-hour lipstick from Paraguay (that's right—the kind that was around all the time in the early '90s). I took it out did a "make" [preserves English word] and went out feeling pretty and RICH, the way we should all feel every day. So my girlfriend asks me: "What pretty lipstick! It's pretty! It's glamour [English word, once again]! IS IT MAC [a line of cosmetics with a very distinct brand, and high prices,

> particularly in Brazil]?" "MAC? Nope—it's my Paraguayan Glamour," I said. And it became my all-time favorite expression. (Facirolli 2012)

Here, the viewer, rather than the buyer, is fooled—thinking that the makeup is expensive only to discover that it's not. The low cost of apparent brandedness then becomes grounds for celebrating. The blog goes on to document clothing, makeup, and music that is right on the border of tacky, including references to the late glam and stadium rock of the 1980s, and pictures from fashion magazines that depict tasteless outfits—many of them involving fur and feathers. Paraguay here becomes a way of addressing anxieties over what something costs, whether or not it is, in some sense, "real," and whether that "reality" translates into an interactive experience wherein its buyer's tastes are then valued. Is the product truly fashionable, or just ridiculous? "Paraguay" points not only to something cheap but also more precisely, to the fear that in this economy, ways of being certain that things actually are what they purport to be are few, and subject to manipulation. In this context, "Paraguay" underscores worries that consumption could, and frequently does, go wrong—and that it does so precisely at places that are deemed important: how you look (your makeup), or your capacity to participate in the sort of technological consumption that leaves you feeling plugged in (your computer or your phone). Crucial to this epistemology of consumption is the notion of possible deceit, mingled, crucially, with too much permeability. Put somewhat differently, this use of the term Paraguayan calls attention to the potential (inevitable?) space between the artifice of a brand, and what it can accomplish. What, precisely, *is* the text, and who are its producers and consumers? We simply don't always know.

What we have seen so far is that the adjoining nation of Paraguay is defined, in Brazil, as an unequal relation, a lawless territory and a sporadic border—one that offers illusory benefits that threaten economic and communicative orthodoxies while at the same time reinforcing them. This cluster of overlapping tropes came to a head in the summer of 2012, as left-wing Paraguayan President Fernando Lugo was dubiously impeached and chased out of office—thus threatening a throwback to the days of military dictatorship that Latin American countries had all too recently attempted to distance themselves from (Brazil redemocratized gradually through the 1980s, and Paraguay, not till the early 1990s).[5] The other nations of the Mercosul Agreement responded by cutting Paraguay out of the trading zone while suddenly admitting Venezuela. When the new right-wing Paraguayan president, who had been put in power by what looked awfully like a coup d'état, finally took charge, he was not at all pleased with Brazil. He issued a statement saying that the world's largest hydroelectric dam, in Paraguay near the Brazilian border, and built in collaboration with Brazil, would no longer be selling its substantial surplus to Brazil. At the time, the dam supplied Paraguay with all the electricity it needed, using up only 7 percent of its total output, with the remaining 93 percent being sold to Brazil. The new Paraguayan leader announced that this excess power would, henceforth, stay home—an odd claim to make since there was no viable way of storing the excess power.

This subsequently retracted threat spurred a Brazilian commentator from a prominent newsweekly to derisive flourishes. First of all, the author put Paraguay down for being small, in contrast to Brazil's larger size and buying power: "Since our neighbor [Paraguay] consumes only 7% of the energy it has a right to—precisely because it is economically stunted, with a population of 6.5 million inhabitants, equivalent to half of the residents of the city of São Paulo—Brazil ends up buying all the remaining electricity, for which it forks over close to R$800 million per year [about US$400 million at that time]" (Cilo 2012). Then, the columnist's tone becomes even more demeaning, and several Brazilian stereotypes take shape, among them: that Paraguay is responsible for flooding Brazilian streets with low-quality merchandise, that it is incapable of collecting taxes or formalizing its economy, that it has a lopsided market with only one export, and that it is incapable of making intelligent policy decisions. The screed is worth quoting at length because it gives a clear idea of how tropes of lawlessness populate Brazilian thinking about Paraguay, returning us to the fears that surround an unregulated and unruly space of digital textuality (the Internet):

> The Paraguayan threat is either a joke in bad taste or an amateurish political bluff. President Franco didn't even blush when he appeared on national television saying that the energy that today comes to Brazil should stay in the

> country. Stay in the country? Sure—to help the economy grow, spur industrialization and stimulate job growth. Look, even if Paraguay started manufacturing in-country all the contraband products that supply the illegal commerce of all of South America, or even if they decided to give out LED lamps and televisions—without receipts, of course—to all the homes in their country, they would never succeed in consuming the seven thousand megawatts they're entitled to at Itaipu [dam]. . . . Without the energy from Itaipu, Brazil would fall short, it's true. . . . On that side of the border, on the other end of the Friendship Bridge, there would be a well-lit country, full of electricity, but without money to pay doctors, police and teachers. A political loss that, in the long run, would cost more than the R$800 million that Paraguay receives. So who are you going to sell your energy to, you Paraguayan horse? (Ibid.)

The answer is Brazil, of course (of course; the reference is to an American talking horse called Mr. Ed; Livingston and Evans 1961).

To sum up, then, Paraguay has here appeared as the weak and lawless territory whose boundaries are capricious, whose modernization is stunted, but which is thereby able to inundate Brazil with goods that allow Brazilian consumers to feel as though they can participate in modern information and fashion economies on nearly equal footing with Europeans and North Americans. But this participation can be deceptive, because these goods can, and frequently do, underperform when compared with their considerably more expensive counterparts. Paraguay is, in some sense, everywhere—not just at Brazil's border. "Paraguay" is the omnipresent anxiety that, in places where your consumption is marked (the technological devices through which you "stay connected," the kinds of music and film preferences you have, or the way you look), it might appear broken or cheap because you paid too little for a fake—a fake that entered the country through a sporadic border.

Coeval Collapsings

Linguist and literary critic Mikhail Bakhtin defined the chronotope with some care as a specific *relation* between time and space *that had particular outcomes for subjectivity.* He argued, for instance, that romantic genres used an orientation to an amorphous past in order to critique a debased present, creating characters that longed for something lost. Or, considering *The Odyssey,* Bakhtin argued that the epic genre involved a series of loosely related events keyed to the outsized qualities of a redeeming hero, Odysseus, who changed very little in the course of the narrative (Bakhtin 1981b). The term "chronotope" was therefore not just a property of text types (or genres), but was, rather, a kind of metric for evaluating those genres, useful for parsing out the specific voicing structures for various kinds of expressive production. Along these lines, we can see that negative judgments about the Internet derive from anxieties about its unsettling of time and space—the sort of firm grounding that many expect from face-to-face conversation—but also, at the very same moment, from functioning borders between functional states or between adequately controlled corporations and empowered public citizens. It is in joining these scales that the chronotopes of law and lawlessness become important. Material and temporal fixity are judged to be loose with the Internet, and this looseness has benefits and dangers for digital textuality.

In the context of this discussion of the Internet, it is crossing that concerns us—the way in which bordering takes place and the ways the demarcation of an "area" itself becomes a problematic undertaking, sporadically policed. What is striking here, both for the Internet's boosters and for its critics, is the way in which strategic features of these seemingly distinct domains of experience begin to transform precisely *through* the process of crossing. It is the capriciousness of the border that unsettles users of an unregulated Internet—an unsettling that, though it has different targets on the Brazilian right and left, nonetheless derives from an isomorphic set of fears. In this Brazilian case we can see that because temporal and spatial problems of the Internet's digital textuality become one and the same, pat distinctions between materiality and the ideational come into question (Keane 2005; Miller 2005). These questions pose localized problems not only for the how and the where of an individual subject on the Internet, but also for the nuts and bolts of what constitutes communication in a digital space. These problems render the customary boundaries of person and property problematic. Common to the cases of Paraguay and the critique of the grasping Brazilian corporation is the way that borders become unstable and, hence, the way that social categories and products conceivable as "owned"—identities and cellular phones, ideas and the texts that contain them—are put at risk by being allowed to mingle indiscriminately.

In the early 1990s—at the very moment that the Internet was beginning to be spoken of as a life-transforming mode of communication—Paraguay becomes important to Brazilians in particular ways. In geopolitical terms, it becomes important as the place where the technology required for participation in the emerging digital textuality becomes suddenly available to a much broader spectrum of the population for much less money—thereby "democratizing" the technology, in the language of its boosters. Significantly, "Paraguay" becomes able to hold this democratizing role precisely because of its inferior status. Connected to this inequality, Paraguay becomes representative of an anxiety about how technology and mediation, unchecked, might threaten one's capacity to read things for what they "really" are. In similar ways, a longstanding public-cultural engagement with the greed of Brazilian corporations, collaborating with international organizations that have no investment in Brazilian consumers, ramps up anxieties about a lack of transparency in Brazilian society—an elaborate system of smoke and mirrors that cannot be penetrated by the average user. Recall digital textuality's frequently radical decontextualizations. Brazilians often say that Brazil is "not for beginners." In this case, in Brazil, slippery mediation creates incertitudes about who's who and what's what. Liquidity and motility can bring people together for creative work and the salutary sharing of information, or it can, in the words of Brazil's Film and Music Antipiracy Association, bring people together who are spread out across the country to trade in pirated goods; these people don't "really" know each other, since they "make contact only via computer" (FMAA 2008)—a debased and "unreal" form of communion, if ever there was one, especially if it isn't supplemented by face-to-face contact. The tensions around these forms of communion will take more detailed shape in the next chapter, as I consider the ways that digital textuality's movement toward cellularity brings pleasures and dangers that are difficult for actors and institutions to manage.

4 PRE-PAPAL PREPARATIONS AND CELLULARITY

IN 1990, BRAZILIAN COUNTRY MUSIC DUO Leandro & Leonardo struck gold with their song "Pense em mim" (Think of me). The national hit, following in the mold of the vast majority of Brazilian country music *(música sertaneja),* featured a male narrator crying to his female love: "Think of me. Cry for me. Call me. No, don't call him" (Leandro and Leonardo 1998). *Música sertaneja,* both a wild national success and, to some, an embarrassment, is sometimes mocked for its whiny male singers (Dent 2009; Leandro and Leonardo 1998); in this case, that male whining referred to calls placed on a traditional landline. As we will see below, the phone was a presence in much popular music in Brazil and abroad. Nonetheless, as is the case with "Think of Me," despite the importance of the call, meditation on the phone's properties does not typically take center stage.

This contrasts sharply with a more recent song from a more contemporary country singer, Thiago Brava, called "Sai do Facebook" (Get off Facebook).[1] In the lyrics, Brava begs his lover: "Please get off Facebook and give me some attention, / I can't believe that you would exchange / An entire life of love with me / for an entire day with your cell phone" (quoted by Ghedin 2014). We can notice the way the male narrator experiences the woman's attention to her phone in a globalizing way: "an entire life . . . " (Ibid.). Furthermore, Brava's problem is not just that his love is spending all her time with the phone; her willingness to go out is shaped by her cellular phone's capacity to access the Internet: "You will only eat dinner where there's wi-fi / And if they don't have it, you say you won't go." The narrator finishes with the lament: "I don't deserve this lack of attention" (Ibid.).

As with Leandro & Leonardo, we can observe a plangent male narrator. But in this case, the phone itself has squarely entered the discussion. Indeed, the phone, the lover's relationship with it, and her organization of her life around its capacity to grant her access to digital spaces and modes of connection have become the substance of the song. The phone has become the object of jealousy, whereas in the Leandro & Leonardo song, it was another man (Ghedin 2014). How can we account for the different way of treating this technology of communication that has developed since the 1990s? And what might this difference tell us about digital textuality?

In chapter 2, we saw that the large, centralized informal markets carrying goods dubbed "pirated" have been heavily policed. This has multiplied the appearance of pirated clothing, music, and movies in peripheral and intimate locations. Now, instead of carrying these kinds of items, the centralized informal markets that tend to cluster near public transportation hubs, for instance, are now sites for the sale and repair of cellular phones. While cellular phone manufacturers are disgruntled by this state of affairs—since the phones for sale are of variable provenance—policing of these informal cellular phone venues remains moderate. Evidently, the necessity for Brazilians to stay "connected" outweighs the potential costs of this particular mode of unauthorized use.

In order to understand this necessity to stay connected, this chapter will examine the ways in which cellularity emerges as a dominant form of digital textuality in current capitalism. Why might the piracy of cellular phones get a kind of "pass" in the piracy wars? Analysis of cellular phones reveals that digital textuality in Brazil destabilizes localized approaches to the boundaries between the public and the private in ways that are both exciting and upsetting. We saw some of this in chapter 1, when the "dirty" pirated goods were brought into the "clean" home by a cheating father. With respect to this book's ongoing critique of technological determinism, notice that this analysis does not rely solely upon the materiality of the device, but highlights its communicative capacities and incitements. This, in turn, requires an intervention in our contemporary understanding of publics. Such an intervention begins by excavating some of the joys and sorrows of telephony in early twentieth-century Brazil. I then elaborate upon a specific case of cellular phone use from Brazil, where the neoliberal government denationalized phone service in the late 1990s. I end the chapter with four pronouncements about cellularity intended to bring the concept into alignment with the three central forms of contextual appropriateness (called "deixis") in linguistics and linguistic anthropology: time, space, and person (Hanks 2001; Lenz 2003).[2]

In order to arrive at these forms of deixis, we should begin with a basic question. What, if anything, is new about cellular telephones? If we break down their apparently novel capacities and injunctions, many appear to have been around for quite some time. Both proponents and detractors of the cellular phone bombard us with the obviousness of the answer: everything is new about the cell phone. Evidence? Your new cell phone just keeps getting "smarter," which makes you more efficient in your labor, while also making you more vulnerable to unwanted scrutiny.[3]

This apparent novelty, however, calls for more careful stipulation than we customarily provide in treatment of cellular phones, both in the news media and in scholarship (for notable exceptions, see Archambault 2017; Horst and Miller 2006). One way to carry out this stipulation is to make use of social theorist Michael Warner's notion of a "public," in which a public is conceived not as a fixed audience of "receivers" but rather as a dynamic mode of subjectivity associated with text production and reception. The conventional approach to a public proposes that it is a group of people, however scattered in space, that is engaged in "reading" a given text (Geertz 1973a, 1973b; Hanks 1989). Most often, this coral reef–like agglutination of sensate bodies is thought of purely in terms of the visual, though sound, smell, touch, and taste are often just as relevant in the composition of a public. Some other aspects of publics bear emphasis. Following philosopher John Austin's argument that human beings "do things with words" (Austin [1962] 1975), Warner stated that publics involved poetic world making, constituting social categories such as gender, generation, and race. He also argued that the somewhat sudden appearance of newspapers in the 1700s ushered in the age often referred to as "modernity." This ushering in takes place in part because publics facilitate virtual modes of group affiliation. For Warner, publics connected users through bonds made of "mere attention" and did not require physical copresence. Indeed, this, for Warner, is why continuing to think of publics as audiences misses much of what is important about contemporary mediation.

Despite their virtual nature, Warner argued that these bonds were extremely real in that they influenced social action—and they were characterized by the odd fact of being both intimate and widely available. Listening to the radio, a romantically involved couple might experience a song as "theirs" while being acutely aware that others could make the same claim. In addition, publics were characterized by expectations of diverse rhythms with respect to call and response. To illustrate: with newspapers, one might read a story on day one, decide to comment on that story by way of a letter to the editor on day two, see that letter printed on day three, and read a response to your letter (in turn) on day four. All publics rely upon unique rhythms.[4]

Brazil is a particularly propitious place to analyze these matters of circulation due to the sheer size of its cellular phone–using populace. According to the International Telecommunication Union of the United Nations, Brazil is the sixth-largest user of cellular phones in the world. The country currently has 263 million active cellular phone numbers, which, for its population of approximately 200 million, suggests that a substantial portion of its subjects is quite connected. In Brazil, a distinctive attribute of cellular phone publics resides in the scale of celebration and indictment that shapes the use of cellular phones. But Brazil's cellular phone publics are distinctive for other reasons, too. They rely on a dialogue between the current cellular phone and the now old-fashioned landline telephone, such that participants experience the newness of cellularity in relation to the limitations of the traditional telephones of yesteryear. This, in turn, gets recruited to discourses of Brazilian backwardness. That is, publics have histories that their users are attuned to, whether those histories lie above each participant's horizon of awareness or below it (Silverstein 1981). In this case, cellular telephony critiques the fixed lines of the previous age—even among users who had no direct experience with landlines. In Brazil, at least, we will see that this critique very much happens across class lines.[5] The modes of subjectivity surrounding cellular telephony rely upon claims to transcend the constraints of the form of mediation that preceded cellularity. And it is this transcendence that proud multitaskers in business, government, and leisure the world over believe makes cellular phones better than mere telephones (Salvucci and Taatgen 2010).

In its negative modalities, however, contemporary users of the cellular phone become unstable with respect to time, space, and person. Cellularity's distancing from the telephone has both positive and negative results, in that cellularity just as often makes Brazilians upset as it makes them giddy. I have examined this tension with respect to digital textuality in numerous locations, and I will discuss it again in chapter 5. Put differently, the attributes of cellular phones that are often touted as improving the lives of users exist in productive tension with tremendous anxieties about the inescapabilty of interruption and interception in channels of communication that are increasingly taken to be unavoidable (Baron 2008). Everyone has to have a cellular phone for their ability to keep us connected, but cellular phones also expose us to risks of broken and unwanted connections. The fact that the modes of subjectivity under analysis here must be mediated through small (and ever smaller, as we shall hear) devices makes all the difference to the modes of subjectivity that are available in those acts of mediation. And because modernity's engagement with inscription has consistently moved toward cellularity, this further reinforces the ways in which digital textuality has brought the relationship between piracy and IP to the forefront of userly awareness. The boundaries between cellular phones, their users, and the texts that users create by and through them have become blurry—a tendency that shows no signs of slowing down.

Early Brazilian Telephony

Cellular phone users in Brazil are in direct dialogue with the mobile device's immediate predecessor, the fixed-line, or landline telephone. Indeed, what we refer to as "technology" is best understood as a set of practices aimed at the solution of a particular problem. This means that the practices associated with a particular technology directly critique the solution to the problem that immediately preceded the current one (Williams 1985). A very early ad for the telephone in Brazil, from 1878, pitches a particular company in Rio as the only Brazilian distributor of the device of that era and refers to its combination of fidelity and distance transcendence as "magical" (Reis and Fagundes 2019). The text continues: "The advantages that telephones . . . offer are well-known, from the promptness of calls to their simplicity, with the great advantage that the telephone transmits words and facilitates the recognition of the voice of the speaker from any distance" (Ibid.). The accompanying artwork appears to have been taken from an ad directed to a US market, since a man talking into a phone in the center of the picture (labeled "New York" and with an outline of a suspension bridge over his head) is surrounded by images of others talking into telephones in Patterson, Newark, and Yonkers. Perhaps these sites were chosen because, at the time, they were centers of industry that were somewhat distant from Manhattan. How these ads might have been read in late nineteenth-century Brazil is unclear.

Jumping more than a hundred years into the future, an ad for the São Paulo phone company, Telesp, trumpets the power of the phone in anticipation of a papal visit in 1980. The ad's text elaborates on the ways that the phone is at the very center of the journalistic process. It is worth quoting at length. The text focuses on the large numbers of technologically advanced communicative modalities (indexed by acronyms), the multimedia potentials of telephony, and the connections that the phone offers to other journalists and sites (including "home"). A picture of the pope smiling and waving occupies the top of the page.

> A communicative pope can count on Telesp. Telesp has made preparations so that millions of people in Brazil and around the world can follow—at home—all the moves that Pope John Paul II will make in our country. In São Paulo: In the Exposition Pavilion of Anhembi, the company will have: a center for interurban, national, and international calls with 30 booths and telephone-operator assistance; 5 telephones with booths for DDD [direct distance dialing]; 5 facsimile machines for the transmission of pictures and documents to any point in Brazil, including the press office in Aparecida do Norte [a religious pilgrimage site, and one of the pope's stops]; 25 booths for the installation of private lines; a service center with PBX [private branch exchange] to attend to calls by the press, and 30 telex machines [teleprinters for sending and receiving text] linked to the National Network—all in the press building. (Ibid.)

So, a hypothetical journalist—another kind of medium, after all—backed by a battery of telephones and incumbent technologies for text and imaging, can be in a state of eternal readiness to transmit the words of God's representative on earth as he visits one of its largest Catholic countries.

In this papal pitch, and other ads from the 1970s, the various companies (most of them state owned, though a few international companies such as Ericson) are at pains to emphasize the sheer number of connections they are facilitating. In a television ad from the early 1970s (Ibid.)—also for Telesp—a couple sits at their kitchen table watching TV and eating lunch. They appear bored, barely moving as they place food in their mouths. The action cuts to a group of police cars and motorcycles racing along a highway, escorting a bright yellow-and-blue Telesp Volkswagen bug. Inside the bug sits a white-haired man in an immaculate double-breasted gray suit with a bright, white telephone on a platter in his lap. He looks down and removes a speck of dust, invisible to viewers, from the phone, as his motorcade races to its destination. We cut back to the couple, who hear a loud knock at their door. When they open it, two police officers flank the phone carrier, who proudly asks if he might have the honor of installing this new phone in their house—the three millionth line in São Paulo. "Three million?" the husband asks, raising an eyebrow, but otherwise deadpan. "Yes," the phone carrier responds. Quietly, the husband loses consciousness and falls to the ground, presumably bowled over by the enormity of the sheer number of connections and the occasion of the installation of his own phone.

We will revisit the various ways in which this advertised fantasy of interconnectivity was at odds with Brazilian experiences of landlines in the 1970s and 1980s in chapter 5. It may be that the advertisers had the husband pass out at the absurdity of having a phone so easily installed in his home—since under normal circumstances getting a phone was incredibly difficult. It is worth a brief detour from these celebrations of telephony, however, to contemplate the darker side of the landline telephone. This detour is by way of the thoughts of famous theoretician of ennui Franz Kafka, and it takes place somewhat after the 1878 advertisement cited, though substantially before the 1980s. In the short story simply called "My Neighbor" (Kafka 1971), the protagonist is in an office building:

> The wretchedly thin walls betray the honorable and capable man, but shield the dishonest. My telephone is fixed to the wall that separates me from my neighbor. . . . Sometimes I absolutely dance with apprehension around the telephone, the receiver at my ear, and yet can't help divulging secrets. . . . If I wanted to exaggerate . . . I might assert that [the man on the other side] does not require a telephone, he uses mine, he pushes his sofa against the wall and listens; while I at the other side must fly to the telephone, listen to all the requests of my customers, come to difficult and grave decisions, carry out long calculations—but worst of all, during all this time, involuntarily give [him] valuable information through the wall. (Ibid.)

This negative image of the phone differs sharply from the Brazilian celebrations of connectivity we examined above. In Kafka's story, we do not get the sense that the telephone has made life better for the protagonist; his capacity to conduct business from the comfort of his own office may facilitate his business, but he is wracked by doubt and fear. He suspects the man next door of deliberately listening to his telephone conversations through the wall. This eavesdropper needn't bother getting a telephone of his own since he can just make illicit use of the protagonist's. The speaker attempts to hold back. He shakes. He obsesses. But he has to answer his phone. He is trapped by the form of mediation that he both requires and reviles.

Bringing together the Brazilian ads and Kafka's story, we can begin to enumerate some claims for the telephone in both laudatory and damning modes. These should appear familiar in the context of an engagement with digital textuality. First, the telephone grants its user a capacity to reach new interlocutors—distant media outlets for the journalists and, for Kafka's narrator, a lurker in the office next door. Second, in both cases the telephone is deemed a necessity of business; the journalists must pass information along to interlocutors, and Kafka's protagonist must attend to his customers. Third, the telephone is thought to put the journalists in control, while putting Kafka's protagonist completely out of control. Fourth, the telephone transforms space and time—both cancelling out the distance around the world for papal observers and converting an office wall into a cover for the neighbor's illicit intentions. All of these points will return in dialogue with the claims that are made for the newness of the cellular phone in Brazil.

The Cellular as Critique of the Fixed

In an effort to further pin down the specificities of the cellular public in Brazil, I now move to a press release over the joy of Brazil's largest cellular provider, Vivo, at bringing out a then faster streaming service for multimedia applications (3G).[6] Notice the ways in which the adulation over cellular telephony partakes of the celebration over fixed telephony from a previous era, while also beginning to move in some new directions. The article in question appears in a British cellular phone trade magazine and cites no author. "For some time, now," the piece triumphantly begins in a nonetheless nonspecific mode,

> Information Technology has been the driving force behind many significant and outstanding economic and social changes all over the world. One of the outcomes and advantages of all this technology is the mobile concept and capability that many experts consider to be the underlying cause of the Third Industrial Revolution. As an integral part of this trend, cellular telephony is one of the markets making the biggest contribution to digital convergence, personalization and, especially, the advance of multimedia applications. (WMOL 2005)

Apparently, in this redemptive modality, the appearance of 3G not only promises more accurate consumption of video and sound but also contributes to a world-historical shift in the mode of production itself. Though the specifics of this revolution go unnamed, the authors do list more localized wonders: "Although the industry in Brazil is not yet experiencing the same phase as in the Asian countries, innovative third-generation services, aligned with world-class technology, are already present," leading to something the authors of this article call "digital inclusion" (Ibid.). The authors continue to state that digital technology has surpassed traditional fixed lines in the rural areas, "taking communication to all levels of the population," opening "gateways of outreach into regions that formerly had not been benefited by the implementation of a fixed telephone system" (Ibid.). New frontiers await.

Furthermore, faster speeds facilitated by 3G technology allow for the consumption of multiple forms of media in an increasingly "enjoyable" way—allowing users to combine television (even "adult material") with music, radio, and, crucially for Brazil, "the best soccer highlights"—all on their cell phones. The authors specify what they might mean by "convergence" in more detail: "We are in the midst of a new era where the cellular telephone is no longer merely an instrument for voice transmission, but has stepped forward to offer clients an almost limitless range of multimedia services. This is an enormous technological leap, especially for the Brazilian marketplace" (Ibid.). Consider the benefits, they continue, which include "velocity, security, quality, efficiency, productivity, and agility" (Ibid.). "Professionals" who spend less time attached to their company's office buildings will benefit. Markets, which, we should recall, constitute a quite particular form of "public," will "expand." Instant pleasure!

Ambiguities abound, however. And in order to consider the form these ambiguities take in Brazil, we should consider what is often thought of as the very first samba—that most Brazilian of musical genres, intimately tied up with ideologies of racial mixture and harmony so important to emerging discourses of nationalism in the early twentieth century (Vianna 1999). Indeed, samba's hegemony as the most consummately Brazilian of musical forms continues to index ideologies of racial mixture and national culture to this day. That first samba was called "Pelo telefone" (By telephone), and it became a tremendous hit during the carnival season of 1917, garnering numerous versions and countless performances. Two early versions of the song's lyric are worth comparing:

Festa da Penha Version (1916)
The chief of police
Told them to call me
Just to say
That we can samba.

Anonymous Version (date unknown)
The chief of police
On the telephone
Calls to advise me
That in the Carioca [an establishment]
There's a gambling wheel
For playing.[7]

In this early Brazilian public-cultural engagement with the telephone, the device—at that time, a rarity—becomes a way for the police to communicate that some activity that had heretofore been considered illegal will now be permitted. In the song's lyrics, the celebration of a consummately modern, though as yet largely unavailable, mode of mediation is filtered through that which the people really want to do but have previously been discouraged from doing (samba, gambling, and samba with gambling). That such a "modern" device had been used to grant this permission from authority made the permission all the more special, tying changes in technology with enlightenment—or at the very least, choice and development. Even more importantly, however, the introduction of the telephone in Brazil implies a blurring between legalities and moralities that is both threatening and positive. This directly indexes Brazilian discourses of racial mixture by way of miscegenation made so famous by Boas-trained Brazilian anthropologist Gilberto Freyre in his classic *The Masters and the Slaves* ([1933] 1992). Indeed, it is the interbreeding of black and white on the sugar plantations of the Northeast that Freyre claims powers the emergence of Brazil—and it is precisely this discourse that propels samba to a position of national prominence. Returning to "Pelo telefone," the medium itself (the phone) becomes not just the occasion, but the means by which previous normative rigidities can be relaxed—a process that is both celebrated and feared. The emerging technology of the phone, coupled with an emerging musical technology of sorts (samba), facilitates new economies and connections—on the dance floor, around the gambling table, or on the phone.

This particular song and the samba genre it represented, circulated far more widely than actual telephones. In any case, the elation the early song reveals for telephones transforms, over the course of the twentieth century, into very different feelings. Indeed, when contemporary Brazilians compare their relationship with telephony to that of North America and Europe, anxieties emerge. Retired telephone researcher and professor of electrical engineering Lucas speaks to me at length on the history of telephony in Brazil at his home in Campinas—one of the hubs of telecommunications research in Brazil. As late as the 1980s, he reports, telephone lines were for wealthy private citizens or businesses, while the rest of the populace shared or used public telephones. This knowledge must have made the papal ad, above, even more noteworthy. Such limited access made telephones seem like luxuries in private settings. Into the 1980s, the government, suspecting it would be privatizing phone companies soon, stopped subsidizing landlines, which drove cost up wildly.

Landlines became so expensive that people would write them into their wills to make sure their children would not lose such a precious possession. This practice continued into the 1990s, Lucas reports, so that when the government finally privatized telephony in 1998, and cellular phones began to become more affordable, they took the nation by storm. By the early twenty-first century, telephony, which had been expensive and fixed during the latter half of the previous century, had suddenly arrived in a portable and cheaper form (though still far from "cheap" in local terms, as we will soon hear). In its lust for the new possibilities, Lucas reported, Brazil then proceeded to "skip" a stage of development, just as it always did.[8] Recall the detemporalizing shame that accompanied the head of NAIF at the end of chapter 1—in which Brazil's piratical impulses are the consequence of its forgetfulness.

Here, we have another set of problems associated with a lack of attention to time. Across this narrative, Lucas was careful to point out the ways in which the Brazilian version of development was a "distortion" of what had happened in North America. In North America in the 1950s, telephones had been much more widely available and affordable than in Brazil. And, in the North American case, cellular telephony came to a populace prepared to receive it through long interactions with the telephone, and also through the implantation of the old-school telephone into the physical landscape of the nation by way of wires and switches. Analogue prepares people for digital. Americans were ready. Brazilians were not.

Lucas drew a parallel with what was happening in Brazilian higher education (I conducted the interviews in December of 2012) to the leapfrogging of Brazilian telephony. These days, he opined, Brazilians knew that if they really wanted their economy to take off, they needed to send more people to university to prepare them for the kinds of technical jobs that the new markets would require. So the government relaxed what had been a restrictive policy on the creation of new universities. A profusion of private colleges has ensued, but most of its degrees were really no good, Lucas stated flatly. Most of the students (including, at various times, his own sons), just weren't getting much of an education, though they were ending up with advanced degrees. According to Lucas, college credentials were being awarded with full knowledge that they were of limited value, in the hopes that the whole process would begin to generate pedagogical momentum and improve graduate preparedness for research and industry. "And that's Brazil! You just jump ahead and hope that it works out. You don't worry about taking the proper steps." He laughed long and hard, suggesting to me that this tactic might succeed or it might fail, but that at the very least, it was audacious. This comical indictment of Brazilian hurriedness brings us back to the fact that different publics carry with them particular histories that shape their use of media. Here, Brazil's inadequacies with respect to following the "right steps" are voiced as a constant refrain not only in the news media but also across class lines, from boardrooms to street-corner bars where interlocutors wonder why their nation is such a mess.

Thus, the massive adoption of cellular phone technology in the nation is seen by many Brazilians as evidence of how tremendously up to date Brazilians can be. At the same time, the technology is a sign of how Brazilians still seem to be incapable of following the rules, such as going through the developmental stages that places such as Europe, Japan, and North America went through to achieve ubiquitous cell phone ownership and use. This more "correct" developmental path involved painstakingly installing fixed lines in homes and businesses *before* building cellular towers. Brazilians have been watching North Americans answer landline phones in movies and on television for several decades, and now their embrace of cellularity allows them to ruefully experience having bypassed that infrastructural step (Larkin 2013). In this way, in Brazil, telephony never became rooted in the intimacy of households, the story goes. For this reason, cellular phone use in Brazil is alternately celebrated and perceived to be too much too soon.

These familiar sensations of developmental inadequacy have been discussed by Brazilian political scientists, economists, and sociologists in analyses of "associated dependent development," and it is in this way that we can see that digital textuality aligns itself with localized historical experiences. Former President Fernando Henrique Cardoso, who is perceived by many to have been the one to stabilize Brazil's currency and bring it out of staggering inflation in the early 1990s (O'Dougherty 2002), wrote extensively about such development (in his left-wing, intellectual days, before a neoliberal career in politics that included auctioning off the Brazilian telephone company in 1998; see chapter 5). Back in his days as an academic, Cardoso suggested that Brazilian development followed neither a Prussian model of massive investment in basic industries nor an American one of incremental growth, but instead had "a different *style*" (Cardoso 1989 301; my emphasis). Associated-dependent development in Brazil was characterized by tragicomic leaps, as seen in the fact that in 1980, for instance, "73% of urban households were linked to the world by television but only 58% had sewage link-ups" (Ibid. 304). Put in broad terms, Brazilian social scientists argued that features that traditional developmentalists would consider to be basic were neglected in favor of what traditional Marxists would call the superstructural: TV before sewage, airplanes before trains, cellular phones before landlines, cars before adequate roads. In sum, Brazilians ate dessert before the main course. The implication of these associated-dependent critiques was that the unfolding of the telephonic has a teleology that ought to have been followed, but was not. Cardoso continues with his argument that Brazil skips steps, noting that Brazilian airlines are more efficient than railroads. And then, he sums it up: "When we wait for the 'inevitable' to happen (in general conceived as a tendency extrapolated from the history of the early developer [the United States or Europe]), the 'unexpected' happens" (Ibid. 304–305). This unexpected "fuses old and new in a contradictory manner and without a guarantee that the contradiction will result in a new synthesis" (Ibid.). In short, Brazilian consciousness of its own progress is characterized by a sense of incompleteness as well as a sense of being a bad copy of an idealized original, returning to anxieties about mimesis and reproduction in Brazil (Schwarz 1992). Cardoso's point was that Brazil relies on imported technology, but the oddities of its unevenly developed infrastructure mean that even its attempts to follow the foreign examples often end up generating something bizarre: a mutation.

Using Cardoso's terminology, we might argue that the cell phone is an example of the "unexpected" that happened while Brazilians were supposed to be dutifully waiting for the inevitable (landlines). If the process of economic development can be thought of as a kind of ritual, the steps of which ought to be followed in detail in order to achieve whatever the ritual goal might be (as in Abramson 1999), Brazil is skipping steps and rewriting incantations. As a result, following Walter Benjamin's simultaneously despairing and hopeful analysis of historical change, a kind of dark angel (Benjamin 1968b, 257–58) hovers over cellular phone use (see, in a different context, the suggestive analysis of Mitchell 2013). Fears that "pirated" headsets had been "cloned" by members of criminal gangs abound (which I will examine in detail in the next chapter). I also heard frequently that Brazilians all had cellular phones and that many of them even had several. However, in words I considered somewhat brutal, the next piece of this critique was that due to the "stupidity" of the population, no one had anything to actually discuss on them.

Along the lines of localized understandings of the inadequacies of the cellular phone and its supporting infrastructures, Ivan, a colleague of Lucas's in the department of telecommunications at a nearby university, enjoys telling friends who are not acquainted with how cellular technology works, about digital sampling. He brings this up when his interlocutor seems overly celebratory of Brazil's brisk adoption of cellular phones. "Do you know what a *tiny* portion of the person's voice you're actually hearing?! It's a miracle that you can even know who's talking. The cellular phone selects tiny pieces of the voice and passes them along—they're little packets. And landlines give you a lot more information than cellular phones do. It's a wonder we can talk on cell phones at all." In this way, for Ivan, cellular telephony relies on approximation, guesswork, and a great deal of faith—much more than land-based telephony would. Too bad most of the nation skipped over the landline, Ivan laments; his discourse is always seasoned by sadness, absurdity, and laughter.

In this way, we can see the overlapping of the two dialogues that are crucial to the cellular mode of digital textuality in Brazil. First, the cellular phone is experienced by young and old, rich and poor, as both wonderful and problematic at the very same time. Yes—the cellular phone has allowed for the quick crossing of space and the transcendence of time. It has also, with the rise of the smartphone, allowed for the unification of media consumption in a device that is highly portable. Further, we can see the ways in which the cellular public relies upon a critique of the landline. This critique emerges in durable Brazilian upset over its jagged developmental biography. Having skipped over the materially rooted history of how this developmental progress was supposed to have been made "in the First World," Brazilians are left with a distinct unease over the cellular phone. Put somewhat differently, the capacity to fully benefit from the telephone's challenges to time, space, and person is here perceived to be contingent upon a "natural" process of telephonic growth beginning with planting (in a sense) copper lines. Understanding these localized anxieties now sets us up to define the cellular public quite broadly and, in that way, to get a further glimpse into the significance of piracy for digital textuality.

Two Plus Two

Recall that this book seeks to contextualize narratives of technological determinism rather than simply undermining them. In this way, the first two attributes of the cellular public I will discuss—the spatiotemporal ones, time and space—predate the cellular phone itself, tracing their roots at least to the earlier landline telephone, if not to the telegraph (Simon 2005). The cellular phone seeks to quicken response time and transcend very large distances, to be sure, but this ability is not entirely new—a fact we can see clearly from the material on the traditional telephone, above; our papal journalists wanted a piece of this. The cellular public's third and fourth attributes—unification and portability—are where the distinctive features of the cellular public begin to emerge most clearly. But we should notice that it is the coming together of all four of these attributes in a small, light, and handheld device that makes cellularity distinct.

It is important to understand that cellularity does not necessarily revolve around a particular type of content—as many print or broadcast publics did and do (see, for example, Bauman 2009). Once again, as I noted with the policing of illegally copied CDs and DVDs in chapter 2, it is the modality of circulation that is subject to scrutiny by pro- and antipirates and which thus extends above the horizon of userly awareness in considerations of circulatory legitimacy. Put somewhat differently, cellularity has in many ways allowed users to customize their own experiences online—as has been discussed in a substantial literature on "media effects" within the discipline of psychology (Valkenburg, Peter, and Walther 2016). Thus, it is the cell phone's material and communicative potentials (Kuipers and Bell 2018) that are the most important defining features of cellularity. These defining features are most easily captured through a union of four attributes.

The *first attribute* of cellularity is a decreased cycle of interaction such that the time between an initiation of communication and a response to that initiation becomes almost instantaneous—approximating face-to-face dyadic speech (between two people).[9] We may think of this first attribute as the diminution of response time or, in Warner's terms, a shortening of the cycles of circulation. Recall that for Warner, participants come to anticipate a certain rhythm of call and response, and this becomes crucial to the way they participate in a given public—even the identity categories they may inhabit. This reduction of response time is often experienced as one of digital textuality's redemptive qualities—most often expressed as a capacity to "communicate instantly" with friends in Brazil while located in Washington, DC, for instance. We may, however, note that this and, indeed, all of these attributes of the cellular public, can also explain pejorative positions as well. For instance, in cases of cyberbullying, the fact that a threat can instantly be posted to a social media site is alarming to many parents, as instantaneous response is often blamed for desperation, doubt, and even suicide (Leung 2013; Zernike 2013).

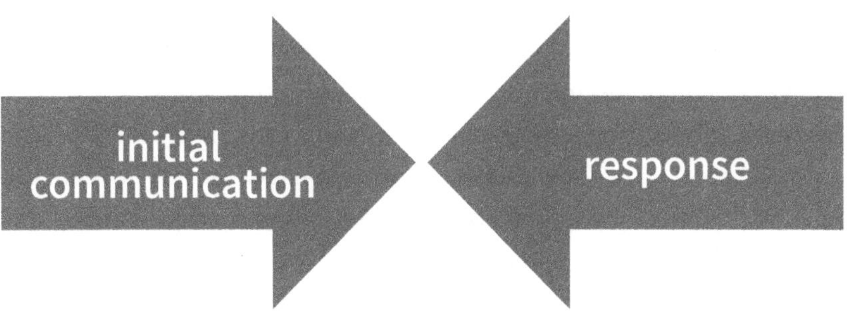

FIGURE 4.1 Cellularity attribute 1. Time: reducing the response.

The *second attribute* of cellularity expands the spatial reach of communication and media consumption. It refers to the potentially tremendous stretch across space (see figure 4.2). Distance has been transcended. Within the context of digital textuality, it is precisely the capacity to cover so much ground that leads not only to the raptures of much cell phone advertising but also to the headiness of much globalization theory, both in mainstream media and in anthropology (see, for instance, Appadurai's excitement about blue jeans, 1996). Brazilian journalists can post an article on police enforcement practices in informal economies in São Paulo and expect audiences fluent in Portuguese to be able to read it in Angola, Portugal, Goa, or the United States. The wonders of digital translation programs increase that reach even more. Incumbent in this sense of transcendence is the notion of the compression of space that has been indexed by so many theorists of globalization (see Harvey 2007; Jameson 2003, for starters). This transcendence and compacting often leads to a kind of vertigo that is sublime (Costa 1994; Nye 1996; Mosco 2005; Masco 2013). In any case, algorithms that pick up on key terms and echo headlines to selected audiences further this process of transcendence. This nearly instantaneous circulation of information is great when you are hoping to "inform" global publics about local best practices (such as crushing illicit DVDs in the street), but notice that, once again, fear applies. Local embarrassment can become a source of international shame with the culturally intimate click of a mouse (Herzfeld 1996). Along these lines, consider the way something called "Brazilian police brutality" during the protests of the summer of 2013 takes shape as national shaming right before the World Cup—when the world is watching (Dent and Pinheiro Machado 2013). Now, the embarrassment is not merely Brazil's own, but can intensify because Germans, British, Japanese, and Ghanaians can see it, too.

Up to this point, occupants of cellular publics have sought to intensify attributes of previous media types with respect to time and space. Recall that telegraphic messages could be sent quite quickly over large distances. With the *third attribute* of cellularity, however, it begins to move in what we might consider new directions: users of cellularity seek to unify as many channels of communication as possible into one single node or device (see figure 4.3). This unification occurs not only when cellular phone makers market their products

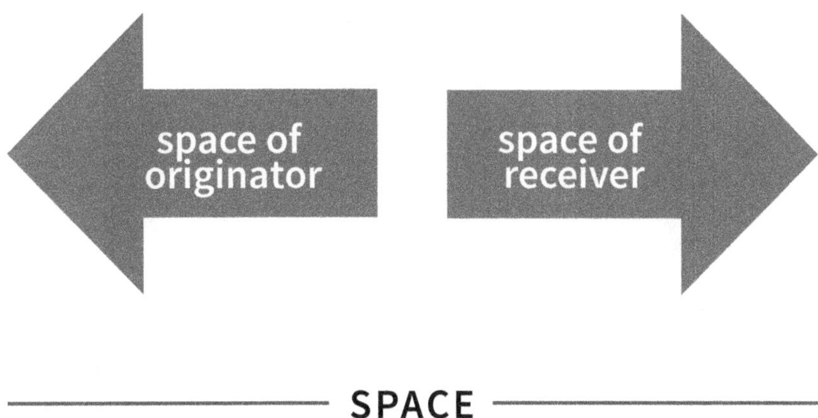

FIGURE 4.2 Cellularity attribute 2. Space: transcending geography.

but also when users celebrate the fact that they can look up a restaurant using their current location, switch to the Internet to read a few reviews of that restaurant, switch to SMS in order to text friends about where to meet, and finally, switch to their camera to immortalize their arrival with a selfie. What is so frequently celebrated by makers and users of smartphones is that just one piece of technology can "do it all." How wonderful to have such a profusion of forms at one's fingertips! Returning, for a moment, to Brazilian magazine advertisements from the 1970s, adulation for the computer, the fax machine, the transistor radio, the television set, and, as noted, the telephone focused on a discrete function, modality, and textuality—not a limitless combination. Cellularity brings it all under one roof. The cellular phone becomes like a communicatively empowered Swiss army knife of considerable thickness—one that contains not only the usual variety of blades but also a magnifying glass, pliers, nail file, Allen wrenches, ruler, and toenail clipper (at least).

Once again, however, notice that there is a dark side to communicative compression, because it can be used to explain oppositional practices that celebrate the simplicity and superiority of "old-fashioned" forms of mediation, too. Due to the fact that the unification of communicative modalities into one device is channeled through cellular networks and the Internet,

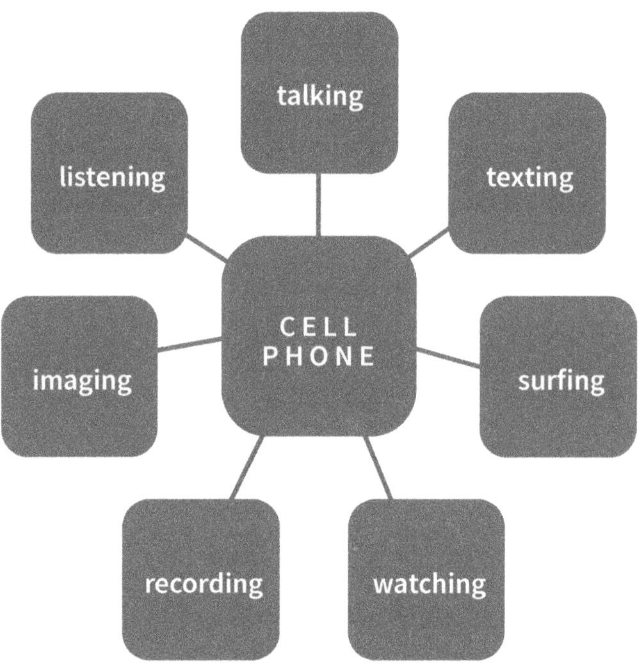

FIGURE 4.3 Cellularity attribute 3. Unification: condensing communication and media.

they are traceable, for example. A recent commuter newspaper circulated on the public transportation network in Washington, DC, advised readers to take pleasure in the fact that their reading of that newspaper could not be watched over by a nosy boss or used against them in the future. Because of the materialities of the newspaper, each reading would reside nowhere outside the reader's memory. No Internet service provider could compile statistics on how your eyes hit the paper as you ride the train. Similarly, devices that only take pictures or make sound recordings are frequently described as more "devoted" than the smartphone. Recall the "promiscuity" that the policing of digital textuality was intended to contain in chapter 2. We can also note a revival of old-school cellular phones that only make calls and simple texts, such as the iconic Nokia 3310.

The final, *fourth attribute* of cellularity is omnipresence, which is often glossed among cellular phone boosters as "portability." This attribute is related

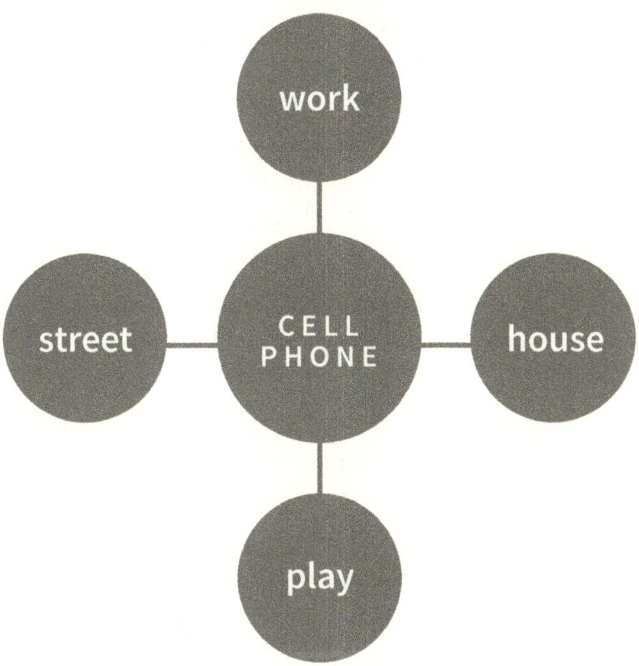

FIGURE 4.4 Cellularity attribute 4. Portability: ubiquitous connections.

to the previous attribute in the sense that portability indexes the capacity of a device to unify as many communicative and receptive modalities as possible (see figure 4.4). Here, however, cellularity uses that capacity for unification in flaunting an actor's ability to move about. To clarify further the distinction between this orientation of portability and unification, it is possible to conceive of a device weighing twenty pounds that can mediate your talking, listening, typing, reading, media making, and consumption. Indeed, such a device is called a desktop computer. This fits our previous attribute (unification) perfectly. The desktop computer, however, has to be used only in a particular location because of its size and weight, and therefore evidences only condensation, not portability. Portability as a mode of digital textuality suggests the paramount importance of being able to take these other three orientations everywhere—the ability to approximate face-to-face interaction quickly, communicate across great distances, and link communicative pathways. As we are often asked to do in cellular advertising campaigns, just think of the possibilities![10] Once again, this omnipresence leads to worries, too—in this case, about the capacity to keep the public and the private distinct. Indeed, documentary filmmakers, authors, and journalists have recently begun to fret over the impossibilities of staying "off the grid" (Hoback 2013; Angwin 2014) precisely because the cellular device is with us everywhere—even, some parents of teens are horrified to find, in bed. Together, these four attributes of cellular publics connect with localized anxieties around time, space, and person—making the boundaries around each more difficult to draw.

This underscores another attribute of cellularity, and of digital textuality broadly speaking, which is that a larger and larger portion of what we communicate is mediated through real-time text (recall Kittler 1999). A wide variety of digital communicative modalities—all of them dependent upon the dialogue between these four attributes of the cellular—result in what linguistic anthropologists Bambi Shieffelin and Graham Jones have called "inscripts" (Shieffelin and Jones 2015). These are not quite like transcripts of oral communication since the communication takes place in the kind of cyclicality that once characterized orality (with turn taking), but with new potentialities and anxieties—such as the anxieties around "ghosting" (taking so long to reply that you are deemed, by your interlocutor, to have disappeared). This sort of accrual within the context of digital textuality also contributes to what Danah Boyd has called the "searchability" of cellular communication (Boyd 2014).

Portability, Unification, and the Wall

Cellularity is further defined by two overlapping dialogues. The first is between current forms of the telephone (mostly "smart" phones, these days) and older, fixed, landlines. In this sense, recall the broader point that each new form of technology is an attempt to improve upon previous forms. However, these improvements are accompanied by anxieties—a fact that emerges clearly in the cyclical nature of accusations of piracy dating back to the advent of the printing press (Johns 2010). In many ways it seems as though every new form of technology has had its panics. In any case, the laptop computer improves upon the desktop computer by diminishing its size. The cellular phone user strives to transcend certain limitations imposed upon the landline user, covering great distances quickly as well as focusing communicative modalities into one small, and ultraportable, device. This seems to fly in the face of a previous age's ideologies of mediation, when things were fixed, univocal, slower, and more geographically bounded (though never completely, as the pope has shown). The unmooring of these fixities is great in some ways, since you can pick up your phone in Washington, DC, and text your Brazilian friend about the MP3 file you just emailed to her from the punk show you're watching. The coming together of these four attributes in a single object therefore creates a whole series of opportunities that advertising for cellular phones has made all too familiar. Recall the benefits touted by the Brazilian cellular phone article above: "velocity, security, quality, efficiency, productivity, and agility"; we might continue this list with happiness, satisfaction, and even pleasure.

The second dialogue that defines the cellular public is between positive orientations to its use and critical ones. Thus, these four qualities of cellularity lead, in equal measure, to fears about "interruptions" in, and "interceptions" of, service. These manifest themselves in anxieties about Brazilian development gone wrong—which, in turn, suggest the ways in which these two dialogues of cellularity must be framed by local histories of technological practice. Along these lines, recall Kafka's protagonist. His perceptions of "the wall" offer the illusion of maintaining a boundary between public and private, while actually allowing dark forces to penetrate his world. The nature of those dark forces will vary from place to place. And here, once again, is where the affordances of the contemporary cellular phone reassert themselves, but always in a local context—cellularity's mingling of quickened time, transcended space, and variety of communication in a package you can (and do) hold in your hand, in the Brazilian context of anxieties about maintaining boundaries between the house and the street. Nowadays, the wall of Kafka's story is more frequently present in the life of the cellular phone user—and its incapacity to truly stop sound from passing through it is even more diffuse. "The wall"—which both separates speakers and listeners and brings them together, both providing and undermining the security of participants—has, thus, become more permeable and ubiquitous, just as it has also become more obligatory. Recall Brazil's border with Paraguay. In this way, digital textuality gives us all cause to celebrate *and* reason to despair. And it is to the nature of that despair that we now turn.

5 DIGITAL TEXTUALITY AS INTERRUPTION

IN THE LATE SUMMER OF 1998, the neoliberal government of then president Fernando Henrique Cardoso (recall, once the theorist of associated-dependent development) sold off the rights to land- and cellular telephone lines in a massive auction (Folha Online 2010). For the purposes of the auction, each state was divided into landline rights and cellular rights, and two companies would be permitted to compete in each of the two markets—making for a total of four companies in each state. As the auction approached, telephony and its future became a regular subject of conversation in the news media, but also on street corners where people wondered what would become of their phone service, lousy as it was. Could it get any worse? Some Brazilians wondered whether cellular rights would amount to much in this nation that seemed technologically challenged. Surely the landlines discussed in the last chapter would continue to reign supreme for some time. Many commented that it would probably take Brazilians a while to adopt cellular phones. As confirmation of these suspicions, in the actual auction, the landline portions of the market fetched higher prices (Filippozzi 1998).[1]

Any doubts about the efficacy of the cellular in Brazil were soon dispelled, however, as cellular phones began to surpass landlines in a matter of two years. Into the 1980s, as we discussed in the last chapter, middle- and working-class families could only dream of having a phone. The definitive arrival of the cell phone had, some argued, thus "democratized" telephony.[2] Yes, Brazilians would tell me in the early years of the twenty-first century, cell phones and cell phone plans were too expensive because the government overtaxed the purchase of phones and Brazilian cell phone companies gouged consumers (recall the corporate rapaciousness indicted by antimaximalist activists in chapter 3). But even with this unnecessary inflation, cell phones were much less expensive and difficult to acquire than landlines had been. Brazil's style of progress worked this way, I was told. It comprised just barely perceptible innovation, all in the context of corporate acquisitiveness and an ineffective, often corrupt, government (as we also heard in chapter 3). But this sudden and expensive connectivity represented modest progress, nonetheless. The confluence of the auction with Brazil's attempts to adhere to TRIPS was not lost on theorists of neoliberalism, despite Brazil's resistance to pharmaceutical patents in its successful treatment of HIV (Kunisawa 2015; Petryna, Lakoff, and Kleinman 2006; Schwartz 2014; Sell 2003; Sundaram 2014).

Begrudging acknowledgments of increased connectivity was about as much celebration of the arrival of the cell phone as I encountered during the years of the cellular phone's Brazilian ascendancy. The euphoria I had expected over a relatively sudden capacity to "connect" was in short supply. Instead, what became frequent were increasingly shrill complaints about mobile phone costs as well as plan prices, lauding of success in "pirating" cell phones, fears that personal phone numbers were being used by criminal gangs ("cloning"), and discussions of how those gangs smuggled cell phones into prisons using desperate though creative means. Why was there so much negative chatter at the very moment when—hopeful technological determinists suggested—Brazilians ought to be jumping up and down at the dawning of a glorious age? Why did Brazilians seem every bit as upset by cell phones as they were pleased by them (if not more)? And how were the different forms of cellular upset related to one another in the context of digital textuality?

This chapter answers these questions by further exploring the dialogue around the four attributes of cellularity analyzed in chapter 4 and their centrality to digital textuality. I argue that we should understand digital textuality, and its incumbent struggle between IP and piracy, as an *embodied* practice, since many Brazilians approach their phones much as they might approach prostheses. This prosthetic sensibility derives from the belief that the phone allows its user to be "always on."

To elucidate this perpetual readiness to initiate and receive communication, we must delve further into the last chapter's arguments for condensation and portability. The cell phone's designers, marketers, and users seek to colonize an extremely wide variety of human communicative behavior. As noted in chapter 4, most forms of mediation up to this point in history have required the employment of a specific physical apparatus in order for interaction to take place—and it is that *specificity* that is most relevant for contrastive purposes here. Writing an old-fashioned letter calls for ink, a pen, and paper. When the telegram still provided an important way to communicate, sending one required a telegraph operator who was connected to other operators by wires and fluent in Morse code. In just these two examples, we should notice that you can't send a telegram with a pen and paper, nor can you write a letter with a telegraphy machine and an operator (unless that operator wants to loan you a pen and give you some paper).

The designers of the current "smart" phone, however, seek to obliterate the specificity of communicative instrumentation—attempting to encompass the media ecologies of participants. The smartphone's designers aspire for it to be the one technology that will be useful in most (if not all) communicative situations. And notice that in addressing this encompassment we are not simply talking about the phone itself, as though, in its materiality, it might be divorced from its contexts of use. Older communicative modalities (such as writing a letter and sending a telegram) relied not only on specific tools, but relatedly, on specific contexts in which those tools were to be employed. We sit down to write a letter (or we did, once upon a time) and, when such a service existed, we traveled to the post office to send a telegraph.

Users and designers of cell phones, by contrast, seek not only the communicative flexibility of the cell phone in a material mode but also its communicative flexibility in a discursive mode. They hope that the phone will call to you (interpolating you) in most of the situations in which you need to communicate (Mankekar 2001). This leads to the increasing prevalence of "inscripts," as discussed in the last chapter (Shieffelin and Jones 2015). It also shifts understandings of communicative genre (Briggs and Bauman 1992;

Hanks 1987). What I mean by this last claim is that at a club in Washington, DC, at 10 p.m. on a Friday, what once might have been conceived of as "listening to a band" shifts, without entirely transforming. During this newer form of hanging out, I could choose to interact in written form by texting, instant messaging, or emailing another friend in São Paulo, Brazil—*while I'm watching/listening.* The communicative genre "watching a band" has, in this way, morphed. It has become sociable and communicative not only in immediate space and time (talking with proximal friends) but also in far-distant spaces and times (texting with distal friends in different time zones; for the ways genres transform, see Hanks 1987).

Digital textuality has brought other transformations, too—ones that index the condensation of media channels. As noted, cell phones present numerous communicative modalities, and the choice of one modality over another may be conceived of as being supported by a belief that one mode of conveyance is better suited to the circumstance than another. I can select not only the purely text based but also the visual, by taking a picture of what is happening at the bar and then sending it by Instagram, SnapChat, or Facebook. If I wanted to talk to and also see my interlocutor, I could use Skype or FaceTime with him. Or, if he does not have a cell phone, I might even make a phone call to a traditional landline. But in each of these cases, my cell phone would provide the channel through which I communicated. And because my phone is always with me (many people take them to bed), a crucial aspect of cellularity results not only from the carefully crafted "affordances" (Gibson 1986) of the phone but also from its associated communicative injunctions, encouraging me to reach out and "pinging" me to want to be the one who is reached out *to.* It is as though I had my own post office and telegraph operator in tow at the bar, complete with flash photographer, tape recorder, and extremely quick courier service (Hermes, perhaps)—all of them clamoring: "Use me!" "No, no . . . use *me*!"

Throughout this analysis of what it means to be "always on," we should notice that we are discussing more than just production—by which I mean the sending of a message. In a receptive mode, cellularity involves a kind of continual openness to the possibility of receiving communications, too. As I am standing in that club, my friends from São Paulo might post on my Facebook page, send me a text, or even give me a call. If I have enabled "notifications" from these various applications, or apps, I may hear a sound that lets me know of such activity, or my phone may vibrate, transmitting a little frisson to my left breast or upper thigh—its customary locations on my person. Strangers don't get to touch me in those places.

From the perspective of participant experience, then, because the cell phone incorporates such a wide variety of communicative modalities, and because it is so portable, cellularity involves the continual potential to initiate communication regardless of time and space, together with the continual potential to receive it—an ongoing pair of injunctions that are, in some senses, initiated by the device but also by the contexts in which I find myself. With my old-fashioned, traditional, landline telephone, I had to be at home to answer it or make a call—and even in a specific room (remember Kafka's office). Not so with my cell.

Recall, from the last chapter, that this omnipresence of cellularity has been trumpeted by cell phone boosters in Brazil as one of its chief positive attributes. The popular 2017 song "Toque do Celular" (Cell phone ring) by the band O Bonde do Brasil (Brazilian streetcar) places the cell phone's ring at the center of an exciting nightlife—in which the ring announces alcohol, dancing, and kissing. A male narrator notes that when his phone rings, it foretells of joys yet to come:

Esse som é envolvente, vai fazer você pirar	That sound grabs you, it'll make you nuts
Vai tocar na sua mente, no toque do celular	It'll ring in your mind, in the cell phone's ring
Vai tocar no paredão, te fazer enlouquecer	It'll play in the DJ booth, and drive you crazy
E mesmo querendo ou não, você vai mexer	And whether you like it or not, you will move

In this way, the ring of the cellular phone is tangled up with the pleasures of having a good time.

We can notice, however, that even within this apparent celebration of the cell phone, there are some ambiguities. The compulsion that the phone must be for "fun" is what blurs the lines between the music and the ring. The ring both signals the fun and makes it happen, by providing access to the DJ (who, presumably, is obliged to take your call on her own cell phone). Later in the song, and even more ambiguously, we can note the deeply gendered nature of this call—in which the female subject of male affections has little control over the kissing that is about to happen; as he's about to kiss her, he counsels, "Don't be afraid." The speaker in this song seems to be celebrating cellularity by way of a "fun" that leaves the woman little room for discussion. And the bartender who gets imperiously called in the second verse has an equally limited say in things; a variety of kinds of alcohol get requested and must "flow." Here, then, is a celebration of the always-on nature of the cell phone that leaves plenty of room for critique by way of gender and power politics. The power of the cell phone mingles with intoxication, and "sonic dominance" (Henriques 2011)—a situation in which agency becomes demarcated by volume, and in this song, numerous types of alcohol (rum, whiskey, and vodka).

Other treatments of the always-on nature of cellularity in Brazil are more immediately and directly critical of compulsion. One article in the online publication *Midiamax* discusses a service in which you can have a particular song play when someone calls you (Libero 2016). Many clients in the state of Mato Grosso do Sul never requested the service, and not only were they repeatedly billed for it, but the music stuck in their heads so obnoxiously that clients compared it to a nervous tick (once again, prosthesis). One of many problems associated with this ringtone feature is that the caller may not necessarily know that only her calls generate a specific song —unless her friend informs her. Clients of the cell phone company Oi have become afraid of touching the wrong key on their phones, since no one seems aware of how the service was activated. Finally, stopping the somewhat expensive service seems to require a quite specific form of complaint.

Yet another incident became famous in the Brazilian blogosphere in June of 2018, when TV news anchor Leilane Neubarth's cell phone went off in the middle of her broadcast. Her ringtone appeared to be a version of the song Pagu, by musicians Rita Lee and Zélia Duncan. When her phone went off as she was talking into the camera, she paused in the middle of her sentence, apologized, and reached for her phone. She had a few problems turning off the loud song, apologized again, and finally silenced the phone, returning to her newscast. Later, she apologized again on Twitter, but reminded viewers that news anchors are constantly using their cell phones to get information in the newsroom: "Just to explain to the grumpy ones—the cellular phone is a fountain of information in the studio, and everyone uses it. . . . May whomever has never had this happen to him throw the first stone" (UOL 2018). She finishes her remarks by saying, in a somewhat desperate tone, that she is "just waiting for the memes"—a primary medium in digital contexts. Tied up in her treatment of the errant ring is a certain amount of shame that the phone went off in the first place, combined with an indictment of those who would shame her because, with their omnipresence, phones have done this to all of us.

Such critiques of cell phones often reduce the myriad anxieties involved in cell phone use to a distinction between "real" and "virtual" lives. The idea here is that the former is slowly being eroded by the latter. Categorically, this erosion becomes an added outrage because the latter should ideally be subservient to the former. These commonly voiced critiques therefore frequently suggest that solving our problems with cellularity should be as simple as restoring the boundaries between the private and the public. Critiques of the cell phone along these lines oversimplify the much more deep-seated anxieties that are often at play in the course of cell phone use—anxieties surrounding the very possibility (more often, the impossibility) of being understood as well as anxieties around the incoherence of identity. They also oversimplify the myriad ways in which lines between privacy and publicness are policed in different contexts.

Indeed, scrutiny of cellularity calls into question the very categories upon which these critiques might be based—privacy, the public, the real, and the virtual. The texture and rhythm of quotidian experience itself are problematized by cellular practice, creating worries about our communicative capacities writ large (see also Baron 2008). My argument is, therefore, that a large part of the discomfort of digital textuality derives from its dismantling of our capacity to police the boundaries of the conversational "turn"—where one person speaks and another listens. Indeed, it can frequently be difficult to determine who the participants are. We are uncomfortable, in large part, because we no longer know when our turn begins and ends—when we should initiate conversation or bring it to a close, or who is "speaking." Because the cell phone is always on, it beckons to us in anticipation of a soon-to-arrive text message or asks us to reply to that important but inexplicably forgotten email. (Shouldn't you, reader, be looking back through your in-box instead of reading this—right now? Surely you've left something undone. You'd better check.) Due to this always-on characteristic of the cell phone, we are constantly living in fear of interruptions and impersonations of various sorts. Pretty much all interactions, public or private, seem to be constantly under threat of being cut short or overheard—not so much blurring the boundary between public and private as constantly pushing the one into the other so as to interrogate the very possibility of their separateness. In other words, the digital constantly intercedes into the "actual," grafting the two onto one another.

All this said, it would be a mistake to view the discomforts of cellularity as simply being about who talks and when. Such discomforts have been well documented by linguistic anthropologists for many years (James and Clarke 1993; Katz and Aakhus 2002; Sacks, Schegloff, and Jefferson 1974; Schegloff 2002a, 2002b), and as disquieting as they are, they do not account for the sorts of malaise that accompany the Brazilian examples we are about to discuss. Rather, as noted, the malaise derives from the way in which the erosion of conversational turn-taking and conversational participants extends to our understanding of the flow of experience itself. Not only has the cellular telephone made it difficult to decide what a turn *is,* making it unclear who initiates and who responds, but it has also shaped the very ideas of initiation and response. More substantively—calling to mind the cognitive anthropology of the 1960s, in which researchers looked for ways that participants sort experience into categories (for example, Conklin 1964; Frake 1964)—digital textuality has challenged our typology of speech events and participants, so that we sometimes suffer from an incapacity to make sense of our communicative affairs. Interactions do not seem to have the beginnings and endings they once did. Who is taking part? When does a conversation start, and when does it stop? These doubts are aggravated not only by the smartphone's portability but also by its multimodality. Users might begin with texting, switch to Facebook, and end with a phone call; response times can be instant or measured in months; and audiences may or may not overlap. This incapacity to draw coherent boundaries around communicative events and the constant fear of interruption mutually reinforce one another and create brooding problems for cell phone users—problems that worm their way into consciousness, finding unexpected paths beyond the "horizons of awareness" that have been underlined by linguistic anthropology (Silverstein 1981).

In this case, I will consider four modes of consciousness that these sorts of ruptures engender. We will see how these anxieties around cellularity take shape in the context of Brazilian approaches to development and governance, distrust of institutions, crafty workarounds (recall *jeitinhos,* see below), apprehensions about organized crime, and beliefs about the circulation of feral animals. In more detail, the argument unfolds in the following way:

(1) Users of cellular telephones in Brazil find phone costs to be absurd. The frequent complaint is that government taxes come between users and cell phones in ways that they do not in places such as North America, Japan, or Europe. In Brazil, phones simply cost too much, the story goes. Many users choose to respond to what they feel is absurd government intervention by availing themselves of "pirated" phones.

(2) In response to this widespread consumer use of illicit phones, manufacturers of cellular telephones promulgate fears that pirated handsets hurt users. Manufacturers circulate these rumors through the news media and antipiracy NGOs; they argue that this cellular piracy contributes to uncertainty in consumer economies by forcing buyers to wonder about the truthfulness of claims regarding a commodity's provenance. Relatedly, manufacturers also promote fretfulness that pirated phones make users subject to poor call quality, and dropped calls—one of the chief complaints about cell phone use around the world.

(3) While many pirated cell phone users celebrate their piracy and vehemently disagree with antipiracy positions in conversations and Internet comments, they also secretly fret that it may well be precisely this piracy that opens up their personal cell phone numbers to being coopted by criminal gangs. Stemming from this concern, users once again bemoan

the inadequacies of the Brazilian state, suggesting that criminal gangs essentially run the nation from behind bars by way of mobile phones.

(4) Users who celebrate, or even simply avail themselves, of pirated phones feel a certain limited empathy for the criminal gang members; we will *all* go to extremes to get a phone. Along these lines, consider a series of stories circulated in 2013 in the media about how members of criminal gangs obtain their phones while in prison. These stories largely revolved around birds or cats with cellular equipment attached to them, underscoring ways that digital textuality requires some distinctly analogue assistance in selected circumstances.

Interrupting the Supply Chain

Unease over digital textuality in Brazil frequently springs from a common sense that the cellular telephone originated "somewhere else," often taking shape in discussions about pricing. Brazilians continually complain about the expense of their phones, in contrast with countries such as the United States, Canada, Japan, and the Eurozone. This sense of high prices in Brazil has led to some local attempts to circumvent the typical supply chain—wherein well-known manufacturers such as Apple, Samsung, and HTC distribute their phones through plan providers who frequently subsidize the cost of a phone in return for a signed contract of a fixed duration (often two years).

Recall that the sense of interruption evidenced here involves a transformation of an expected routine or sequence. That is, interruption happens not only when one participant in conversation cuts off another but also when an expected supply chain is cut into—for example, when a shipment of phones circumvents customs as a result of a bribe, when illegally copied iPhones are shipped, or when reconditioned (sometimes stolen) phones are passed off as new ones (all of these are referred to as "piracy" by cell phone manufacturers).

Many of these circumventions of the supply chain come to fruition in street markets, driven by open hostility to Brazilian pricing schemes. For example, Rogério, a retired community college administrator from São Paulo, wanted to replace his old flip phone with a contemporary smartphone that came with an excellent camera, the ability to surf the Internet while listening to music, an acceptable keyboard for texting, and the capacity to quickly see Facebook pictures of his niece and nephew. He felt the licit prices were "absurd." So, it was off to the camelô (or street market) he went.

These street markets were prepared to receive him. The police repression of pirated CDs, DVDs, software, and games discussed in chapter 2 have prepared these markets for the selling of illicit cell phones.[3] Some of the largest informal economies in Latin America nowadays feel like cell phone megastores and repair centers all rolled into one. Though cell phone prices are three to four times less at the informal market than they would be at the licit shopping mall on the outskirts of town, stall owners still profess to be happy with the recent change from selling less expensive goods (such as DVDs) to cell phones and accessories (phone cases and headphones, for example) because they feel they can reap larger profits. Perhaps this change in attitude is about sheer volume of sales. Brazilian cell phone consumption has risen dramatically in recent years, and at least 13 percent of that rise was in the informal market (probably more, given the difficulty of gathering data in informal circumstances).

The contemporary manifestation of subjectivity known as a "consumer" has made a particular kind of decision when she decides to stop by the camelô to buy a phone. She is engaging in a sort of critical practice whereby she casts off the typical supply chain and embraces a whole series of interruptions in what licit economy proponents present as a seamless, albeit expensive, process. For starters, as noted above, the phones she is able to buy at the street markets trace their origins variously—though, once again, all of these variations are dubbed "piracy" by cell phone manufacturers and antipiracy advocates. This variation individualizes each commodity in a circumscribed way—not by disenchanting its fetish and signaling that each phone is a bundle of social relations (as Marx would have appreciated), but rather, through the fact that at the camelô you learn that what you thought was a simple supply chain is actually complex.

This complexity manifests itself in terms of the actual phone you may purchase—"a good one" or perhaps "a lemon." Recall from chapter 3 that the Brazilian term for something that perennially breaks is "Paraguayan," a usage that points to the ostensibly lawless nation through which cheap electronics from China come into Brazil (Pinheiro Machado 2017). This moment of shopping is a dissonant one for the consumer, since the shopping mall across town will have much higher prices and, presumably, goods that are uniform in their behavior. Here at the camelô, however, the consistency of the production and supply become at least potentially suspect, and, hence, the future behavior of the device opens up to possibilities that are not as knowable at the moment of purchase. In these illicit street markets, what you buy might break tomorrow, or it might work "more or less," or it might work "much better than my friend's 'original' iPhone," as one excited shopper for a new protective phone case informed me, repeating the most common Brazilian term to denote something that is not pirated or counterfeit: "original." When she factored in her far lower outlay, she was elated that she had chosen not to buy the real thing.

The act of purchasing a phone in the informal economy requires an acuity not needed at shopping malls or official cellular stores. Here, the consumer must make a series of careful reads, calibrated by circulatory legitimacy, in order to determine what she might be buying. Is it, for instance, an iPhone—made to look and work like an iPhone, and sporting the same name, but not actually made by Apple? Or is it a copy of an iPhone employing identical design but without the trademark bitten apple on the back? Could it be a rip-off that approximates the target brand but attempts to improve on its design, such as the popular HiPhone, which allows the user to install two SIM cards instead of one, watch analogue television using an antenna, and do simple videoconferencing? Is it, in fact, made in the same factory as the Apple phone, but "after regular factory hours," when lower levels of quality control might be in effect? Or last, is it the real deal, but a unit that entered Brazil without its importer having paid the tremendous duties (more than 40 percent, and likely circumvented through a series of bribes to customs officials)? Though all of these are referred to as "piracy" by IP maximalists and even shoppers at the camelô, a purchase could go any number of ways, with an incumbent variety of possibilities for the phone's eventual performance in communicative terms.

Contrary to the portrayals of this loosely informal economy by the cell phone manufacturers—who, as we are about to see, want consumers to think that the phones they buy at street markets will lead to all sorts of interruptions—the camelôs of Campinas and São Paulo contain buyers prepared to celebrate the customer service they have received there. Discussing these satisfactions from chapter 1 reinscribes the unsuitability of North American or Japanese models of circulation and repair for Brazilian practices. In this context, then, the interruption in the regular supply chain process that we may call "piracy" is not just about getting a lower price. It is a simple necessity of the Brazilian context due to the inaccessibility of branded customer service available in the North. This "personalization" of the repair system was even described to me by a retired social scientist as reinforcing Brazil's self-understanding as the land of "the cordial man" (Holanda [1936] 1995), a famous sociological take on Brazil's odd mixture of familiarity and structure published in the 1950s and popular to this day.

Whatever strategy is used to find a phone that costs less than it might at a licit dealer, customer service representatives of the major cell phone carriers in Brazil do not bat an eye when you show up with your patently pirated purchase and wish to place it on your licit plan. Indeed, that you upgraded to a smartphone requiring more data charges is good for them. Though they won't necessarily make money on your actual phone, they will make money on your phone *plan* in the long run, so it's a win for them. In the cell phone provider's store, on the day when you're adding your new phone, it might take customer service operatives several hours to attend to you because the store is so crowded and there are not enough employees to wait on customers. But when they finally get to you, as long as you can produce a receipt for your new phone (which is simple enough, since receipts are easily falsified), its addition to your phone plan is simple.

Manufacturer (and Participant) Fears

Manufacturers of cellular phones are displeased with this state of affairs, in which what they call piracy receives all kinds of tacit support. A commonplace explanation of this displeasure might point to the way pirated headsets hurt the manufacturers' bottom line. But a fuller account of their upset acknowledges their fear of the kinds of interruption we have been discussing and the implications of those sorts of interruptions for social life. Indeed, even proud users of pirated cell phones can, in quiet moments, be heard to mirror some of these "industry" concerns.

Such industry concerns about dropped calls or interloping cell phone pirates emerge most clearly in discussions of regulation in Brazil. Though cell phone manufacturers have been unable to get the police to close down the sale of illegal copies of their products in the same way the music and film industries have, they do seem to have persuaded the Brazilian telecom regulator, ANATEL, to begin the process of barring illicit cell phones from the nation's networks. The reasons they offer for such prohibitions are few. "Because these uncertified phones are of such low quality, they end up making problems in the network [*rede;* literally, the web] and contributing to a rise in the number of dropped calls, which causes complaints against the cell phone operators," Eduardo Levy, executive director of the National Union of Telephone Companies and Mobile Cellular and Personal Services (Sinditel) told online news source *O Globo* (quoted in Amato 2012, together with the quotations that follow). Such arguments for connectivity, however, offer no supporting data. Furthermore, they suggest that the pirated phones are simply "of poor quality." As one journalist and blogger reported, with pirated phones, "there is no guarantee that the unit will meet the required technical functioning specifications that the country requires" (Ibid.).[4] Neither the journalists nor the companies for which they so often speak provide details as to which standards might go unmet. They also fail to propose what this "failure" might mean for user experience.[5]

Some respondents to the news of these imminent regulations (both shoppers and store owners within the informal economies of São Paulo and Campinas) doubted that ANATEL's filtering network would really work, or else trusted that they would be able to find a clever, Brazilian-style workaround—much as they have found workarounds for problems such as the high price of cell phones. After all, one stall owner asked me didactically, what could be more Brazilian than the *jeitinho* or clever alternative?[6] But others recalled the effectiveness of the military dictatorship (which ended in 1985) and suspected that the new limitations might well work. This potential efficacy led them to rail against the corruption of a government that would abet such ridiculous prices and then penalize those who were able to bring products to market more competitively (i.e., pirates). Some online responses to articles containing news of the impending block on illicit phones included harsh language, frequently employing the term used to describe illegal phones made in China—*xing ling* (a phonetic variation on the Portuguese pronunciation of "China"). The comments evidenced a universal distrust of large institutions, targeting the cell phone plan providers, the phone makers, and the governmental institutions that collaborated with them. One user complained:

> This must be a joke—the providers wanting to lay the blame for the terrible service at the feet of xing-ling telephones. ANATEL wants to fine providers who allow xing-ling telephones, and the providers, in turn, retaliate by banning xing-ling telephones. What will this change do? Nothing. We're going to keep having xing-ling [which is to say, bad] service, provided by all of them, until they invent a new excuse for this xing-ling service we're getting. (Ibid.)

This commenter believes that the providers are using the illicit phones as an excuse for the dropped calls and patchy network access (interruptions). Faulty pirated phones are perceived by this user to be a smokescreen for the incompetence of the cell phone providers. Returning to the previous chapter's discussion of infrastructure, the use of pirated phones cannot be entirely to blame for trouble with network connectivity. Instead, in their view, pirated phones are being used to displace responsibility for poor service from providers and manufacturers to those simply attempting to get by within contemporary capitalism.

In a slightly different vein, there are frequent indictments of the particular absurdity of Brazil in terms of making excuses, deflecting responsibility, and failing to protect the majority of its citizens:

> ANATEL is good for nothing but regulating the irregular, and we get to pay the bill! I'm sorry, but what a lame excuse for the fact that the providers don't have the necessary competence to offer a telephone service with the minimum of quality that clients require. It is only in this crazy place called Brazil that these sorts of things happen, and the government gives its full support to them. (Ibid.)

In another variation, echoing the above remarks about customer service, a commenter suggests that the only sensible way to *be* Brazilian is to be a pirate: "If Brazil didn't have so many taxes on the price of the phone, [the phone] would actually be viable for a majority of the population. FOR THIS REASON, I USE A PIRATED PHONE WITH GREAT PLEASURE!" (Ibid.). And last, the cell phone companies are compared with organized crime:

> These businesses are a real mafia! They rob Brazil's money with absurd prices and illegal taxes that Fernando Henrique Cardoso [the aforementioned president who presided over the sale of the phone company in 1998] allowed. This must be to pull access away from the poorest, and to keep the providers from investing in infrastructure. What we *should* do is make a pirated cell phone *network*! With a great, cheap price. Hahaha. (Ibid.)

This user believes that, in Brazil, the practices of piracy should actually be extended from the illegal copying and importing of handsets to the provision of an entire network.

In two of these comments, and in others that I heard or read but did not include here, piracy is framed as a practice critical of contemporary Brazilian capitalism. In contexts where users crow about their piracy, they are proud of having bought illicit cell phones and actually wish that such piratical logic could be applied not only to the price of handsets but also to the cellular plans themselves. In framing piracy as a critique, users reviled the state as a collaborator with the companies that provided bad service and sought to destroy a working solution to faulty pricing. In such contexts, the companies and the state were compared to criminal gangs who were believed by many Brazilians to be running the country from behind bars—by way of cellular phones, mind you. Notice that it is precisely here that crowing about the joys of piracy starts to double back on itself, because it is the perceived failure of the state to protect consumers, as well as the strength of a desire to pirate phones and cell phone plans, that fuels fears that someone else—perhaps some *actual* criminal gang—is itself pirating the phones and plans of law-abiding users. Such imagined scenarios, in turn, reveal ways in which users are not as completely at ease with their pirated solutions as their criticisms of the industry would suggest. Indeed, their piracy might be opening them up to much more serious interruptions than simply dropped calls.

Cloning

The cell phone's challenge to land-based telephony's handling of time, space, and communication has created anxieties about interruption. In the previous section, cell phone manufacturers fretted that their profits were being eroded by phone pirates who sacrificed authenticity for lower prices, and also that consumers would stop respecting their brands. Underlying this concern was an epistemological apprehension that no one will know what consumables "really" are if piracy continues. Is it a real iPhone, or a fake? Related to this investigation of realness, precisely because of the uncertain provenance of all these phones, their communicative efficacies opened up doubts. On the other hand, users railed against the government and the cell phone providers, comparing them to organized crime. This is not to say, however, that users are completely without the sorts of fears that phone manufacturers seek to inculcate. Indeed, they do experience considerable anxiety about using "pirated" phones. Sometimes the cheaper phones break and can't be fixed. At other moments, users wonder if their lousy service—with its dropped calls and slow Internet speed—could, indeed, be attributable to the cheap nature of their phone (contravening the outrage in the above quotations). From time to time, users were also sheepishly aware of their phone's lack of features, or its inadequate "design" (often preserving the English term) when compared with fully branded counterparts. Thus, cell phone piracy did come with some disquiet on the part of informal economy shoppers.

Even more urgent was another fear that was never voiced in commentary about the absurdity of ANATEL's new policy. This fear only emerged in more hushed tones after anger at the cell phone providers had dissipated. Many users dreaded that their handset and phone number might end up being "cloned," and many wondered if buying their phone from a camelô made this possibility more likely. *Cloning* is a process whereby the identification number of a handset, together with its telephone number, gets appropriated by an outside party who then uses it as though it were their own (Singh, Bhargava, and Kain 2007). We should underscore precisely what is taking place here. For cloning to work, your particular cell phone's identification number must be paired with your phone number, thus individualizing not only your device, but your relation to that device by way of your relation to your carrier.[7] It is this *set of relationships*, therefore, that can then be sold to someone who could use their own cellular device while accessing your telephone plan. Later (usually at the end of the month), you get the bill for this cloned device. You might also get a few people calling your phone and asking if "the package was delivered"—a potential clue that your cell has been cloned.

Sometimes, cell phone users explain their anxiety about this eventuality of cloning in financial terms: it will take many hours to get the bill set straight. In these sorts of anticipatory narratives, stories are mobilized, once again, about the way Brazilian phone companies are not responsive to consumer needs, refusing to accept customer stories about having been cloned, and attempting to collect enormous sums of money for calls that were made by another party. Lucas explained the anxiety about the cellular plan provider's lack of attention to customers in cases of cloning this way: "Brazilians just don't trust institutions. We don't. And the bigger they are, the less we trust them. It's the opposite of you guys [North Americans, who, apparently, *do* trust them—a case I later argued with him]." A case in point is what one blog termed the "soap opera" survived by lawyer Francisco Roberto da Silva, a case that became somewhat famous on the Brazilian Internet. Apparently, the lawyer's phone was cloned twice, and it took him two years to fix the situation—in the end, through a lawsuit. "Vivo [the largest carrier in Brazil] was sentenced to pay me close to R$5,000 (about US$2,500) at the time, but this didn't come close to the business I lost because of the cloning of my phone." Silva noted that, at first, he got some minor clues that made him nervous: "I would hear someone say 'look, the package is already at the location,' those kinds of things" (Sousa 2011). Eventually, though, his monthly R$80 bill became thousands of reais, letting him know definitively what was going on. For this reason, advice columns on the Internet (one of them attached to his story) warn readers to avoid using your telephones close to bus stations or airports (where phones are thought to become more vulnerable), to never leave your phone for repair at an unofficial store, to never buy a pirated handset, and to immediately call the provider if you start getting a lot of calls in which the interlocutor is looking for someone else. In these ways, the providers suggest, you can protect yourself from, or at least minimize, these kinds of interruptions.

In these sorts of cloning narratives, it is not just the cost and time associated with addressing this discrepancy that create worries. A dominant fear is that a continually looming criminality is to blame for cloning, not only in the actual moment when your phone's identification numbers are stolen but also in who eventually profits from that moment of theft. Colloquial explanations of the phenomenon always state that the buyer of this cloned relation of numbers is a member of a criminal gang who is in prison—frequently, a "gang leader." The idea—a popular one in the Brazilian news media, at the Brazilian box office, and on television—is that criminal gangs use these cloned phones to conduct their affairs both inside and outside of prison. Top-grossing Brazilian film *Tropa de Elite II* (Elite Squad II) is noteworthy in this respect, in that the opening scene has members of three separate criminal gangs conversing on cell phones with people outside the prison as well as people inside it—in separate wings of a jail that has been specially designed to keep the three gangs physically separate. And it is through these cellular communications that one gang stages a takeover of another gang's prison wing, setting fire to its leader and killing many of its members. In this way, the flexibility of the free and law-abiding consumer subject that results from cellularity is also enjoyed by the gang boss, allowing him to give orders and receive real-time updates that transcend the prison's walls. The gang member, therefore, by way of the appropriation of another's cell phone, becomes mobile—at least for the purposes of carrying out consequential actions back in the real world. The phone does not get him out of prison, but it does allow his criminality to continue as though he were—temporarily suspending his sentence in selected ways.

What is deemed particularly pernicious with respect to cloning is that the user, in some sense, becomes tainted by these illegal activities. "It is *my* phone that could be being used for such things," I heard frequently. These fears are abetted by the phone's ability to go everywhere with you—its efficacy as a kind of cybernetic appendage. According to its fans, your phone is so customizable that it comes to represent *you*. And yet, in this terrifying moment of cloning, it becomes someone else. Note that the term for this practice is not "copying." "Cloning" partakes of the biological. It is one phone masquerading as an individualized other. In this way, its always-on qualities become toxic, while, in a mode reminiscent of science fiction or Franz Kafka, adding to the security and force of an unseen enemy.

By detailing what gang leaders do while on the cloned phone, reports in the news media feed fears about the state's incapacity to contain crime. In one graphic tale, a hit man nicknamed Greenhorn walked his employer—who was, of course, in prison at the time—through an assassination. "I'm stabbing him now, I'm stabbing him," Greenhorn is reported to have said (presumably, he was using headphones so his hands were free; "Assassino" 2012). Later in the call—recorded by police using precisely the same technology gangs use to clone the phones in the first place—shots were heard. The next day, a young man was found shot and stabbed in a location that, the authorities speculated, was likely to have been the one from which Greenhorn had called. In other reports, gang leaders are described as taking part in multiparticipant "conferences" on cloned phones, some of them lasting as long as ten hours. The subjects discussed, we are told, are drugs, murder, and the investment of gang money. Cristiano Jacques de Lima, of the Special Operations Group within the civil police, reported that two leaders in particular were about to be remanded to federal custody, since their existing prison evidently did not meaningfully hold them: "It has been proven that these prisons don't restrain them, that they can continue to be active *outside* of them. They make these prisons into criminal dormitories, giving orders by phone and even listening in to the death of rivals by cellular" (Ibid.). Their access to the cell phone allows these prisoners to transcend the space–time limitations prison is thought to impose.

We should pause for a moment to notice the compound nature of the anxieties at play in this discussion of cloning. Consummate lurkers—criminal gangs—might at any given moment be using you (by way of your phone) to do bad things in the world. This is layer number one—a sense of dread that unpleasant things are happening *through* you, influencing not only your capacity to communicate without interruption but also your resultant sense of self. But there is more to it than that, because these crimes are happening through you despite the criminal in question being locked up. Thus, this interruption in cellular communication is possible because of the inefficacy of the Brazilian criminal justice system—a downfall that affects your use of digital textuality by driving prices for licit cell phones so high. Buying pirated goods in the first place is the initial interruption in the chain of production and that which facilitated all subsequent risk. You did it to yourself. And the fact that the phone is always on and always with you only makes it worse.

Birds, Beasts, and Medieval Weapons

Through all this process of cloning, the physical necessity of the device required for this trick of being always on is not to be denied. Indeed, we might say that readers of the news media understand the desire of criminals to have cell phones precisely because they, themselves, want to have them so much. Cell phones are the only way to get the condensation and portability discussed in chapter 4. And you, as a user, are acutely aware of how absurd prices make you turn to piracy. So of course criminals will turn to desperate means to insert themselves into the supply chain. This leads to much-discussed stories about getting the cell phones into the prisons. At least in the media tellings, this smuggling procedure is rarely a matter of simply bribing prison guards who then find ways to bring them in on their own persons (Affonso 2010). Journalists covering instances of prison guard corruption spend no time at all describing the actual practices the guard might have employed to carry the phones into prisons. Much more captivating and common are news reports on how a device must actually be made to fly or slink in order to reach its new user. These stories juxtapose old technologies of transfer with new ones, once more collapsing simple distinctions between the virtual and the real. Thus, in one case, a team of four men was apprehended outside a São Paulo state prison with a crossbow and two arrows with cell phone parts taped to them. The group was to be paid R$6,000 (about US$3,000 at that time) to get some cell phones into the prison (Trindade 2011). They had purchased the archery equipment for R$350 (US$175) and had been practicing for two weeks on a farm located close to the penitentiary. Their efforts, including the taped arrows, were worthy of photographic documentation and recirculation in the news story. This visual reinforcement once again focused readers on the physical device of the cell phone itself.

In other locations, animals have been employed in the ostensibly difficult smuggling process, we are told. In one story, for example, a gang used doves to take cell phones to inmates. Tiny backpacks were constructed to hold the phones and phone parts. The journalist for the local paper reporting the story proposed that the birds' customarily peaceful associations conflicted with this new purpose—the support of organized crime:

> In Prajuí (58 kilometers from Bauru), doves, traditionally symbols of peace, are being "recruited" for a function that is anything but peaceful. Since the beginning of this month, birds that have access to Penitentiary I (PI) are being apprehended with a kind of "backpack" attached to their backs, where cellular phones and drugs are stored. . . . In one case, a dove smashed into one of the cell windows in Building 3—probably because it couldn't support the weight of its baggage—and ended up dying. . . . [The city paper] confirms that the viewing of doves flying with difficulty in the environs of the prison has become an almost daily occurrence. In some situations, prison workers tried to attract the birds to see what they might be carrying on their backs, but to no avail. (Grasiela 2012)

The pictures included with the articles argue for the feasibility of fitting a dove with a backpack and then actually placing a real flip phone into that backpack. Apparently, the birds were raised inside the prison, smuggled out, and then released with the backpacks filled. Because of their peculiar homing device—still largely obscure to ornithologists—the birds found their way back "home" to the prisons.

And finally, a story circulated widely on the Internet in early 2013 about a cat being used to transport phones and drugs into and out of Brazilian prisons. Apparently, someone had duct-taped cell phone parts, chargers, drill bits, and hacksaw blades around the cat's midsection and tried to send it into a medium-security prison in Arapiaca, in the interior state of Alagoas. The phone would transcend space by way of cellularity; the drills and saw blades would be used to dismantle the prison in more traditional ways. The unfortunate beast carrying both semiotic and material liberation was apprehended on its way back into the prison's main gate—apparently having forgotten its clandestine path (perhaps it was upset by all the tape around its midsection). One spokesman for the prison is reported to have said, "it will be hard to discover who is responsible since the cat does not speak" (Alvarez

2013). And cats have committed other crimes, too, aside from attempted smuggling. One cat was described as having "taught" inmates at another prison how to tunnel to the outside and escape (Reis 2013). The inmates noticed that the cat came and left the prison without using the expected entrances and exits and eventually discovered how the beast's capacity to ignore human-planned routes yielded other pathways. Cats thus become available as a form of mediation for mediation.

These beasts of burden and repurposed weapons represent the other side of cloning. First, someone needs to capture a device and telephone number, and sell that number to another customer. But importantly, the user needs to actually have a phone. This final stage, in particular, seems to require a good deal of work in arcane domains. Handlers must practice fitting tiny backpacks to squirming birds. Just the right, prison-savvy cat, must be procured. And archers must make sure their arrows can arc high enough to get over prison walls. Comments on the digital articles covering these tales of digital qua anachronistic ingenuity point to the desperation of criminals—the way they will stop at nothing to keep doing the bad things they want to do. But one comment cuts to the chase: "Now *this* really IS technology reaching all levels of society!" (Alvarez 2013).

Desperation

The cats, crossbows, and birds return us to the decision to buy a pirated phone in the first place. It is likely that only a very small percentage of the phones that make it into prisons get there by such old-fashioned means. Nonetheless, the number of reader comments on articles about these alternative smuggling techniques suggest that readers, themselves attracted to different means of acquisition and use, understand the allure of the cell phone and the extent users will go to in order to acquire one.

Buying a pirated phone is something that not all Brazilians do—though my personal experience suggests that reports of pirated phones accounting for about 15 percent of mobile phones in Brazil are far too low; I met no one in the course of my fieldwork who did not have at least one pirated phone. Nonetheless, the uneven distribution of incomes in Brazil that allows few to afford full-priced phones, forcing the majority to consider some more reasonably priced facsimile, is ever present. In other words, plenty of Brazilians buy pirated phones, but even those who don't are acutely aware of those who do, both envying their ability to pay less and fearing that their piracy has unnecessarily encumbered the network which everyone must partake of—putting call quality in jeopardy and subjecting everyone to risks of cloning and, potentially, criminal activity.

Brazilians very much have a sense that the system is not working as it should—a sense they have developed in dialogue with users in countries where they believe phones are always working and also in dialogue about fundamental properties of cellularity. In this sense, the always-on qualities of the phone, and its incumbent inabilities to, in fact, *be* always on, lead to fears of interruption and interception all over the world. But in this specific case, these fears take shape in quite particular ways, attentive to the unevenness of development, an unequal distribution of income, the necessity of clever workarounds, and the distrust of large institutions—corporate, governmental, and criminal. In Brazil, these fears conspire to force practicing with crossbows as well as reliance upon the mysterious capacity of pigeons to find their way home and of cats to find the paths that humans are too large and habit bound to tread. In this way, in Brazil, being always on in the way that digital textuality promises requires considerable ingenuity, while resulting in substantial discomfort, too.

CONCLUSION
STATIONARY INDIANS AND CORPORATE RAIDERS

What powers of mediation does mimesis embody and unleash at the site of exchange?

Steven Feld, "Pygmy Pop" (1996)

My conclusion is divided into three parts. In the first section I will restate, in point form, some broad arguments that pertain to the policing of IP in which I am critical both of IP policing and of its critiques. In the second section, I will tie this book's investigation of digital textuality to broader concerns about reproduction, underscoring the way in which digital textuality unites inscription (the portability of the text) with broadcast (the text's promulgation). In the third section, I will synthesize a localized understanding of digital textuality and piracy's role in its constitution.

I. A Few Pithy Statements about Policing IP and Piracy

(a) IP does not exist as a category unto itself. It has always been constituted by its dialogic relation with its violations—violations that are often glossed as "piracy." For this reason, any book, article, or class that purports to analyze IP in any of its legalistic guises (as trademark, patent, or copyright, as well as brand) without considering its historical constitution in relation to piracy is, at best, partial. At worst, such an argument seeks to obscure the dynamics at play in the maintenance of IP regimes.

(b) It is productive to analyze the field of actors, institutions, and practices within which the dialogue between IP and piracy plays out. In our current moment, this field is best understood by way of digital textuality, which is in turn best explained using the concept of intertextual gaps.

(c) Policing of IP relies upon an apparatus that seeks to make private use of public funds—privatizing policing, in a sense. The policing of IP relies upon privately funded NGOs that seek to "incentivize" government-funded law enforcement.
(d) Policing of IP also relies upon local actors seeking to align themselves with internationally oriented legal and policy frameworks, such as TRIPS.
(e) This said, the policing of IP serves distinctly local ends, too. Law enforcers draw upon aspects of digital textuality and integrate them with ideologies of circulatory legitimacy. In other words, policing takes place because people on the ground map longstanding anxieties about gender, race, social class, and materiality onto the properties of digital textuality. This has important implications for cultural perceptions of time, space, and person.
(f) If its aim has been to stop or even slow piracy, then IP policing has been staggeringly ineffective. This is especially so if we consider the costs that have been involved in the war on piracy—not just financial costs but social costs as well. Policing of IP has made piracy simultaneously more urgent and more intimate, while amplifying its reach. It has also made the lives of those seeking to work in informal economies more dangerous.
(g) Attempts to critique IP policing have often—though not categorically—partaken of an almost theological belief in the "freedom" of something called "information." This has obscured the importance of digital textuality. The result has been to fetishize the digital, once again eliding the complex practices that surround local uptakes of digital textuality.
(h) The championing of piracy frequently rests upon a naive vilification of "corporations" and "capitalism"—a vilification that fails to consider the complexities of how contemporary capitalism draws upon propertization. It also fails to consider cultural reasons for policing piracy.
(i) The interplay between IP and piracy is useful for global governance, maintaining outdated conceptions of "first" versus "third" worlds by way of orientations to unauthorized use of texts. Even as international governing institutions and corporations seek to banish terms such as

"First World" and "Third World," they maintain such distinctions in practice by making use of IP as tool for instilling shame. In the context of these ostensibly outdated global categorizations, what used to be the "second" world has become a kind of piratical one. Plus ça change . . .

(j) The interplay between IP and piracy is useful to policy makers, governments, and corporations in deciding who gets to participate fully in the global economy and who does not.

II. Digital Textuality and Reproduction

Whereas previous modes of textuality often kept broadcast and inscription distinct, uniting them from time to time (as in mimesis; see Davis 1999), the always-on nature of digital textuality fuses broadcast and inscription as a matter of course. This has concrete consequences. In Walter Benjamin's classic essay on mechanical reproduction, the removal of the conventional limitations on circulation facilitated by mechanical reproduction—limitations Benjamin framed in terms of the work of art's "aura"—creates violence under capitalism (Benjamin [1935] 1968b). In the final paragraphs of the essay, he argues that the potentially revolutionary aspects of film—altering perception in circumstances of group enjoyment—will create fascism. Unless we transform the underlying class structure, Benjamin concludes, the appetites created by mechanical reproduction will lead to wreckage. Anxieties about reproduction unite Benjamin's thinking about film with his seemingly more abstract musings on history—where what he terms "messianic time" (as opposed to more traditional chronological time) creates both redemption and crisis in its elision of aspects of the past (Benjamin [1940] 1968a). In other words, in being decoupled from previous events and primarily serving the needs of the present (losing the accountability of chronology), messianic time risks great harm in the hopes of redemption. The permissibility of reproduction thus becomes a historical question, as we have seen throughout these chapters (see also Taussig 1993).

Translated for our current purpose of understanding the elastic space between piracy and IP, the way contemporary users of digital textuality experience the potential limitlessness of circulation, coupled with the dehistoricizing and despatializing evident in its radical decontextualizing, lead to the exhilaration and horror of the boundless. Put more plainly, IP's capacity to transcend the past era's scaling of time, space, and person (Carr and Lempert 2016) are both exciting and terrifying. Circulatory legitimacy is IP maximalism's way to redress overlarge intertextual gaps. Without circulatory legitimacy, the story goes, the compression of time and transcendence of space inherent in digital textuality solicit a kind of sublime; they do so because they seem simultaneously too big and too small to contemplate (Burke 2014; Costa 1994; Ferguson 1984; Mosco 2005; Nye 1996; Schiller 2001).

Propiracy and "commons" advocates rail against the "castration" of this possible transcendence. According to this propiratical discourse, circulatory legitimacy forecloses the redemptive aspects of digital textuality. This foreclosure once again echoes the Critical Theory of Benjamin—though this time by way of Theodor Adorno's indictment of self-undermined critique inherent in ostensibly revolutionary cultural forms (his target was Tin Pan Alley's popular music; Adorno 1938). Adorno was bothered by how jazz seemed to promise a critique of popular music by way of syncopation, but it then destroyed that critique through standardization. Constructs from psychoanalysis also prove useful here. To use anthropologist Steven Feld's language in his analysis of the ways in which the Pygmies are continually displaced through their reverberations in popular music of the 1960s–1990s, we can frame digital textuality as radicalizing "schizophonic mimesis" (Feld 1996). Its users frequently pull its subjects and objects apart and scatter them far and wide without regard for their current location in time and space.

Feld's remarks were penned at the dawn of the technique and vehicle for this pulling apart and scattering: the liquid space of the Internet—temporarily made comprehensible through metaphors such as the high seas or unequal political borders between nations (such as Paraguay and Brazil). Notice that no single "technology" is responsible for the deeply individuated nature of digital textuality. Cellularity, as a consummate example of some of digital textuality's most important properties, resides as much in contemporary capitalism and longstanding practices of mediation as it does in any particular device.

All of this decoupling, promulgating, and individuating gets localized in ways I hope this book has made clear. Brazilian upset over digital textuality dovetails with the recursive nature (as in Kelty 2008) of what Roberto Schwarz called the incessant reinvention of culture by each generation according to a poor facsimile of Europe or the United States (see also Junge 2018; Schwarz 1992). For Schwarz, the problem is not just that Brazil engages in "nationalism by elimination," but that it does so repetitively. An inability to understand the way these anxieties about digital textuality lead to polarizing discourses about the self and its boundaries is certainly playing out repetitively in contemporary discussions of IP. A final incident demonstrates this.

III. Final Thoughts on Digital Textuality in Brazil

On October 26th, 2011, the City of São Paulo's public defender gathered representatives from the content industry—such as book publishers, music industry lawyers, and studio representatives, together with spokespeople for NGOs soliciting open access—for a debate at the municipal courthouse. Her idea was to get conventionally opposed perspectives on IP in the same room to see if their proponents could agree on some terms. The laudable project failed because the participants had not considered digital textuality's centrality to contemporary capitalism and, in particular, the way it played out in Brazil, inciting quite localized fears about time, space, and person.

Here's what I mean when I say the day failed: The first panel began with a speaker from the Instituto Brasileiro de Defesa do Consumidor (IDEC; Brazilian Institute for the Defense of the Consumer), who singled out Brazil as one of the worst nations in the world for what he termed "access to knowledge" (by which he meant music, film, software, and books). His argument, supported by charts and graphs in a polished PowerPoint, was that draconian IP laws and capricious though tightening enforcement made it difficult for low-income Brazilians to get access to public-cultural texts—more difficult than it was in nations whose laws and enforcement were more relaxed and whose pricing was calibrated to costs of living. Brazilians were essentially forced to resort to piracy; it wasn't some perverse choice. In this way, the speaker sought to localize Brazilian IP practice and, as we saw in chapters 3 and 5, to indict rapacious Brazilian corporations that were able to influence lawmakers to support grasping policies. In this presentation, IP maximalism appeared as a form of social control with deep roots in Brazil's colonial governance.

Responding to this first speaker was a charismatic lawyer who represented the music industry. Considerably older than the first speaker, the lawyer used no PowerPoint and referred to no notes—simply speaking off the cuff in an engaging style. He, too, sought to localize Brazilian IP practice, but he began with a much simpler metaphor, meant to draw his audience in by translating the potentially difficult legal matters under discussion into the simplest terms. He turned to the panelist sitting next to him and handed over his pen. The slightly nonplussed recipient accepted it, but almost immediately, the lawyer asked for it back. "It's my pen," he stated flatly. "Don't touch what's not yours," he admonished, accepting the returned pen from his smiling interlocutor. A laugh went through the audience, since the reprimand was obviously a joke intended to make a more serious point. The lawyer continued with his final broad illustration before getting decidedly local. IP law is to protect artists, pure and simple: "Mozart should not have died poor," he intoned, pausing between his words. "And yet he did. And that sort of injustice is what IP law is designed to prevent."

Beyond this simple illustration of *what's mine is mine,* together with an invocation of the unjust treatment of an internationally loved composer, this skilled orator went on to make more local points. Using a term from indigenous Latin America for describing a native chief he said, "the caciques [chiefs] off in the United States are telling the Indians [by which he meant Brazilians] to jump. But the Indians won't jump." He was proposing that the incitement for Brazil to loosen its IP laws and relax its policing came from elsewhere: from a bunch of foreign fat cats whose bossiness was familiar. In this way, the music industry lawyer sought to play on his Brazilian audience's sympathy for the notion that Brazil gets pushed around by larger economic powers from the North, and always has. Indeed, his speech skillfully made use of the trope of cultural imperialism—the idea that nations of the Global South are forced to play by rules established in the Global North. Except here, the indictment of Northern interventionism was being turned on its head. "We have already seen this movie several times," the lawyer repeated throughout his remarks as a way to indicate that being dictated to by the North was nothing new. Who in the audience could disagree?

An attached strategy for localizing the lawyer's perspective involved aligning his discussion with Brazilian musical nationalism, declaring his familiarity with numerous famous Brazilian musicians (whom he addressed, as though they were interlocutors right there in the wood-paneled room, by their first names). Perhaps he had actually represented them, I wondered as I listened. It certainly sounded as though he knew these cherished stars well. In stark contrast to Brazil's highly localized IP practice, of which he was clearly a representative, Creative Commons (see chapter 3), he continued, was a scheme financed by American technology companies. If Brazil instituted open-licensing initiatives such as Creative Commons, it would render the nation "fragile," he opined. Google had helped with the drafting of these sorts of "sharing" (as opposed to paying) policies, and Google was clearly *not* a Brazilian company.[1] Google did not have Brazil's interests at heart.

The music industry lawyer was not proposing draconian measures, he clarified. "The best law is the law that seeks equilibrium," he said, which sounded eminently sensible. He was not seeking to go after students in dorm rooms who made individual copies for themselves; "don't criminalize the kid," he stated flatly, in good-cop mode. The true villains were the pirates—the middlemen—who profited from the creativity of others by making copies and then selling them in large numbers. Piracy was a derivative industry, parasitic and criminal. And lest we should conceive of the difference between the opinions he was now espousing and those espoused by the younger (and less experienced) representative from IDEC as the result of some generational divide, he wished for us to understand that his own sons were IP lawyers, too. This was not a case of young people feeling differently from an older generation. He was offering a multigenerational perspective, not some dusty policy of the elderly. "There, in the United States, they have copyright problems. Not here," where Brazilian copyright law was the result of many local actors having been extensively consulted over the years, he opined.

The Sweet Sound of Sensibility

This lawyer's discourse was the most sonorous and calming rendition of IP maximalism I had ever heard. But most importantly, its alignment with Brazilian nationalist arguments for the distinctiveness of Brazilian music and the risks posed to Brazil by cultural imperialism made me dizzy. I was accustomed to IP maximalism appearing foreign. The CopyLeft Brazilians who were my friends (one of whom was scheduled to speak later that afternoon) had made this foreignness seem self-evident. Nonetheless, this lawyer's discourse had brought IP maximalism exquisitely to earth, here in downtown São Paulo.

A direct response to the music industry lawyer's remarks about the eminent sensibility of Brazil's IP laws, which sought to "protect" artists and "punish" pirates, by historian and activist, and my friend, Pablo Ortellado, had to wait till the afternoon. While sharing his research on the vast public funds that went into the preparation of textbooks that were eventually bought by private corporations and then priced out of reach of low-income students (Craveiro, Machado, and Ortellado 2010), Ortellado paused. "I can't help responding to the remarks we heard earlier today about the history of Brazil's IP laws," he began. In Ortellado's opinion, the claim that Brazilian IP law had been the result of consulting Brazilian stakeholders—from artists, to consumers to record companies and publishers—was preposterous. He cited particular copyright laws with dates and the ways in which they had been dictated by first British and later American corporations. He compared the specific language of the Brazilian laws to their American and British counterparts, demonstrating that in his view, Brazil's IP maximalist laws—the same ones that the lawyer had defended—had largely been dictated by corporations. Far from the indigenous outgrowth of Brazilian arts, letters, and technology, Brazilian copyright law had, in fact, been cobbled together through a mixture of British and American impositions onto the Brazilian legal code. It turns out that the Indians *had* jumped—with vigor and obedience. Before continuing with an exposition of his research on textbooks and scientific articles, Ortellado completed his reply to the music industry lawyer (who was no longer in the building) by stating that the idea that the Brazilian copyright system was inherently suited to the Brazilian context was a canard—a typical attempt of the IP maximalists to distract Brazilians from the coercive nature of their IP regime. Indeed, echoing the indictment of record companies, studios, and publishers voiced by prosharing activists in chapter 3, such a clearly foreign copyright system threatened the very health of Brazil by restricting knowledge to the wealthiest.

The Return of Digital Textuality

Across both approaches we find conflicting arguments for the locality of IP law. In the first case, voiced by the music industry lawyer, maximalist laws were the natural outgrowth of Brazilian arts and letters. In the second case, voiced by Ortellado (and also, note, by the speaker from IDEC), Brazil's long history of capitulating to international governments and corporations continued to play out. My overall point, however, as it has been throughout this book, is that in both cases, the local inflections of digital textuality remain the constant subtext: the elephant in the room. And the inability to identify this elephant renders this discussion of IP as a variation on a theme—a replaying of an age-old conflict between proponents of IP and their piratical enemies that dates back to the printing press (Johns 2010).

This book has aimed to show how this oppositional theme elides something deeper: the way contemporary social practices associated with digital textuality play out in plural contexts, making participants both giddy and uneasy about potentially limitless circulation. The argument has been that digital textuality engages with localized practices associated with circulation, materiality, purity, sexuality, memory, personhood, and space. To borrow from chemistry—it is as though digital textuality is an element that, upon entering a particular space, adheres to certain existing elements, forming new compounds but leaving other elements untouched. In doing so, digital textuality creates a dialectic between piracy and IP that users get caught up in. Proponents of brands, associated advertisements, and the sort of IP maximalist scoldings discussed in chapter 1 incite consumers to scan their purchases for circulatory legitimacy. Consumers are enjoined to align their purchases with an originator, much as Christians across the ages have prayed to pieces of the one true cross (Geary 1978; Gillingham 2010; Knight 2010; Pereira de Sá, et al. 2008; Turner and Turner 2011); the problem is that nowadays, this prayer is also experienced as an unnecessarily expensive genuflection—an inefficiency that is bad for the local economy because the commodity in question can be produced for less. Buying the brand is therefore also construable as waste, especially when pains must be taken to show the ways that the copy is different from its original. This sameness of original and copy under digital textuality incites localized discourses of cleanliness and promiscuity in handling the materialization of digital texts. Police must be trained to "see" the differences between pirated and legitimate texts, all as a way of counteracting what is perceived to be a perennially Brazilian forgetfulness (Ortiz 1999). And this policing becomes as consequential for its demonstrative force as for its stated aim of stopping piracy. Indeed, it has proven most effective at displaying the scrutiny of piracy while atomizing piracy's practice and rendering it both more common and more intimate.

Within this ambit, the spatiotemporal amorphousness of the modes of circulation of digital texts complicates the work of consuming and policing. The anxieties around the necessity for expensive digital products (recall how expensive "originals" are in Brazil and thus the limited subaltern capacity to experience originality in Brazil) becomes legible by way of an unequal border between Brazil and Paraguay. In this sense, the mechanical reproducibility of the text—its seeming likeness to its "original"—is filtered through the concern that, in breaking, it becomes neither Brazilian nor Chinese, but Paraguayan (Pinheiro Machado 2017). And the guilt associated with this cheaper mode of consumption becomes the fodder for policies that would feed a typically Brazilian corporate rapaciousness—in which localized representatives of international corporations do the bidding of corporate bosses (caciques) abroad.

As a moment in what is often termed "modernity," digital textuality has moved ineluctably toward the cellular—which itself relies upon neoliberalism's theology of individual actions accruing to a larger and beneficent whole. We can come to understand cellularity, then, not only in terms of the material devices that facilitate it (smartphones, as of this writing), but as a cluster of concurrent exhortations to reduce response time, transcend space, condense communicative channels, and establish portability. It is this union of exhortations that loosens the subjects of contemporary capitalism, potentially distributing them globally, while also putting them at risk by, once again, interrupting their media ecologies. These days, Brazilians experience this fragmenting as an undermining of the protective capacities of the state, voiced by the public-cultural ubiquity of discussion of "gangs." In a spectacular irony of digital mediation, which continually presents itself as reliant upon ephemeral entities such as "clouds," these ostensibly limitless textualities require cats, birds, and arrows to reach users who are enclosed (and protected) by physical boundaries meant to isolate them—boundaries such as prison walls. The same liberation that the cell phone offers to the corporate executive is also offered to the gang boss in prison.

The failure to see the centrality of digital textuality to contemporary capitalism and, in turn, the highly localized entailments of digital textuality, maintains the discussion of IP and piracy as a polarized field. An attached tendency to see the digital as a transformer of everything assists in this elision (see Kittler 1999). In particular, what often goes undiscussed is the way in which digital textuality brings together what were once distinct aspects of mediation: inscription—which seeks to entextualize, rendering a text portable—and broadcast—which seeks to promulgate that text as widely as possible. Once upon a time these were largely distinct, but with inscripts and cellularity, they fuse.

The tensions that this fusion creates lead to a discussion of IP, wherein IP maximalists (portrayed as industry lackeys by their opponents) square off against proponents of the "open" and the "commons" (portrayed as thieves and dreamers by maximalists). The result is a series of co-monologues in which participants extrapolate their reaction to digital textuality to a global context, ignoring locality and oversimplifying their interlocutors.

Perhaps by attending to the multiple locations of digital textuality under contemporary capitalism, we might begin the sort of dialogue in which opinions actually thaw and shift.

NOTES

Introduction: The Joys and Sorrows of Digital Textuality

1. Focusing on textuality carries certain risks, since textuality received suggestive critiques in anthropological circles in the 1980s (see, for example, Asad 1983). Some of these critiques had a point. Many indictments of text-centered approaches to culture and language suggested that by fixating on texts we focused too much on authors and too little on readers. Critics also suggested that we lost sight of the processes that create texts, eliding the ways in which dialogue involves contestation—smuggling orientalist narratives into our analyses in the bargain. Linguistic anthropology has nonetheless maintained an engagement with textuality, addressing the criticisms about change and contestation by focusing on processes and actors in fluid ways. For a different approach, see the work of James Boon (2000), which treats texts more "chromatically" than linguistic anthropologists often do.

2. Even if it were true that, as Peruvian economist Hernando de Soto (1989) argues, everyone just wants to be a good capitalist, "piracy" often prevents them from becoming one.

3. I do not wish to exonerate the largely North American insistence on attacking the supply side of illegal ingestibles; many people have died in that conflict—something that cannot be said to the same extent of the war on piracy. I merely wish to point out the reciprocal absurdities of criminalizing the production of ostensibly dangerous texts-as-substances while leaving largely untouched the incentives for their consumption (Muehlmann 2018). To be clear, I am not, in some sense, blaming consumers. Rather, I am pointing to the hidden incentives to consume as part of the problem. Put somewhat differently, a war on drugs that fails to tackle the reasons why consumers might wish to consume drugs—escaping various elements of contemporary capitalism, in so doing—is a war in vain.

4. I applaud the attempt to reframe performance as "animation" (Gershon 2015; Silvio 2011). I draw on these critiques in order to reframe my continued use of the old-fashioned term, supplemented by notions of role inhabitance suggested by Silverstein (2004).

5. Gavin Mueller (2019) does an excellent job of critiquing such constructions in the context of work on piracy, choosing, instead, to embed it in contemporary labor practices.

6. The application of rational choice theory has reached contemporary popularity in Freakonomics—which was originally a book but nowadays is a *New York Times* column and NPR podcast that seeks to apply economistic thinking to the most intimate and nonfinancial domains. Freakonomics is proudly about everything.

7. We should notice that contemporary indictments of piracy seek to muddle together these distinct forms of IP—a form of semantic warfare I will address in chapter 1.

8. The overlap with Donald Trump's aggressive use of Twitter was striking.

9. These were the same redemptive ideologies of digital textuality that surrounded the use of multiple sources in apprehending the Boston Marathon's bombers. In the North American case, investigators were able to stitch together chunks of security camera and cellular phone footage to follow the bombers and discover their identities.

10. TRIPS is clearly a crucial backdrop for this book, as it attempts to set a tone for IP protection. This tone continues to be debated by IP maximalists who think TRIPS protections are too weak—an opinion that has fueled a whole series of TRIPS-PLUS measures such as ACTA and the TPP. However, because this is a book about the cultural life of IP as it lives and breathes in quotidian affairs, I have avoided a detailed discussion about the niceties of TRIPS—including the ins and outs of the Doha Declaration, in which many of the flexibilities were established. This policy material has already been much better handled by political scientists, historians, and activists such as Susan Sell (2003, 2010), Mariana Giorgetti Valente and Pedro Nicoletti Mizukami (2014), and Joe Karaganis (2011, 2019).

Chapter 1: "Magical" Consumption and the Violence of Informality

1. All proper names are pseudonyms.

2. The *real* is the Brazilian currency, currently valued at about twenty-five US cents. At the time of my research that value hovered around fifty cents. The plural is *reais.*

3. Piracy has also existed for reasons not associated with mediation, such as loose governance regimes with little concrete investment in enforcement (Simone 2006).

4. Fast tape-duplication machines could copy a full-length album to cassette in just a few minutes, though this higher speed created more background "hiss" than a reproduction done more slowly (Moore 2004).

5. In support of Sterne's argument, I would note that in numerous conferences where IP was being debated by a broad array of stakeholders, representatives from the companies that sell cellular phones, tablets, and laptops always pushed for a more open approach to IP. It was squarely in their interest that users be able to acquire texts quickly and cheaply. To call representatives from this device industry "piratical" would perhaps be too radical. One of their lawyers, however, proposed that the IP maximalists might be subsidized by the US government for simply allowing their texts to be pirated—since the broad popularity of US-made public culture clearly represented American "soft" power abroad.

6. In addition to using pseudonyms for all individuals I interviewed, I have also changed the names of the Brazilian NGOs; I have retained the names of NGOs based in the United States (such as the International Chamber of Commerce).

7. The presidency of the organization changed in 2010, though Roberto continues to play an active role.

8. Numerous Brazilians have done superb sociological research on this informal economy, among them, Marcio Pochmann, a professor of sociology and economics at

Campinas's largest university, UNICAMP. Professor Pochmann has published widely on labor and social justice in what he terms the "periphery" of capitalism (Pochmann 2004, 2007). He also collaborated with Amilton Moretto, also of UNICAMP, together with Campinas's General Technical Services branch (SETEC) to produce a detailed report on the market itself in 2001: "Workers of the Ambulant Commerce in Campinas: A Diagnostic of Work Conditions" (SETEC 2001).

9. For more on the layout of the Campinas camelódromo, see Camilo Albuquerque de Braz's excellent thesis (2002)

10. Note that this relaxed attitude shifted over the period of my research. The scrutiny that circulatory legitimacy brought almost entirely wiped out films and music in large, centralized markets by 2012. I will discuss this in more detail in the next chapter. Note, also, that digital cameras became vanishingly rare with the hegemony of smartphones by 2012; more about this in chapter 4.

11. There is currently a battle over the STEIC acronym. The older organization is now the Society (or *Sociedade*) of Workers of the Informal Economy of Campinas, while the new union calls itself the Union (or *Sindicato*) of Workers of the Informal Economy of Campinas. Both spell STEIC.

Chapter 2: The Materialities of Digital Texts

1. Because the FMAA became so secretive in its later years, I have been unable to determine the circumstances of its dismantling.

2. The US Government Accountability Office has exposed these numbers in the United States as largely unfounded (USGAO 2010). The methodologies used to make the kinds of claims that the USGAO has put into question are identical in the Brazilian case. These sorts of claims are not only equivocal, but downright misleading. For more information, see Karaganis (2011).

3. I derive this from an anonymous interview with a spokesman for "Balanced IPR Organization," conducted on March 2, 2011. It is likely that, nowadays, bribery mostly takes the form of renovating police stations, with little actual cash changing hands (Ibid.).

4. Conventional theories of democratization would suggest that violent policing should decrease when democratic participation increases. This has not been the case. Under Brazilian democratization, policing has risen. Violent policing has been around for a very long time in Brazil. What seems to be new, under redemocratization, is the prevalence of such practices, as well as their broad acceptance (Holston and Caldeira 1999). This fact, however, tells us little about how IP became one of the underlying justifications for this rise in policing.

5. This invocation of promiscuity becomes even clearer in the context of Brazilian autocriticism about inconstancy—which indicts Indians for taking on multiple religions and deities. Eduardo Viveiros de Castro (2011) has argued that the figure of the unconvertible Indian encountered by early Catholic missionaries had an important influence on national consciousness. Castro reveals that the early Indians would express a strong desire for Jesus, but would then return to cannibal practices, "indecent" sexuality, and ceremonial warfare at the first opportunity.

6. These controversies resemble the sort that have arisen over forged religious relics in terms of anxieties over provenance (Geary 1986; Gillingham 2010).

7. See, in particular, the thorough treatment of such critiques in Joseph (2013).

8. We may also detect such an ethos underwriting any arguments for why "the IP thing doesn't work here" (as in the rigorous work of Boatema Boateng 2011).

Chapter 3: Bordering, the Internet, and Paraguayan Horses

1. The irony of the negative reaction to Stevens's statement is that the term "pipe" is often used by those who construct physical digital networks in order to explain aspects of connectivity (in other words, those who "light up" buildings by "pulling cable"). Stevens was moderately quick to point this out. But the damage had already been done.

2. In fact, a great deal of Chinese merchandise enters through Brazilian ports—some of it legitimately, much of it, not. See the detailed work of Pinheiro Machado (2017).

3. Significantly, AI-5 did not require fixed identity in situations where that identity was not clear, but, as discussed briefly in the last chapter, required that newspapers either self-censor (most common) or submit all their material each day to the censors (least common; see Smith 1997; Carneiro 2002; Kushnir 2004; Reimão 2008).

4. For a detailed analysis of the Marco Civil itself, as well as scrutiny of the paradoxes of its implementation, see the work of Jeffrey Omari (2018).

5. I would like to thank Raquel Machaqueiro for pointing out that the US ambassador to Paraguay at the time of the coup ousting its left-wing leader was Liliana Ayalde. She was later transferred to Brazil, right at the moment in which Brazil's left-wing successor to Lula—Dilma Roussef—was being impeached.

Chapter 4: Pre-Papal Preparations and Cellularity

1. Brava is a singer of a form of Brazilian county music called "college country" (Dent 2016c). I am indebted to Rodrigo Ghedin's (2014) analysis of the role of the cell phone in contemporary Brazilian music. Brava's song does not appear to have been recorded on his major records, but rather, was distributed in 2012 as an individual release, and as of May of 2019 has received over 500,000 views on YouTube. Indeed, Brava's career was shaped by YouTube. In 2011, after many years playing in various bands of different genres, he had given up music when one of his videos suddenly became popular on YouTube, and collaboration offers from famous musicians began streaming in.

2. Dana Boyd also attempts to simplify the discussion of cellular telephony by selecting four affordances: visibility, searchability, spreadability, and durability (Boyd 2014). Though I attempt to incorporate Boyd's characterizations of youth cellular phone use into my four attributes of cellular publics, her affordances combine space, time, and person in ways that make it difficult for me to determine what is really new about the cellular phone. Her notion of visibility, for instance, would seem to privilege the eyes (sidelining the ears, as is customary; hear Feld and Brenneis 2004). And "durability" would seem to have applied to archives even more than cellular phones. To be clear, Boyd has done a superb job interfacing with audiences outside of the academy. My aim,

here, however, is to get at the underlying nature of cellularity by way of time, space, and person.

3. Examples of redemption and perdition by way of the cell phone abound. Here are two, briefly: Technology blog *Asian Efficiency*—started by a pair of friends whose acquaintances noticed how they got massive amounts of work done fast, and without stress—argued that "technology is a wonderful thing" because "it makes you more efficient" (Lynn 2012). By the same token, technology blog *Gizmodo* and the *New York Times* report that a "new" SIM card hack could make your phone "vulnerable" (Newman 2013; O'Brien 2013).

4. For a variation on this type of thinking, see the famous formulation of "imagined communities" by Benedict Anderson (1991).

5. Protests in 2013 over Brazil's transportation problems revolved around a similar idea—namely, that in leaping to the ownership of cars before the transportation network was sufficiently developed, the country brought itself to a standstill. This comparative and developmentalist critique was voiced by both the poor and the middle class in interviews, social media, and street signs during the protests of the summer of 2013 (Caldeira 2013; Holston 2013).

6. As of this writing, 5G is all the rage, with almost identical discourses being brought to bear in its celebration.

7. Both versions, including the IP storm elicited by the registration of the 1916 version of the song, are well documented by Marc Hertzman (2013).

8. For more on Brazilian attempts to become supramodern, see James Holston's *The Modernist City* (1989).

9. The hegemony of ideologies of face-to-face interaction in digital spheres, where quite different models of initiation and reception are called for, requires further research. The underlying power of the talking heads to animate discussions of communication in myriad circumstances is addressed by Lee (1997).

10. For example, technology bloggers for *Envisioning Technology* write, in awestruck tones, about "The Smartphone of the Future—An Explosive Wealth of Possibilities," wherein the explosion in question seems to be a good thing (Envisaging Technology 2012)

Chapter 5: Digital Textuality as Interruption

1. The circumstances of the auction have been critiqued by Brazilian journalist Amaury Ribeiro, Jr., in a book in the title of which *privatização* (privatization) and *pirataria* (piracy) are joined to create a word in Portuguese equivalent to "Piratization": *A Privataria Tucana* (2011). Ribeiro analyzes hundreds of pages of documents to support his claims that Fernando Henrique Cardoso's minister of planning (later, his minister of health), José Serra, received substantial kickbacks from the companies participating in the auction.

2. As an example of such "democratization" language, take the Committee for the Democratization of Information, based in Rio de Janeiro, which seeks to bring technology to underrepresented communities throughout Brazil as a way of empowering

them. See https://www.devex.com/organizations/committee-for-the-democratization-of-information-technology-comite-para-la-democratizacion-de-la-informatica-cdi-chile-130994.

3. As we have seen, the proliferation of cellular phones has taken place only in the larger and centralized alternative markets and has not meant an end to these other types of pirated goods, which now simply appear in smaller kiosks clustered in peripheral neighborhoods and residential areas.

4. Another report suggests that the new measures by ANATEL will make it easier to stop cell phone "cloning," which we will examine below. The report offered no evidence to support this contention. See also: https://www.bnamericas.com/en/news/brazil-watchdog-to-resume-irregular-phones-blocking-in-15-states.

5. Proregulation advocates perhaps risk a massive backlash from customers well-heeled enough to have bought their phones abroad. (Unlocked foreign phones that are already working in the Brazilian network, however, would be left alone by this new policy and would still be able to make and receive calls.)

6. From chapter 3, recall that *jeito* is Portuguese for "way" and *inho* is the diminutive—resulting in *jeitinho.* Roberto DaMatta has extensively explored the politics and poetics of this common practice, suggesting that it is the result of a society in which laws do not match social reality (DaMatta 1979, 1984; DaMatta and Hess 1995).

7. For more on the way in which machines involve complex, discursively managed relationships, see Julian Orr's underappreciated *Talking about Machines* (1996).

Conclusion: Stationary Indians and Corporate Raiders

1. At the risk of interrupting the lawyer's flow, I should point out that Google had nothing to do with drafting Creative Commons.

BIBLIOGRAPHY

Abramson, Allen. 1999. "Sacred Cows of 'Development': The Ritual Incorporation of a Dairy Project in the Eastern Interior of Fiji (c. 1980–1997)." *Oceania* 69 (4).

Adorno, Theodor. 1938. "On the Fetish Character in Music and the Regression of Listening." In *The Essential Frankfurt School Reader*, edited by Andrew Arato and Eike Gephart, 270–99. New York: Continuum.

Adorno, Theodor. 1989. "Perennial Fashion—Jazz." In *Critical Theory and Society*, edited by Stephen Bronner and Douglas Kellner, 199–209. New York: Routledge.

Affonso, Cicero. 2010. "Agentes que levariam celulares para o PCC São presos em SP." *Jornal do Brasil*, June 2, 2010.

Agha, Asif. 2015. "Tropes of Branding in Forms of Life." *Signs and Society* 3 (S1):S174–94.

Aguiar, José Carlos G. 2010. "Stretching the Border: Smuggling Practices and the Control of Illegality in South America." *Global Consortium on Security Transformation: New Voices Series*, no. 6 December 10, 2010.

Allison, Anne. 2000. *Permitted and Prohibited Desires: Mothers, Comics, and Censorship in Japan*. Berkeley: University of California Press.

Alvarez, Alex. 2013. "Cat Smuggles Saw, Phone into Brazil Prison." *ABC News*. January 7, 2013. https://abcnews.go.com/ABC_Univision/News/brazilian-prison-cat-smuggle-tools-phone/story?id=18150784.

Amato, Fábio. 2012. "Operadoras investem em sistema para barrar celular pirata no país." *Globo* 1, November 11, 2012.

Anderson, Benedict. 1991. *Imagined Communities: Reflections on the Origin and Spread of Nationalism*. London: Verso.

Angwin, Julia. 2014. *Dragnet Nation: A Quest for Privacy, Security, and Freedom in a World of Relentless Surveillance*. New York: Times Books.

Ansell, Aaron. 2018. "Impeaching Dilma Rousseff: The Double Life of Corruption Allegations on Brazil's Political Right." *Culture Theory and Critique* 59 (4):312–31.

Aoki, Keith. 2008. *Seed Wars: Controversies and Cases on Plant Genetic Resources and Intellectual Property*. Durham NC: Duke University Press.

Appadurai, Arjun. 1996. *Modernity at Large: Cultural Dimensions of Globalization*. Cambridge, UK: Cambridge University Press.

Archambault, Julie. 2017. *Mobile Secrets: Youth, Intimacy, and the Politics of Secrecy in Mozambique*. Chicago: University of Chicago Press.

Asad, Talal. 1983. "Anthropological Conceptions of Religion: Reflections on Clifford Geertz." *Man* 18 (2):237–59.

"Assassino narra homicídio por telefone para 'chefe' preso na Paraíba." December 12, 2012. *G1 Paraíba*. http://g1.globo.com/pb/paraiba/noticia/2012/12/assassino-narra-homicidio-por-telefone-para-chefe-preso-na-paraiba.html.

Austin, John Langshaw. [1962] 1975. *How to Do Things with Words*, 2nd ed., edited by J. O. Urmson and Marina Sbisà. Cambridge, MA: Harvard University Press.

Avelar, Idelber. 2006. "A Internet do Sr. Eduardo Azevedo." *O biscoito fino e a massa* (blog). http://idelberavelar.com/index.php/2006/11/10/a-internet-do-sr-eduardo-azeredo/.

Bakhtin, M. M. 1981a. "Discourse in the Novel." In *The Dialogic Imagination: Four Essays*, edited by Michael Holquist, 259–423. Austin: University of Texas Press.

Bakhtin, M. M. 1981b. "Forms of Time and of the Chronotope in the Novel: Notes Towards a Historical Poetics." In *The Dialogic Imagination: Four Essays*, edited by Michael Holquist, 84–258. Austin: University of Texas Press.

Bakhtin, M. 1986. *Speech Genres and Other Late Essays*. Translated by Caryl Emerson and Michael Holquist. Austin: University of Texas Press.

Bandyopadhyay, Ranjan, and Karina Nascimento. 2010. "'Where Fantasy Becomes Reality': How Tourism Forces Made Brazil a Sexual Playground." *Journal of Sustainable Tourism* 18 (8):933–49.

Bannon, Elizabeth Cutter. 1990. "Revisiting the Rational Basis of Trademark Protection: Control of Quality and Dilution—Estranged Bedfellows." *John Marshall Law Review* 24: 65–117.

Barney, Darin, Gabriella Coleman, Christine Ross, Jonathan Sterne, and Tamar Tembeck, eds. 2016. *The Participatory Condition in the Digital Age*. Minneapolis: University of Minnesota Press.

Baron, Naomi. 2008. *Always On: Language in an Online and Mobile World*. New York: Oxford University Press.

Bauman, Richard. 2009. "'It's Not a Telescope, It's a Telephone': Encounters with the Telephone in Early Commercial Sound Recordings." In *Language Ideologies and Media Discourse: Texts, Practices, Politics*, edited by Sally Johnson and Tommaso Milani, 252–77. London: Bloomsbury Academic.

Bauman, Richard, and Charles Briggs. 1990. "Poetics and Performance as Critical Perspectives on Language and Social Life." *Annual Review of Anthropology* 19:59–88.

Benchley, Peter. 1974. *Jaws*. New York: Doubleday.

Benjamin, Walter. [1935] 1968a. "The Work of Art in the Age of Mechanical Reproduction." In *Illuminations: Essays and Reflections*, edited by Hanna Arendt, translated by Harry Zohn, 217–51. New York: Schocken Books.

Benjamin, Walter. [1940] 1968b. "Theses on the Philosophy of History." In *Illuminations: Essays and Reflections*, edited by Hannah Arendt, translated by Harry Zohn, 253–64. New York: Schocken Books.

Berlant, Lauren. 2011. *Cruel Optimism*. Durham, NC: Duke University Press.

Besteman, Catherine, and Hugh Gusterson, eds. 2019. *Life by Algorithms: How Roboprocesses Are Remaking Our World*. Chicago: University of Chicago Press.

Bester, Alfred, and Jack Burnley. 1941. *The Menace of the Invisible Raiders*. Starman comic series, edited by Whitney Ellsworth, Starman. Burbank, CA: DC Comics.

Bica-Huiu, Alina, Jeffrey Aresty, Karen Hudes, and Leon Irish. 2007. "White Paper: Building a Culture of Respect for the Rule of Law," pp. 1–16. American Bar Association.

Biehl, João. 2006. "Pharmaceutical Governance." In *Global Pharmaceuticals: Ethics, Markets, and Practices*, edited by Adriana Petryna, Andrew Lakoff and Arthur Kleinman, 206–39. Durham, NC: Duke University Press.

Biondi, Karina. 2016. *Sharing This Walk: An Ethnography of Prison Life and the PCC in Brazil*. Edited and translated by John F. Collins. Chapel Hill: University of North Carolina Press.

Boas, Franz. [1929] 1982. "The Classification of American Indian Languages." In *Race, Language and Culture*, 219–25. Chicago: University of Chicago Press.

Boateng, Boatema. 2011. *The Copyright Thing Doesn't Work Here: Adinkra and Kente Cloth and Intellectual Property in Ghana, First Peoples*. Minneapolis: University of Minnesota Press.

Boon, James. 2000. "Showbiz as a Cross-Cultural System: Circus and Song, Garland and Geertz, Rushdie, Mordden, . . . and More." *Cultural Anthropology* 15 (3):424–56.

Bourdieu, Pierre. 1977. *Outline of a Theory of Practice*. Translated by Richard Nice. Edited by Jack Goody Ernest Gellner, Stephen Gudeman, Michael Herzfeld, and Jonathan Parry. Cambridge Studies in Social and Cultural Anthropology, Book 16. Cambridge, UK: Cambridge University Press.

Bourdieu, Pierre. 1984. *Distinction: A Social Critique of the Judgment of Pure Taste*. Translated by Richard Nice. Cambridge, MA: Harvard University Press.

Bourdieu, Pierre. 1993. *The Field of Cultural Production: Essays on Art and Culture*. Translated by Randal Johnson. New York: Columbia University Press.

Boyd, Danah. 2014. *It's Complicated: The Social Lives of Networked Teens*. New Haven, CT: Yale University Press.

Boyer, Dominic. 2003. "Censorship as a Vocation: The Institutions, Practices, and Cultural Logic of Media Control in the German Democratic Republic." *Comparative Studies in Society and History* 45 (3):511–45.

Braz, Camilo Albuquerque de. 2002. "Camelôs no sindicato: Etnografia de um conflito no universo do trabalho." Dissertation, Instituto de Filosofia e Ciências Humanas, Departamento de Antropologia, UNICAMP, Campinas, SP.

Brenneis, Don. 1987. "Performing Passions: Aesthetics and Politics in an Occasionally Egalitarian Community." *American Ethnologist* 14 (2):236–50.

Briggs, Charles L., and Richard Bauman. 1992. "Genre, Intertextuality, and Social Power." *Journal of Linguistic Anthropology* 2 (2):131–72.

Brown, Michael. 2003. *Who Owns Native Culture?* Cambridge, MA: Harvard University Press.

Burke, Edmund. 2014. *A Philosophical Inquiry into the Origin of Our Ideas of the Sublime and Beautiful*. Cambridge, UK: Cambridge University Press.

Caldeira, Teresa Pires do Rio. 2001. *City of Walls: Crime, Segregation, and Citizenship in São Paulo*. Berkeley: University of California Press.

Caldeira, Teresa. 2013. "São Paulo: The City and Its Protest." https://www.opendemocracy.net/en/opensecurity/sao-paulo-city-and-its-protest/.

Caldwell, Steven, and Thomas Holt, eds. 2018. *Digital Piracy: A Global, Multidisciplinary Account*. London: Routledge.

Cardoso, Fernando Henrique. 1989. "Associated-Dependent Development and Democratic Theory." In *Democratizing Brazil: Problems of Transition and Consolidation*, edited by Alfred Stepan, 299–326. New York: Oxford University Press.

Cardoso, Fernando Henrique. 2001. *Charting a New Course: The Politics of Globalization and Social Transformation*. Lanham, MD: Rowman & Littlefield.

Cardoso, Ismael. 2012. "Azeredo: Discutir lei sobre crimes na Internet do zero é um atraso." *Terra*. https://www.terra.com.br/noticias/tecnologia/internet/azeredo-discutir-lei-sobre-crimes-na-internet-do-zero-e-um-atraso,9fb9fe32cdbda310VgnCLD200000bbcceb0aRCRD.html.

Cardoso, Leonardo. 2019. *Sound-Politics in São Paulo*. New York: Oxford University Press.

Carneiro, Maria Luiza Tucci. 2002. *Livros proibidos, idéias malditas: O DEOPS e as minorias silenciadas*. São Paulo: Estação Liberdade.

Carr, E. Summerson, and Michael Lempert, eds. 2016. *Scale: Discourse and Dimensions of Social Life*. Oakland: University of California Press.

Castells, Manuel, and Gustavo Cardoso, eds. 2013. *Piracy Cultures: How a Growing Portion of the Global Population Is Building Media Relationships Through Alternate Channels of Obtaining Content*. Los Angeles: USC Annenberg Press.

Castro, Eduardo Viveiros de. 2011. *The Inconstancy of the Indian Soul: The Encounter of Catholics and Cannibals in 16th-Century Brazil*. Translated by Gregory Duff Morton. Chicago: Prickly Paradigm Press.

Caulfield, Sueann. 1993. "Getting into Trouble: Dishonest Women, Modern Girls, and Women-Men in the Conceptual Language of 'Vida Policial,' 1925–1927." *Signs* 19 (1):146–76.

"CD pirata estraga o aparelho de som." *Veja*, December 15, 1999.

Centeno, Miguel Angel, and Alejandro Portes. 2006. "The Informal Economy in the Shadow of the State." In *Out of the Shadows: The Informal Economy and Political Movements in Latin America*, edited by Patricia Fernández-Kelly and Jon Sheffner. Princeton, NJ: Princeton University Press.

Cesarino, Leitícia. 2019. "On Digital Populism in Brazil." Political and Legal Anthropology Review (*PoLAR*). April 15, 2019. https://polarjournal.org/2019/04/15/on-jair-bolsonaros-digital-populism/.

Chan, Anita Say. 2014. *Networking Peripheries: Technological Futures and the Myth of Digital Universalism*. Cambridge, MA: MIT Press.

Cilo, Hugo. 2012. "O fôlego do cavalo paraguaio." *Isto É*, Dinheiro section, August 10, 2012.

Coleman, E. Gabriella. 2010. "Ethnographic Approaches to Digital Media." *Annual Review of Anthropology* 39:487–505.

Collins, John. 2004. "'X Marks the Spot': Protestant Ethics and Bedeviling Mixtures in a

Brazilian Cultural Heritage Center." In *Off Stage/On Display: Intimacy and Ethnography in the Age of Public Culture*, edited by Andrew Shryock, 191–224. Redwood City, CA: Stanford University Press.

Collins, John. 2015. *Revolt of the Saints: Memory and Redemption in the Twilight of Brazilian Racial Democracy*. Durham, NC: Duke University Press.

Conklin, Harold. 1964. "Hanunoo Color Categories." In *Language in Culture and Society: Reader in Linguistics and Anthropology*, edited by Dell Hymes, 189–92. New York: Harper & Row.

Connor, Steven. 2001. "Edison's Teeth: Touching Hearing." Wenner-Gren Foundation—Hearing Culture conference (canceled), Morelia, Mexico, October 4–12, 2001. http://stevenconnor.com/edsteeth.html.

Coombe, Rosemary. 1998. *The Cultural Life of Intellectual Properties: Authorship, Appropriation, and the Law*. Post-Contemporary Interventions. Durham, NC: Duke University Press.

Coombe, Rosemary. 2009. "The Expanding Purview of Cultural Properties and Their Politics." *Annual Review of Law and Social Science* 5:393–412.

Costa, Mario. 1994. *Le sublime technologique*. Lausanne: Idérive.

Cox, Rupert, Andrew Irving, and Christopher Wright, eds. 2016. *Beyond Text? Critical Practices and Sensory Anthropology*. Manchester, UK: Manchester University Press.

Craveiro, Gisele, Jorge Machado, and Pablo Ortellado, coords. 2010. "A cadeia de produção de artigos científicos no Brasil: Financiamento público e acesso ao conhecimento." *GPOPAI/USP*. http://www.forum-global.de/jm/2008-2009/relatorio-artigos-publicado-book_05-cadernosGPOPAI.pdf.

Cunha, Euclides da. [1902] 1944. *Rebellion in the Backlands*. Translated by Samuel Putnam. Chicago: University of Chicago Press.

DaMatta, Roberto. 1979. *Carnivals, Rogues, and Heroes: An Interpretation of the Brazilian Dilemma*. Notre Dame, IN: University of Notre Dame Press.

DaMatta, Roberto. 1982. "Esporte na Sociedade: Um Ensaio sobre o Futebol Brasileiro." In *Universo do futebol: Esporte e sociedade brasileira*, edited by Roberto DaMatta, Luiz Felipe Baêta Neves Flores, Simoni Lahud Guedes, and Arno Vogel, 19–42. Rio de Janeiro: Pinakotheke.

DaMatta, Roberto. 1984. *O que faz o brasil, brasil?* Rio de Janeiro: Rocco.

DaMatta, Roberto. 1997. *Carnavais, malandros e heróis: Para uma sociologia do dilema brasileiro*. 6th ed. Rio de Janeiro: Rocco.

DaMatta, Roberto, and David Hess, eds. 1995. *The Brazilian Puzzle: Culture on the Borderlands of the Western World*. New York: Columbia University Press.

Danino, Roberto. 2006. "The Importance of the Rule of Law and Respect for Contractual Rights in Transition Countries." *European Business Law Review* 17 (2):327–35.

Darnton, Robert. 2003. "The Science of Piracy: A Crucial Ingredient in Eighteenth-Century Publishing." In *Studies on Voltaire and the Eighteenth Century*, 3–29. Oxford, UK: Voltaire Foundation.

Davis, Michael. 1999. *The Poetry of Philosophy: On Aristotle's Poetics*. South Bend, IN: St. Augustine's Press.

Davison, Janet. 2012. "Why It's So Hard to Catch Online Predators." *Canadian Broadcasting Corporation—CBC.* https://www.cbc.ca/news/technology/why-it-s-so-hard-to-catch-online-predators-1.1207481.

Dawdy, Shannon. 2011. "Why Pirates Are Back." *Annual Review of Law and Social Science* 7:361–85.

Delueze, Gilles, and Félix Guattari. 2004. *Anti-Oedipus: Capitalism and Schizophrenia.* Translated by Robert Hurley, Mark Seem, and Helen Lane. London: Continuum.

Dent, Alexander S. 2009. *River of Tears: Country Music, Memory, and Modernity in Brazil.* Durham, NC: Duke University Press.

Dent, Alexander S. 2010. "Flouting the Elmo Necessity and Denying the Local Roots of Interpretation: Anthropology's Quarrel with ACTA and Authoritarian IP Regimes." Program on Information Justice and Intellectual Property (PIJIP) Research Paper no. 3, Washington, DC: Washington College of Law, American University.

Dent, Alexander S. 2012. "Understanding the War on Piracy, or, Why We Need More Anthropology of Pirates." *Anthropological Quarterly* 83 (3):659–72.

Dent, Alexander S. 2013. "Intellectual Property in Practice: Filtering Testimony at the United States Trade Representative." *Journal of Linguistic Anthropology* 23 (2):48–65.

Dent, Alexander. 2016a. "'Hey! If I Should Grab Ya': 'College Country' and the Ruralization of Urban Brazil." In *Country Boys and Redneck Women: New Essays in Gender and Country Music*, edited by Diane Pecknold and Kristine McCusker, 26–43. Jackson: University Press of Mississippi.

Dent, Alexander S. 2016b. "Intellectual Property, Piracy, and Counterfeiting." *Annual Review of Anthropology* 45:17–31.

Dent, Alexander S. 2016c. "Policing the Unstable Materialities of Digital-Media Piracy in Brazil." *American Ethnologist,* 43 (3). https://americanethnologist.org/read/journal/volume-43-issue-3-august-2016/policing-the-unstable-materialities-of-digital media-piracy-in-brazil.

Dent, Alexander, and Rosana Pinheiro Machado. 2013. "Protesting Democracy in Brazil." *Editors' Forum/Hot Spots,* Society for Cultural Anthropology website, December 20, 2013. https://culanth.org/fieldsights/series/protesting-democracy-in-brazil.

Douglas, Mary. 2003. *Purity and Danger: An Analysis of Concepts of Pollution and Taboo.* London: Routledge.

Duarte, Fernanda. 2006. "Exploring the Interpersonal Transaction of the Brazilian Jeitinho in Bureaucratic Contexts." *Organization* 13 (4):509–27.

Eckstein, Lars, and Anja Schwarz, eds. 2014. *Postcolonial Piracy: Media Distribution and Cultural Production in the Global South.* London: Bloomsbury.

Edmonds, Alex. 2010. *Pretty Modern: Beauty, Sex and Plastic Surgery in Brazil.* Durham, NC: Duke University Press.

Envisaging Technology. 2012. "The Smartphone of the Future: An Explosion of Possibilities." http://envisioningtech.com/envisioning-the-smartphone-of-the-future/.

ESPN Brasil. 2014. "Pergunte ao PVC: Qual é a maior 'cavalo paraguaio' do brasileiro? Algum time caiu no ano do centenário?" http://www.espn.com.br/video/435928

_pergunte-ao-pvc-qual-e-o-maior-cavalo-paraguaio-do-brasileiro-algum-time-caiu-no-ano-do-centenario.

Facirolli, Livia. 2012. "Glamour paraguaio é." In *Glamour Paraguaio* (blog). https://glamourparaguaio.wordpress.com.

Fassin, Didier. 2011. "Policing Borders, Producing Boundaries: The Governmentality of Immigration in Dark Times." *Annual Review of Anthropology* 40:213–26.

Fausto, Boris. 1999. *A Concise History of Brazil.* Cambridge, UK: Cambridge University Press.

Feld, Steve, and Donald Brenneis. 2004. "Doing Anthropology in Sound." *American Ethnologist* 31 (4):461–74.

Feld, Steven. 1996. "Pygmy POP: A Case of Schizophonic Mimesis." *Yearbook for Traditional Music* 28:1–35.

Ferguson, Francis. 1984. "The Nuclear Sublime." *Diacritics* 14 (2):4–10.

Fernández-Kelly, Patricia, and Jon Shefner, eds. 2002. *Out of the Shadows: Political Action and the Informal Economy in Latin America.* State College, PA: Penn State University Press.

Ferreira, Maria Cristina, Ronald Fischer, Juliana Berreiros Porto, Ronaldo Pilati, and Taciano Milfont. 2012. "Unraveling the Mystery of Brazilian Jeitinho: A Cultural Exploration of Social Norms." *Personality and Social Psychology Bulletin* 38 (3):331–44.

Filippozzi, Eliana Maria. 1998. "Brazil: Second Largest Telecoms Privatization in the World." *International Financial Law Review* 17 (9):61.

Fisher, Susan. 2014. "Optimizing the Digital Farm: The Right Combination of Technology and Expertise Improves the Accuracy of On-Farm Management Decisions." *Syngenta Thrive* (Summer). http://www.syngenta-us.com/thrive/production/optimizing-the-digital-farm.html.

FMAA. 2008. "Pirataria audiovisual e fonográfica: Estatísticas, aspectos técnicos e jurídicos." PowerPoint presentation. São Paulo: Film and Music Antipiracy Association.

Folha Online. 2010. "Saiba como foi a privatização da Telebrás em 1998." *Folha UOL.* https://www1.folha.uol.com.br/mercado/2008/07/427127-saiba-como-foi-a-privatizacao-da-telebras-em-1998.shtml.

Foucault, Michel. 1971. *The Order of Things: An Archaeology of the Human Sciences.* New York: Pantheon Books.

Foucault, Michel. 1991. "Governmentality." In *The Foucault Effect: Studies in Governmentality,* edited by Graham Burchell, Colin Gordon, and Peter Miller, 87–104. Chicago: University of Chicago Press.

Frake, Charles O. 1964. "Notes on Queries in Ethnography." In *Cognitive Anthropology,* edited by Stephen Tyler, 123–37. New York: Holt, Rinehart & Winston.

Freyre, Gilberto. [1933] 1992. *Casa grande e senzala: Formação da família brasileira sob o regime da economia patriarcal.* 34th ed. Rio de Janeiro: Record.

Fry, Peter. 1982. *Para inglês ver: Identidade e política na cultura brasileira.* Rio de Janeiro: Zahar.

Galemba, Rebecca. 2017. *Contraband Corridor: Making a Living at the Mexico-Guatemala Border*. Redwood City, CA: Stanford University Press.

Ganti, Tejaswini. 2014. "Neoliberalism." *Annual Review of Anthropology* 43:89–103.

Geary, Patrick. 1986. "Sacred Commodities: The Circulation of Medieval Relics." In *The Social Life of Things*, edited by Arjun Appadurai, 169–91. Minneapolis, MN: University of Minnesota Press.

Geary, Patrick J. 1978. *Furta Sacra: Thefts of Relics in the Central Middle Ages*. Princeton, NJ: Princeton University Press.

Geertz, Clifford. 1973a. "Deep Play: Notes on the Balinese Cockfight." In *The Interpretation of Cultures*, 412–53. New York: Basic Books.

Geertz, Clifford. 1973b. "Thick Description: Toward an Interpretive Theory of Culture." In *The Interpretation of Cultures: Selected Essays*, 3–30. New York: Basic Books.

Gell, Alfred. 1996. "Vogel's Net: Traps as Artworks, and Artworks as Traps." *Journal of Material Culture*, 1 (1): 15–38.

Genestreti, Guilherme. 2012. "Preço baixo, variedade e tradição atraem 1 milhão de pessoas por dia à 25 de março." *Folha de São Paulo*, Especial Compras, December 9, 2012. https://m.folha.uol.com.br/saopaulo/2012/12/1197747-preco-baixo-variedade-e-tradicao-atraem-1-milhao-de-pessoas-por-dia-a-25-de-marco.shtml?mobile.

Gershon, Ilana. 2011. "Neoliberal Agency." *Current Anthropology* 52 (4):537–55.

Gershon, Ilana. 2015. "What Do We Talk about When We Talk about Animation." *Social Media Society* (April–June):1–2.

Gershon, Ilana. 2017. *Down and Out in the New Economy: How People Find (or Don't Find) Work Today*. Chicago: University of Chicago Press.

Ghedin, Rodrigo. 2014. "Do Orkut ao WhatsApp, como a música brasileira retrata os apps e redes sociais que todos usamos." October 30, 2014. https://manualdousuario.net/musica-brasileira-whatsapp-facebook/.

Gibson, James J. 1986. "The Theory of Affordances." In *Perceiving, Acting, and Knowing: Toward an Ecological Psychology*, edited by Robert Shaw and John Bransford, 127–37. Hillsdale, NJ: Lawrence Erlbaum.

Gillingham, Paul. 2010. "The Strange Business of Memory: Relic Forgery in Latin America." *Past & Present* 206 (5):199–226.

Glanz, James. 2012. "Power, Pollution and the Internet." *New York Times*, September 22, 2012. http://www.nytimes.com/2012/09/23/technology/data-centers-waste-vast-amounts-of-energy-belying-industry-image.html?pagewanted=all&_r=0.

Goldstein, Donna. 1999. "'Interracial' Sex and Racial Democracy in Brazil: Twin Concepts?" *American Anthropologist* 101 (3):563–78.

Goldstein, Donna, and K. Drybread. 2018. "The Social Life of Corruption in Latin America." *Culture Theory and Critique* 59 (4):299–311.

Golub, Alex. 2004. "Copyright and Taboo." *Anthropological Quarterly* 77 (4):521–30.

Goodman, Steve. 2010. *Sonic Warfare: Sound, Affect, and the Ecology of Fear*. Cambridge, MA: MIT Press.

Grasiela, Lilian. 2012. Pomba leva celular para detentos. *Jornal da Cidade*, Regional section, May 29, 2012. http://www.jcnet.com.br/Regional/2012/05/pombo-leva-celular-para-detentos.html.

Green, W. John. 2015. *A History of Political Murder in Latin America: Killing the Messengers of Change*. New York: SUNY Press.

Greenfield, Adam. 2017. *Radical Technologies: The Design of Everyday Life*. London: Verso.

Guertin, Carolyn. 2012. *Digital Prohibition: Piracy and Authorship in New Media Art*. London: Continuum.

Hacking, Ian. 2002. *Historical Ontology*. Cambridge, MA: Harvard University Press.

Hacking, Ian. [1975] 2006. *The Emergence of Probability: A Philosophical Study of Early Ideas about Probability, Induction and Statistical Inference*. Cambridge Series on Statistical and Probabilistic Mathematics. Cambridge, UK: Cambridge University Press.

Hanks, William. 1987. "Discourse Genres in a Theory of Practice." *American Ethnologist* 14 (4):668–92.

Hanks, William. 1989. "Text and Textuality." *Annual Review of Anthropology* 18:95–127.

Hanks, William. 2001. "Indexicality." In *Key Terms in Language and Culture*, edited by Alessandro Duranti, 119–22. Malden, MA: Blackwell.

Harkness, Nicholas. 2015. "The Pragmatics of Qualia in Practice." *Annual Review of Anthropology* 44 (2015):573–89.

Harvey, David. 2007. *A Brief History of Neoliberalism*. Oxford, UK: Oxford University Press.

Heidegger, Martin. [1954] 1993. "The Question Concerning Technology." In *Basic Writings: From Being and Time (1927) to The Task of Thinking (1964)*, edited by David Farrell Krell, 311–41. San Francisco: HarperSanFrancisco.

Helenius, Timo. 2016. *Ricoeur, Culture, and Recognition*. Lanham, MD: Lexington Books.

Henriques, Julian. 2011. *Sonic Bodies: Reggae Sound Systems, Performance Techniques, and Ways of Knowing*. New York: Bloomsbury.

Hertzman, Marc. 2013. *Making Samba: A New History of Race and Music in Brazil*. Durham, NC: Duke University Press.

Herzfeld, Michael. 1996. *Cultural Intimacy: Social Poetics in the Nation State*. London: Routledge.

Hoback, Cullen, dir. 2013. *Terms and Conditions May Apply*. Documentary. New York and Los Angeles: Hyrax Films.

Hobsbawm, Eric. 2000. *Social Banditry*. Revised ed. New York: New Press.

Holanda, Sérgio Buarque de. [1936] 1995. *Raízes do brasil*. 4th ed. São Paulo: Companhia das Letras.

Holston, James. 1989. *The Modernist City*. Chicago: University of Chicago Press.

Holston, James. 2009. *Insurgent Citizenship: Disjunctions of Democracy and Modernity in Brazil*, In-formation series. Princeton, NJ: Princeton University Press.

Holston, James. 2013. "'Come to the Street': Urban Protest, Brazil 2013." *Cultural Anthropology* (Hot Spots). https://culanth.org/fieldsights/come-to-the-street-urban-protest-brazil-2013.

Holston, James, and Teresa Caldeira. 1999. "Democracy and Violence in Brazil." *Comparative Studies in Society and History* 41 (4):691–729.

Homer. [ca. 700 BCE] 1909. *The Odyssey*. Translated by S. H. Butcher and Andrew Lang. New York: Collier & Son.

Horst, Heather, and Daniel Miller. 2006. *The Cell Phone: An Anthropology of Communication*. Oxford, UK: Berg.

"How Fashion Became a Digital Industry." 2018. *Textile World*. TW Special Report, March 29, 2018. https://www.textileworld.com/textile-world/features/2018/03/how-fashion-became-a-digital-industry/.

Ingarden, Roman. 1973. *The Literary Work of Art: An Investigation on the Borderlines of Ontology, Logic, and Theory of Literature—With an Appendix on the Functions of Language in Theater*. Evanston, IL: Northwestern University Press.

Jakobson, Roman. 1960. "Closing Statement: Linguistics and Poetics." In *Style in Language*, edited by T. A. Sebeok, 350–77. Cambridge, MA: MIT University Press.

James, Deborah, and Sandra Clarke. 1993. "Women, Men, and Interruptions: A Critical Review." In *Gender and Conversational Interaction*, edited by Deborah Tannen. New York: Oxford University Press.

Jameson, Fredric. 2003. "The End of Temporality." *Critical Inquiry* 29 (4):695–718.

Johns, Adrian. 2010. *Piracy: The Intellectual Property Wars from Gutenberg to Gates*. Chicago: University of Chicago Press.

Joseph, Sarah. 2013. *Blame It on the WTO? A Human Rights Critique*. New York: Oxford University Press.

Junge, Benjamin. 2018. *Cynical Citizenship: Gender, Regionalism, and Political Subjectivity in Porto Alegre, Brazil*. Albuquerque: University of New Mexico Press.

Kafka, Franz. [1924] 1971. *The Complete Stories*. New York: Schocken Books. Karaganis, Joe, ed. 2007. *Structures of Participation in Digital Culture*. New York: Social Science Research Council.

Karaganis, Joe, ed. 2011. *Media Piracy in Emerging Economies*. New York: Social Science Research Council.

Karaganis, Joe. 2019. The Piracy Wars Are Over. Let's Talk about Data Incumbency. *Wired*, March 5, 2019. https://www.wired.com/story/the-piracy-wars-are-over-lets-talk-about-data-incumbency/.

Katz, James, and Mark Aakhus, eds. 2002. *Perpetual Contact: Mobile Communication, Private Talk, Public Performance*. Cambridge, UK: Cambridge University Press.

Katz, Mark. 2004. *Capturing Sound: How Technology Changed Music*. Berkeley: University of California Press.

Keane, Webb. 2005. "Signs Are Not the Garb of Meaning: On the Social Analysis of Material Things." In *Materiality*, edited by Daniel Miller, 182–205. Durham, NC: Duke University Press.

Keane, Webb. 2013. "On Spirit Writing: Materialities of Language and the Religious Work of Transduction." *Journal of the Royal Anthropological Institute* 19 (1):1–17.

Kelty, Christopher. 2008. *Two Bits: The Cultural Significance of Free Software*. Durham, NC: Duke University Press.

Kittler, Friedrick. 1999. *Gramophone, Film, Typewriter*. Translated by Goeffrey Winthrop-Young and Michael Wutz. Redwood City, CA: Stanford University Press.

Kleinfeld, Rachel. 2006. "Competing Definitions of the Rule of Law." In *Promoting the Rule of Law Abroad*, edited by T. Carothers. Washington, DC: Carnegie Endowment for International Peace.

Knight, Alan. 2010. "The Several Legs of Santa Anna: A Saga of Secular Relics." *Past and Present* 206 (5):227–55.

Knight, Peter. 2011. "e-Development in Brazil." *Journal of the Knowledge Economy* 2 (1):77–116.

Kockleman, Paul. 2017. *The Art of Interpretation in the Age of Computation*. New York: Oxford.

Kuipers, Joel. 1990. *The Power in Performance: The Creation of Textual Authority in Weyewa Ritual Speech*. University of Pennsylvania Publications in Conduct and Communication. Pittsburgh: University of Pennsylvania Press.

Kuipers, Joel, and Josh Bell, eds. 2018. *The Linguistic and Material Intimacies of Cell Phones*. London: Routledge.

Kulick, Don. 1998. *Travesti: Sex, Gender, and Culture among Brazilian Transgendered Prostitutes*. Worlds of Desire: The Chicago Series on Sexuality, Gender, and Culture. Chicago: The University of Chicago Press.

Kunisawa, Viviane Yumy Mitsuuchi. 2015. *The TRIPS Agreement Implementation in Brazil*. Munich: Nomos Verlagsgesellschaft.

Kushnir, Beatriz. 2004. *Cães de guarda: Jornalistas e censores, do AI-5 à constituição de 1988*. São Paulo: Boitempo.

Larkin, Brian. 2008. *Signal and Noise: Media, Infrastructure, and Urban Culture in Nigeria*. Durham, NC: Duke University Press.

Larkin, Brian. 2013. "The Politics and Poetics of Infrastructure." *Annual Review of Anthropology* 42:327–43.

Larkin, Brian. 2014. "Techniques of Inattention: The Mediality of Loudspeakers in Nigeria." *Anthropological Quarterly* 87 (4):989–1015.

Lavinas, Lena. 2017. "How Social Developmentalism Reframed Social Policy in Brazil." *New Political Economy* 22 (6):628–44.

Leandro and Leonardo. 1998. *Sonho por sonho*. Warner Music Brasil. Sound recording.

Lee, Benjamin. 1997. *Talking Heads: Language, Metalanguage, and the Semiotics of Subjectivity*. Durham, NC: Duke University Press.

Lemos, Ronaldo, and Oona Castro. 2008. *Tecnobrega: O Pará reinventando o negócio da música*. Vol. 9, Coleção tramas urbanas. Rio de Janeiro: Aeroplano.

Lenz, Friedrich, ed. 2003. *Deictic Conceptualisation of Space, Time, and Person*. Amsterdam: John Benjamins.

Lessig, Lawrence. 1999. *Code and other Laws of Cyberspace*. New York: Basic Books.

Lessig, Lawrence. 2004. *Free Culture: How Big Media Uses Technology and the Law to Lock Down Culture and Control Creativity*. New York: Penguin Press.

Lessig, Lawrence. 2009. *Remix: Making Art and Commerce Thrive in the New Hybrid Economy*. New York: Penguin.

Leung, Wendy. 2013. "Vigilantes or Heroes? How Anonymous Is Reshaping Its Image with the Rehtaeh Parsons Case." *The Globe and Mail*, April 15, 2013. https://www.theglobeandmail.com/life/the-hot-button/vigilantes-or-heroes-how-anonymous-is-reshaping-its-image-with-the-rehtaeh-parsons-case/article11211575/?cmpid=rss1.

Lévi-Strauss, Claude. 1966. "The Science of the Concrete." In *The Savage Mind*, 1–33. Chicago: University of Chicago Press.

Leyshon, Andrew, Roger Lee, and Colin Williams, eds. 2003. *Alternative Economic Spaces*. London: Sage Publishing.

Libero, Daiane. 2016. Clientes reclamam de música no celular e sofrem para cancelar cobrança. *Midiamax*. March 7, 2016. https://www.midiamax.com.br/brasil/2016/clientes-reclamam-de-musica-no-celular-e-sofrem-para-cancelar-cobranca.

Lindtner, Silvia. 2014. "Hackerspaces and the Internet of Things in China: How Makers Are Reinventing Industrial Production, Innovation, and the Self." *China Information* 28 (2):145–67.

Lippman, Alexandra. 2014. "Cannibalizing Copyright? Vernacularizing open Intellectual Property in Brazil." *Anthropology Today* 30 (5):11–14.

Livingston, Jay, and Ray Evans. 1961. *Mr. Ed.* Theme Song. New York: Universal/MCA Music Publishing and Warner/Chappell Music.

Lobato, Ramon, and Julian Thomas. 2015. *The Informal Media Economy*. London: Polity Press.

Lynn, Aaron. 2012. "Synch: How Technology Makes Us More Efficient." Formerly on *Asian Efficiency* (blog). http://www.asianefficiency.com/start-here/.

Malinowski, Branislaw. 1935. *Coral Gardens and Their Magic: A Study of the Methods of Tilling the Soil and of Agricultural Rites in the Trobriand Islands*. London: Routledge.

Mankekar, Purnima. 2001. *Screening Culture, Viewing Politics: An Ethnography of Television, Womanhood, and Nation in Postcolonial India*. Durham, NC: Duke University Press.

Manuel, Peter. 1993. *Cassette Culture: Popular Music and Technology in North India*. Chicago: University of Chicago Press.

Manzo, Paolo. 2011. "In Paraguay, a Quaint Inn with a Dark Nazi Past." *Time*, November 3, 2011.

Martin, Jeff. 2018. "Police and Policing." *Annual Review of Anthropology* 47:133–48.

Marx, Karl. [1867] 1977. *Capital*. 3 vols. Vol. 1. Translated by Ben Fowkes. Edited and Introduction by Ernest Mandel. New York: Vintage.

Masco, Joseph. 2013. *Nuclear Borderlands*. Princeton, NJ: Princeton University Press.

Matory, Lorand. 2004. "Sexual Secrets: Candomblé, Brazil, and the Multiple Intimacies of the African Diaspora." In *Off Stage/On Display: Intimacy and Ethnography in the Age of Public Culture*, edited by Andrew Shryock, 157–90. Redwood City, CA: Stanford University Press.

Maurer, Bill, Stephen Rea, and Taylor Nelms. 2013. "Bridges to Cash: Channeling Agency in Mobile Money." *Journal of the Royal Anthropological Institute* 19 (1):52–74.

Mazzarella, William. 2014. *Censorium: Cinema and the Open Edge of Mass Publicity*. Durham, NC: Duke University Press.

McCartney, Andra. 2016. "Ethical Questions about Working with Soundscapes." *Organized Sound* 21 (2):160–65.

McLeod, Kembrew. 2005. *Freedom of Expression: Overzealous Copyright Bozos and Other Enemies of Creativity*. New York: Doubleday.

Medioli, Vittorio. 2009. "A deliquência no mundo virtual." *O Tempo*, March 19, 2009. http://www.otempo.com.br/opiniao/vittorio-medioli/a-deliquencia-no-mundo-virtual-1.208184.

Miller, Daniel. 2005. "Materiality: An Introduction." In *Materiality*, edited by Daniel Miller, 1–50. Durham, NC: Duke University Press.

Miller, W. Flagg. 2001. "Inscribing the Muse: Political Poetry and the Discourse of Circulation in the Yemeni Cassette Industry." PhD Dissertation, Cultural Anthropology, University of Michigan.

Mitchell, Dan. 2006. "Tail Is Wagging the Internet Dog." *New York Times*, July 8, 2006, Business. http://www.nytimes.com/2006/07/08/business/08online.html.

Mitchell, Sean. 2013. "Space, Sovereignty, Inequality: Interpreting the Explosion of Brazil's VLS Rocket." *The Journal of Latin American and Caribbean Anthropology* 18 (3):395–412.

Moehn, Frederick. 2012. *Contemporary Carioca: Technologies of Mixing in a Brazilian Music Scene*. Durham, NC: Duke University Press.

Moore, Thurston. 2004. *Mix Tape: The Art of Cassette Culture*. New York: Universe.

Mosco, Vincent. 2005. *The Digital Sublime: Myth, Power, and Cyberspace*. Cambridge, MA: MIT Press.

Muehlmann, Shaylih. 2018. "The Gender of the War on Drugs." *Annual Review of Anthropology* 47:315–30.

Mueller, Gavin. 2019. *Media Piracy in the Cultural Economy: Intellectual Property and Labor under Neoliberal Restructuring*. London: Routledge.

Nakassis, Constantine. 2013. "Counterfeiting What? Willful Ignorance and the Brand in Tamil Nadu, India." *Anthropological Quarterly* 85 (3):701–22.

Nazzari, Muriel. 1996. "Concubinage in Colonial Brazil: The Inequalities of Race, Class, and Gender." *Journal of Family History* 21 (2):107–24.

Needell, Jeffrey D. 1987. *A Tropical Belle Epoque: Elite Culture and Society in Turn-of-the-Century Rio de Janeiro*. Cambridge Latin American Studies. Cambridge, UK: Cambridge University Press.

Newell, Sasha. 2012. *The Modernity Bluff: Crime, Consumption, and Citizenship in Côte d'Ivoire*. Chicago: University of Chicago Press.

Newman, Lily Hay. 2013. "Millions of Cell Phones Could Be Vulnerable to This SIM Card Hack." *Gizmodo*, July 21, 2013. https://gizmodo.com/sim-cards-are-hackable-and-researchers-have-found-the-v-860779912.

Nye, David E. 1996. *American Technological Sublime*. Cambridge, MA: MIT Press.

O'Brien, Kevin. 2013. "Encryption Flaw Makes Phones Possible Accomplices in Theft." *New York Times*, July 22, 2013. http://www.nytimes.com/2013/07/22/technology/encryption-flaw-makes-phones-possible-accomplices-in-theft.html?pagewanted=all&_r=0.

O'Dougherty, Maureen. 2002. *Consumption Intensified: The Politics of Middle-Class Daily Life in Brazil*. Durham, NC: Duke University Press.

Omari, Jeffrey. 2018. "Digital Access Amongst the Marginalized: Democracy and Internet Governance in Rio de Janeiro." *Political and Legal Anthropology Review (PoLAR)* 41 (2):277–82.

Orr, Julian. 1996. *Talking about Machines: An Ethnography of a Modern Job*. Ithaca, NY: Cornell University Press.

Ortiz, Renato. 1999. *A moderna tradição brasileira: Cultura brasileira e indústria cultural*. 5th ed. São Paulo: Brasiliense.

Otis, Sarah. 2015. "Mídia Ninja: The *Rede*, Impartiality, and Critiques of the Public Sphere." Paper, B.A., Anthropology, George Washington University.

Palmade, Vincent, and Andrea Anayiotos. 2005. "Rising Informality—Reversing the Tide." In *Public Policy for the Private Sector*. Washington, DC: Foreign Investment Advisory Service, World Bank.

Pardue, Derek. 2004. "Putting *Mano* to Music: The Mediation of Race in Brazilian Rap." *Ethnomusicology Forum* 13 (2):253–86.

Parker, Richard. 2009. *Bodies, Pleasures, and Passions: Sexual Culture in Contemporary Brazil*. 2nd ed. Nashville, TN: Vanderbilt University Press.

Patry, William. 2009. *Moral Panics and the Copyright Wars*. New York: Oxford University Press.

Pereira de Sá, Celso, Ricardo Vieiralves de Castro, Renato Cesar Moller, and Juliana Aieta Perez. 2008. "A memória histórica de Getúlio Vargas e o palácio do Catete." *Estudos de psicologia* 13 (1):49–56.

Peters, John Durham. 1999. *Speaking into the Air: A History of the Idea of Communication*. Chicago: University of Chicago Press.

Petryna, Adriana, Andrew Lakoff, and Arthur Kleinman, eds. 2006. *Global Pharmaceuticals: Ethics, Markets, Practices*. Durham, NC: Duke University Press.

Philip, Kavita. 2014. "Keep on Copyin' in the Free World? Genealogies of the Postcolonial Pirate Figure." In *Postcolonial Piracy: Media Distribution and Cultural Production in the Global South*, edited by Lars Eckstein and Anja Schwarz. London: Bloomsbury.

Picketty, Thomas. 2014. *Capital in the Twenty-First Century*. Cambridge, MA: Harvard University Press.

Pinheiro Machado, Rosana. 2009. "Made in China: Produção e circulação de mercadorias no circuito china-paraguai-brasil." PhD, Social Anthropology, Instituto de Filosofia e Ciências Humanas, Universidade Federal do Rio Grande do Sul.

Pinheiro Machado, Rosana. 2017. *Counterfeit Itineraries in the Global South: The Human Consequences of Piracy in China and Brazil*. London: Routledge.

Pinheiro Machado, Rosana, and Adriano de Freixo, eds. 2019. *Brasil em transe: Bolsonarismo, nova direita e desdemocratização*. Rio de Janeiro: Oficina Raquel.

Pochmann, Marcio. 2004. "Proteção social na periferia do capitalismo: Considerações sobre o Brasil." *São Paulo Perspectivas* 18 (2):3–16.

Pochmann, Marcio. 2007. "Política social na periferia do capitalismo: A situação recente no Brasil." *Ciência e Saúde Coletiva* 12 (6):1477–89.

Portes, Alejandro, and William Haller. 2005. "The Informal Economy." In *The Handbook of Economic Sociology*, edited by Neil J. Smelser and Richard Swedberg, 403–28. Princeton, NJ: Princeton University Press.

Poster, Mark. 2006. *Information Please: Culture and Politics in the Age of Digital Machines*. Durham, NC: Duke University Press.

Postill, John. 2011. *Localizing the Internet*. New York: Berghahn Books.

Povinelli, Elizabeth. 2011. *Economies of Abandonment: Social Belonging and Endurance in Late Liberalism*. Durham, NC: Duke University Press.

Rabossi, Fernando. 2004. "Nas ruas de Ciudad del Este: Vidas e vendas num mercado de fronteira." PhD, Social Anthropology, Universidade Federal do Rio de Janeiro, Museu Nacional.

Rabossi, Fernando. 2007. "Árabes e muçulmanos em Foz do Iguaçu e Ciudad del Este: Notas para uma re-interpretação." In *Mundos em movimento: Ensaios sobre migrações*, edited by Giralda Seyferth, Hélion Póvoa, M. C. Sanini, and M. Santos. Santa Maria, RS: Editora da Universidade Federal de Santa Maria.

Rabossi, Fernando. 2012. "Ciudad del Este and Brazilian Circuits of Commercial Distribution." In *Globalization from Below: The World's Other Economy*, edited by Gordon Mathews, Gustavo Lins Ribeiro, and Carlos Alba Vega, 54–69. London: Routledge.

Rebhun, L. A. 1999. *The Heart Is Unknown Country: Love in the Changing Economy of Northeast Brazil*. Redwood City, CA: Stanford University Press.

Reimão, Sandra. 2008. "Reagindo à censura: Criatividade em tempos sombrios. O caso do concurso de contos da revista status." *Comunicação & Inovação* 9 (16).

Reis, Dalmir, and Augusto Fagundes, administrators. 2019. "Propagandas Históricas." Website. https://www.propagandashistoricas.com.br/.

Reis, Odilon. 2013. "Gato é 'preso' por levar serras e celulares a detentos em Alagoas." *O Globo*. https://oglobo.globo.com/brasil/gato-preso-por-levar-serras-celulares-detentos-em-alagoas-7200798.

Ribeiro, Amaury, Jr. 2011. *A pirataria tucana*. São Paulo: Gerção Editorial.

Ricoeur, Paul. 2004. *Memory, History, Forgetting*. Translated by Kathleen Blamey and David Pellauer. Chicago: University of Chicago Press.

Romero, Simon. 2013. "On YouTube, Comedy Troupe Tickles Brazil and Ruffles Feathers." *New York Times*, September 1, 2013. http://www.nytimes.com/2013/09/01/world/americas/on-youtube-comedy-troupe-tickles-brazil-and-ruffles-feathers.html?pagewanted=2&_r=0.

Rosaldo, Michelle. 1982. "The Things We Do with Words: Ilongot Speech Acts and Speech Act Theory in Philosophy." In *Language in Society*, 203–37. Cambridge, UK: Cambridge University Press.

Ruen, Chris. 2012. *Freeloading: How Our Insatiable Appetite for Free Content Starves Creativity*. New York: OR Books.

Sa, Vanessa Mendes Moreira de. 2011. "Internet Piracy as a Hobby: What Happens

When the Brazilian *Jeitinho* Meets Television Downloading?" *Global Media Journal*, Australian Edition 5 (1):1–9.

Saad-Filho, Alfredo. 2010. "Neoliberalism, Democracy, and Development Policy in Brazil." *Development and Society* 39 (1):1–28.

Sacks, Harvey, Emanuel Schegloff, and Gail Jefferson. 1974. "A Simplest Systematics for the Organization of Turn-Taking in Conversation." *Language* 50 (4):696–735.

Sahlins, Marshall. 1993. "Goodbye to Tristes Tropes: Ethnography in the Context of Modern World History." *Journal of Modern World History* 65 (March):1–25.

Sahlins, Marshall. 1996. "The Sadness of Sweetness: The Native Anthropology of Western Cosmology." *Current Anthropology* 37 (3):395–428.

Salvucci, Dario, and Niels Taatgen. 2010. *The Multitasking Mind*. Oxford Studies on Cognitive Models and Architectures. Oxford, UK: Oxford University Press.

Sansi-Roca, Roger. 2007. *Fetishes and Monuments: Afro-Brazilian Art and Culture in the 20th Century*. New York: Berghahn Books.

Sapir, Edward. 1949. *Language: An Introduction to the Study of Speech*. New York: Harvest/Harcourt Brace Jovanovich.

Schafer, R. Murray. 1993. *The Soundscape: The Sonic Environment and the Tuning of the World*. Rochester, VT: Inner Traditions/Bear.

Schechter, Frank I. 1927. "The Rational Basis of Trademark Protection." *Harvard Law Review* 40 (6):813–33.

Schegloff, Emanuel. 2002a. "Appendix A: On 'Opening Sequencing'—A Framing Statement." In *Perpetual Contact: Mobile Communication, Private Talk, Public Performance*, edited by James Katz and Mark Aakhus, 321–25. Cambridge, UK: Cambridge University Press.

Schegloff, Emanuel. 2002b. "Appendix B: Opening Sequencing." In *Perpetual Contact: Mobile Communication, Private Talk, Public Performance*, edited by James Katz and Mark Aakhus, 326–85. Cambridge, UK: Cambridge University Press.

Schiller, Friedrich. 2001. "Concerning the Sublime." In *Friedrich Schiller—Essays*, edited by Walter Hinderer and Daniel Dahlstrom, 70–85. New York: Continuum.

Schneider, Jane, and Peter Schneider. 2008. "The Anthropology of Crime and Criminalization." *Annual Review of Anthropology* 37:351–73.

Schuster, Caroline. 2012. "Social Collateral: Microcredit Development and the Politics of Interdependency in Paraguay." PhD dissertation, Anthropology, University of Chicago.

Schwartz, Ariel. 2014. What It's Like to Live with HIV in Brazil, the World's Greatest HIV/AIDS Success Story. *Fast Company*, December 1, 2014. https://www.fastcompany.com/3037599/what-its-like-to-live-with-hiv-in-brazil-the-worlds-greatest-hiv-aids-success-story.

Schwarz, Roberto. 1992. "Brazilian Culture: Nationalism by Elimination." In *Misplaced Ideas*, 1–19. London: Verso.

Seabrook, John. 2016. *The Song Machine: Inside the Hit Factory*. New York: Norton.

Sell, Susan. 2003. *Private Power, Public Law: The Globalization of Intellectual Property Rights*. West Nyack, NY: Cambridge University Press.

Sell, Susan. 2010. *The Global IP Upward Ratchet, Anti-Counterfeiting and Piracy En-*

forcement Efforts: The State of Play. Program on Information Justice and Intellectual Property Research Paper Series, no. 15. Washington, DC: American University Washington College of Law.

Seri, Guillermina. 2012. "On the 'Triple Frontier' and the 'Borderization' of Argentina: A Tale of Zones." In *Sovereign Lives: Power in Local Politics*, edited by Jenny Edkins, Michael J. Shapiro and Veronique Pin-Fat, 79–100. London: Taylor and Francis.

SETEC. 2001. *Diagnóstico sobre as condições dos trabalhadores do comércio ambulante na região central de Campinas*. Campinas, SP: Serviços Técnicos Gerais.

Sheriff, Ribin E. 2000. "Exposing Silence as Cultural Censorship: A Brazilian Case." *American Anthropologist* 102 (1):114–32.

Shieffelin, Bambi, and Graham Jones. 2015. "The Ethnography of Inscripted Speech." In *eFieldnotes: The Makings of Anthropology in the Digital World*, edited by Roger Sanjek and Stuart Tratner. Philadelphia: University of Pennsylvania Press.

Silva, Sílvia Cortez. 2001. "Gilberto Freyre, 'O Pornógrafo de Recife.'" In *Minorias silenciadas: História da censura no Brasil*, edited by Maria Luiza Tucci Carneiro, 183–206. São Paulo: Editora da Universidade de São Paulo.

Silverstein, Michael. 1981. "The Limits of Awareness." *Working Paper in Sociolinguistics*, no. 84. National Institution of Education: Washington, DC. 31 pp.

Silverstein, Michael. 2001. "Function." In *Key Terms in Language and Culture*, edited by Alessandro Duranti. Hoboken, NJ: Blackwell.

Silverstein, Michael. 2004. "'Cultural' Concepts and the Language-Culture Nexus." *Current Anthropology* 45 (5):621–52.

Silvio, Terry. 2011. "Animation: The New Performance?" *Journal of Linguistic Anthropology* 20:422–38.

Simon, Linda. 2005. *Dark Light: Electricity and Anxiety from the Telegraph to the X-Ray*. New York: Harcourt.

Simone, Abdou Maliq. 2006. "Pirate Towns: Reworking Social and Symbolic Infrastructures in Johannesburg and Douala." *Urban Studies* 43 (2):357–70.

Singh, Ramesh, Preeti Bhargava, and Samta Kain. 2007. "Cell Phone Cloning: A Perspective on GSM Security." *Ubiquity* 8 (26).

Sinnreich, Aram. 2013. *The Piracy Crusade: How the Music Industry's War on Sharing Destroys Markets and Erodes Civil Liberties*. Amherst: University of Massachusetts Press.

Smith, Adam. [1776] 1976. *The Wealth of Nations*. Vols. 1 and 2. Chicago: University of Chicago Press.

Smith, Anne-Marie. 1997. *A Forced Agreement: Press Acquiescence to Censorship in Brazil*. Pittsburgh, PA: University of Pittsburgh Press.

Soto, Hernando de. 1989. *The Other Path: The Economic Answer to Terrorism*. New York: Basic Books.

Sousa, Marcelo Valladão de. 2011. "Clonagem de Celulares: Informações que Você Precisa Saber." *Superdownloads*, December 20, 2011. http://www.superdownloads.com.br/materias/4279-clonagem-de-celulares-informacoes-que-precisa-saber.htm.

Spence, Jonathan. 1985. *The Memory Palace of Matteo Ricci*. New York: Penguin Books.

Sterne, Jonathan. 2006. "The MP3 as Cultural Artifact." *New Media & Society* 8 (5):825–42.

Sterne, Jonathan. 2007. "Out with the Trash, On with the Future of New Media." In *Residual Media*, edited by Charles R. Acland, 16–31. Minneapolis: University of Minnesota Press.

Stewart, Kathleen. 1996. *A Space on the Side of the Road: Cultural Poetics in an "Other" America*. Princeton, NJ: Princeton University Press.

Strangelove, Michael. 2005. *The Empire of the Mind: Digital Piracy and the Anti-Capitalist Movement*. Toronto: University of Toronto Press.

Striphas, Ted. 2015. "Algorithmic Culture." *Journal of European Cultural Studies* 18 (4–5):395–412.

Sundaram, Jae. 2014. "Brazil's Implementation of TRIPS Flexibilities: Ambitious Missions, Early Implementation, and the Plans for Reform." *Information and Communications Technology Law* 23 (2):81–116.

Sundaram, Ravi. 2010. *Pirate Modernity: Delhi's Media Urbanism*. New York: Routledge.

Tafur, Juliana. 2009. Gringo—What's in a Word? *Rio Times Online*, October 27, 2009. https://riotimesonline.com/brazil-news/rio-business/whats-in-a-name-the-term-gringo-explained/.

Taussig, Michael. 1993. *Mimesis and Alterity: A Particular History of the Senses*. New York: Psychology Press.

Taussig, Michael. 2005. *Law in a Lawless Land: Diary of a Limpieza in Columbia*. Chicago: University of Chicago Press.

Thomas, Kedron. 2015. "Economic Regulation and the Value of Concealment in Highland Guatemala." *Critique of Anthropology* 35 (1):12–29.

Thomas, Kedron. 2016. *Regulating Style: Intellectual Property Law and the Business of Fashion in Guatemala*. Berkeley: University of California Press.

Thomas, Nicholas. 1991. *Entangled Objects: Exchange, Material Culture, and Colonialism in the Pacific*. Cambridge, MA: Harvard University Press.

Trindade, Priscilla. 2011. "Menores São apreendidos tentando arremessar celular para presídio no interior de SP." *Estadão de São Paulo*, August 18, 2011. https://sao-paulo.estadao.com.br/noticias/geral,menores-sao-apreendidos-tentando-arremessar-celular-para-presidio-no-interior-de-sp,760391.

Tsing, Anna. 2011. *Friction: An Ethnography of Global Connection*. Princeton, NJ: Princeton University Press.

Turkle, Sherry. 2011. *Alone Together: Why We Expect More from Technology and Less from Each Other.* New York: Basic Books.

Turner, Ben. 2018. "The Limits of Culture in Political Theory: A Critique of Multiculturalism from the Perspective of Anthropology's Ontological Turn." *European Journal of Political Theory*, January 17, 2018.

Turner, Terence. 1993. "Anthropology and Multiculturalism: What Is Anthropology that Multiculturalists Should Be Mindful of It?" *Cultural Anthropology* 8 (4):411–29.

Turner, Terence. 1996. "Indigenous Rights vs. Neo-Liberal Developmentalism in Brazil." *Dissent* (Summer):67–69.

Turner, Victor, and Edith Turner. 2011. *Image and Pilgrimage in Christian Culture: Anthropological Perspectives*. New York: Columbia University Press.

UOL. 2018. "Celular toca no meio de telejornal e âncora da Globo News se desespera." *TV e Famososos, Televisão*, June 1, 2018. https://tvefamosos.uol.com.br/noticias/redacao/2018/06/01/celular-toca-no-meio-de-telejornal-e-apresentadora-da-globo-se-desespera.htm.

Urton, Gary. 2003. *Signs of the Inka Khipu: Binary Coding in the Andean Knotted String Records*. Austin: University of Texas Press.

USGAO. 2010. *Intellectual Property: Observations on Efforts to Quantify the Economic Effects of Counterfeit and Pirated Goods*. USGAO Report to Congressional Committees, GAO-10-243, April 12, 2010. Washington, DC: United States Government Accountability Office.

Valente, Mariana Giorgetti, and Pedro Nicoletti Mizukami. 2014. "Copyright Week: What Happened to the Brazilian Copyright Reform?" *Infojustice* (blog), January 18, 2014. http://infojustice.org/archives/31993.

Valkenburg, Patti, Jochen Peter, and Joseph Walther. 2016. "Media Effects: Theory and Research." *Annual Review of Psychology* 67:315–38.

Vianna, Hermano. 1999. *The Mystery of Samba: Popular Music and National Identity in Brazil*. Translated by John Charles Chasteen. Chapel Hill: University of North Carolina Press.

Vonnegut, Kurt. [1969] 2010. *Slaughterhouse Five*. New York: RosettaBooks.

Warner, Michael. 2002. "Publics and Counterpublics." *Public Culture* 14 (1):49–90.

Weber, Max. [1905] 1958. *The Protestant Ethic and the Spirit of Capitalism*. Translated by Talcott Parsons. New York: Charles Scribner's.

Weston, Kath. 2008. *Traveling Light: On the Road with America's Poor*. New York: Beacon Press.

Whorf, Benjamin Lee. 1956. "The Relation of Habitual Thought and Behavior to Language." In *Language, Thought, and Reality*, edited by John B. Carroll, 134–60. Cambridge, MA: MIT Press.

Williams, Raymond. 1985. *Keywords: A Vocabulary of Culture and Society*. Oxford, UK: Oxford University Press.

Williams, Raymond, and Ederyn Williams. 2003. *Television: Technology and Cultural Form*. London: Psychology Press—Taylor and Francis.

Willis, Graham Denyer. 2015. *The Killing Consensus: Police, Organized Crime, and the Regulation of Life and Death in Urban Brazil*. Berkeley: University of California Press.

Wilson, Peter Lamborn. 2003. *Pirate Utopias: Moorish Corsairs and European Renegades*. Brooklyn, NY: Autonomedia.

Winner, Langdon. 1980. "Do Objects Have a Politics?" *Daeedalus* 109:121–36.

WMOL. 2005. "VIVO Brings 3G to Brazil and Provides Access to Multimedia Content." *Wireless Telecoms*. São Paulo: World Media Online.

Zaloom, Caitlin. 2004. "The Productive Life of Risk." *Cultural Anthropology* 19 (3):365–91.

Zernike, Kate. 2013. "Son's Suicide Leads to Aid for Students." *New York Times*, February 2, Section A, p. 18.

Zuboff, Shoshana. 2019. *The Age of Surveillance Capitalism: The Fight for a Human Future at the New Frontier of Power*. New York: PublicAffairs.

INDEX

The authorized representative in the EU for product safety and compliance is:
Mare Nostrum Group
B.V Doelen 72
4831 GR Breda
The Netherlands

www.ingramcontent.com/pod-product-compliance
Lightning Source LLC
Chambersburg PA
CBHW030830270326
41928CB00007B/989

* 9 7 8 1 5 0 3 6 1 2 9 7 6 *